PENN'S WOODS WEST

PENN'S WOODS WEST

ONE OF A LIST OF BOOKS IN THE CULTURAL
HISTORY OF WESTERN PENNSYLVANIA MADE
POSSIBLE THROUGH A GRANT-IN-AID FROM
THE BUHL FOUNDATION OF PITTSBURGH

PENN'S WOODS WEST

EDWIN L. PETERSON

PHOTOGRAPHER
THOMAS M. JARRETT

INTRODUCTION BY
A. W. ROBERTSON

UNIVERSITY OF PITTSBURGH PRESS

LIBRARY OF CONGRESS CATALOG CARD NUMBER: 58-6262
©1958, UNIVERSITY OF PITTSBURGH PRESS
SECOND EDITION 1959

PRINTED IN THE UNITED STATES OF AMERICA

To John G. Bowman
who knew the trees and the water of
Penn's Woods West before I was born, and

To Peggy, my daughter,
who will know them, I hope,
for many years after I am gone

". . . A good land, a land of brooks of water, of fountains and depths that spring out of valleys and hills; a land of wheat, and barley, and vines, and fig trees; a land of olive oil and honey; a land wherein thou shalt eat bread without scarceness, thou shalt not lack anything in it; a land where stones are iron, and out of whose hills thou mayest dig brass. When thou hast eaten and are filled, then thou shalt bless the Lord thy God for the good land which he hath given thee."—DEUTERONOMY 8:7–10

CONTENTS

PENN'S WOODS WEST

FALLEN LEAVES

The fallen leaf is but re-born
A gayer, freer thing.
Without stem anchor, it courts the wind
And flies with it,
No longer coy and branch-bound.

Its green dress gone, it wears a rainbow,
A wingless bird of Paradise.
In its new life, it speaks
With gustful rustle.

At last, it joins the restless myriads on the ground.
They chorus an invitation
To heavy feet and troubled mind,
"Come walk, ankle-deep, and forget the years.
Come walk in leaves and find youth's dream."

A. W. R.

PENN'S WOODS WEST

THE TREES STOOD, THE VALLEYS SURROUNDED BY wooded hills remained unchanged. The four seasons followed in an endless sequence. There was no one to gather them into years, or to bundle the years into centuries.

The earliest pioneers on this continent crashed through the forests to the waters of the three great rivers—the Allegheny pouring down from the highlands of the St. Lawrence basin, the Monongahela flowing from the watersheds of the Potomac and Chickamauga to the south, and the Ohio, formed by their union. These for many years were the highways of new settlers. In time, the treasures were discovered hidden deep in the rocks beneath the surface; and gas and oil and coal fired the boilers in ever-growing mills and factories. Great wealth came to the enterprising citizens who built workshops and homes along the rivers and up the many tributaries which branched from them. Then railroads followed the rivers and the streams. A great center of civilization developed around the junction of the three rivers and spread out for miles along the shores. The automobile came; hard-surfaced roads and broad trunk highways connected cities and villages and crossed the broad valleys, around and over encircling hills.

The country was rediscovered. Men and women saw again the trees left standing; saw the valleys and hills; and world travelers declared that no lovelier valleys were to be found. The Vale of Kashmir might be more romantic, and rugged peaks of loftier mountains mightier, but none lovelier.

The peculiar magic of the climate at the junction of the three great rivers was noted and reappraised. In this favored spot there appeared to be a perfect blending of the four seasons. The seasons were well defined and graciously disposed, one to the other. The snows of winter were not accompanied by Arctic blasts of frozen fury, but rather provided a blanket, sealing in the warmth of the earth. Spring arrived early, and summer appeared to be only a mature springtime. Autumn was clothed in gorgeous cardinal robes of brilliant color, yellow and gold, scarlet and red, woven magically from the green leaves of summer. Here, in Western Pennsylvania, the climate of the southland met and mingled with the temperate zone, and fruits and flowers, shrubs and trees, indigenous to both regions, mingled in luxuriant growth. Magnolias and holly bloomed beneath the oak trees. Persimmons and apples flourished as if each challenged the other in a contest of Epicurean delight.

It was thought that this renewed interest in the territory west of the Alleghenies to the Great Plains warranted the writing and publishing of this book, called *Penn's Woods West.*

It is our land to love and enjoy. We shall, as is the custom among men, henceforth gather the seasons into years, the years into centuries, each bearing a number and a name—Twentieth Century, Fortieth Century, Two Hundredth Century. If man does not despoil it, this so lovely a country shall endure until "the earth is laid waste and the heavens are overturned." Each year for all time the earth will be awakened at springtime, and after the summer sunshine, be wrapped in the scarlet robes of autumn, and fall asleep beneath the white blanket of winter.

❋   ❋   ❋

The sun moves toward the horizon of the South!
Its arc is low; its daily journey brief.
Morning is crowding close on night, and
Day retreats toward advancing shadows.
The frigid North presses ever southward.
As the sun fades, all life feigns death;
Leaves fall, birds go, grass withers, life retreats,
    death advances.
At last, a white shroud covers the cold, rigid earth.
It is the end!
The sun returns, riding glorious in the high sky,
Pushing morning and evening far apart,
Driving back the night, driving north the cold,
Lifting the white shroud and kissing the earth awake.
The new-born Spring arises, smiling with blue skies,
And life triumphant renews itself to all eternity!

November 7, 1957   A. W. ROBERTSON
Pittsburgh, Pennsylvania

1

BEGINNINGS

PENNSYLVANIA MEANS MANY THINGS TO DIFFERENT people. To one it means the glow of steel mills along the Monongahela at night or strip mines in Venango County or the milky water of the Clarion at Johnsonburg. To another it means the trout streams of Centre County, duck hunting at Pymatuning, a cabin on the upper Allegheny, maple trees at Myersdale in autumn, the long beach bordered by cottonwoods at Presque Isle, or the ski slopes at Ligonier when the snow lies deep upon the mountains. Or it means an eagle seen from Mt. Davis fighting its way through a thunderstorm, a deer starved and winter-killed in Elk County, acres of trillium along Thorn Creek, or the pink mountains of Bedford County when the wild azaleas bloom. For each of us there is a favorite picture or recollection. Mine takes me back a good many years.

I was in Miss Murphy's class in the sixth grade when I first learned the etymological meaning of the word *Pennsylvania*. It was a spring day, I think, for I remember on her desk a yellow mixing bowl filled with violets. We would not have picked them for any other teacher, but Miss Murphy was different. She didn't paddle us, and she explained things we wanted to know about squirrel nests and flowers and the tracks of animals in the sand along the creek. She always had green things growing on her window sills—geraniums and ferns and moss with little red blossoms under a turned-over fish bowl. We were glad to water the green things when we washed the blackboard.

On this morning that I remember, she said, "Do any of you know what the word *Pennsylvania* means?"

No hands went up.

Miss Murphy had a way of looking at something we never saw. She did that now, looked far off past the green things on the window sills.

"It means," she said, "Penn's Woods. It means a green forest that once belonged to William Penn, a green forest that covered all the mountains and all the valleys from New Jersey to Ohio. It even covered this hill where our schoolhouse stands."

She went on to tell about the land of William Penn, its maples and oaks and tall pines, its streams and rivers that anyone could drink from, its deer and passenger pigeons and wild turkey and bison roaming in great herds, and the dark loam that covered the forest floor and that stored the water for the days of drought. While she talked, she looked out of the window much of the time as though she could see there the things she told us about, and soon all of us in the room began to see with her.

I could see the mysterious shadows of the forest and among them the ferns and little hemlocks. I could hear buffalo padding along their paths, could hear pine cones tumbling to the soft earth, could smell the scent of pine in the air. There were Indians around with bows and arrows and with eagle feathers in their hair, but they were friendly Indians who didn't scalp people and who got along very well with trees, arbutus, and elk.

"In many ways," she said, "the Indians were more intelligent than we are. They used only what they needed. They killed only what they had to kill. That was the way God expected everyone to be, or maybe He wouldn't have made us."

I thought she was talking specially to me. The week before, I had killed an owl and had told Miss Murphy about it.

She had looked at me a moment and then had looked out the window. After awhile, she said, "Why? Why? did you do it?"

I did not know why, and since I was suddenly ashamed, I said nothing.

She laid her cool hand on mine. She said, "The owl is your friend. It's good to you. It helps you. You killed a friend. Maybe, if you think it over, you'll be sorry. Tell me about that, too." Then she took her hand away.

But now she was talking about the land again, the trees and streams, and I could feel the greenness and coolness of them and the peace of the earth the way God wanted it to be. I began to feel sorry for the kind of people who killed owls and dug out

3

green forest once covered the mountains and all the valleys

Jack-in-the-pulpits and threw sunfish on the bank to die. I would never again kill an owl. I even wondered about picking violets.

"Penn's Woods," she said, looking at the yellow bowl of blue violets. "You live in Penn's Woods West. Be good to it today, tomorrow, and when you grow up. Then it will be good to you. You will be happier if you are good to it." She touched the violets gently with her hand. "And now," she said, "let us open our history books."

✿　　　✿　　　✿

About ten years ago I had a letter from Miss Murphy, but she was no longer Miss Murphy. She was living in the mountains of North Carolina with her son and his wife. She had just read a book I had written, and she was glad that I no longer killed owls for the fun of doing it. I wrote back and told her about the morning she talked of Penn's Woods. That was a beginning.

I wish I could write to her now and tell her about the book Tom and I are going to do, this book, in which we hope to become better acquainted with our home—with its goodness to us, and with our responsibilities to it.

Next week we make our first trip together. Ray may go along. We want to learn more about this beautiful part of Pennsylvania we live in—the old mountains and green valleys, the bright rivers, the mountain laurel and rhododendron blooming in late spring, the wildflowers, the birds and animals and moths and butterflies, and the peace that comes over the forests early of a summer evening. We want to know more about these things around us and about our relation to them.

Are they only luxuries, or are they important to us, practically, psychologically, esthetically, philosophically, and are we important to them? How long will they last? How long will we last if they go?

SPRING

LEO

THE LION

THERE HAVE BEEN MANY SIGNS LATELY THAT SPRING has crept in upon us, almost imperceptibly, as it usually does in Penn's Woods West. Though the days and nights are still cold, and though in the northern counties snow still lingers in shaded valleys, the sun shines with a warmer light than it did a month ago and the earth is soft underfoot. Weeks ago in Butler County the skunk cabbages, those exquisite beauties with the vulgar name, were lifting their purple hoods above the snow. On almost any hillside, if I stand very still, I can hear the unseen trickle of water from wet-weather springs and can guess at their location by tufts of grass that are already green.

A few weeks ago there were sucker fishermen along the Conoquenessing. In Somerset County the sugar farmers have tapped their maple trees, and the sap is dripping even now into buckets or plastic bags. Yesterday in Fayette County, on the edge of a cornfield, I watched a ringneck pheasant with outstretched wing courting five hens indiscriminately, and on the way home a flight of robins overtook me, flying in a shifting but northeasterly direction.

Early this evening I went down into Jackson's hollow, hoping to hear the first, uncertain notes of the peepers, but there was none. Last year at this time they filled the hollow with a shrill announcement that, however cold the swamp water and however tardy the rest of the world, spring had arrived, and life for the cold-blooded vertebrates was beginning again with bright music and with primal love. But this evening the peepers were unwilling to commit themselves to music, to love, or to the calendar.

The truth of the matter is that if one wishes to be certain about spring he must look not to the earth but to the skies. And so tonight I walked up to the top of Anderson's hill to see an old friend, Leo, the Lion. Ordinarily, I do not seek the companionship of lions, but this lion is different. He does not even look like a lion. At the end of every winter he comes creeping up out of the eastern horizon early in the evening.

For a moment I could not find him. Then I took the two stars that form the *inner* edge of the bowl of the Big Dipper and followed their line southward for about eight times their distance apart. That led me, looking south, to Regulus, the bright star that forms the very end of the handle of a sickle. Above it are the rest of the handle and the blade itself, its cutting edge facing the south in the early part of the evening, the west at about midnight.

To the east of Regulus and a little higher in the sky is a lopsided quadrangle of stars (a triangle if your eyes are bad), and these represent the hindquarters of Leo, just as the sickle represents his head and chest. The distance from Regulus to the point of the sickle is about the same as the distance from Regulus to the first star in the quadrangle. Or, if you prefer, you can locate Leo's hindquarters by following the line made by the two *outer* stars in the bowl of the Big Dipper and extending it southward. It will take you to a point just a little westward of the quadrangle.

Out of the cold night of the east Leo climbs the heavens quietly to search for spring and warmth, to tell us of good things soon to come or already here—bluebirds and spring peepers and nesting rabbits and snow trillium and skunk cabbage and trailing arbutus and sap dripping from the maple trees in Somerset County. Some constellations are mysterious or profound or filled with things immortal. But Leo is a friendly constellation, searching for kindly, mortal things, warmth and love and the smell of April and all its wonderful beginnings, no cousin, no relation at all to

Tiger, tiger, burning bright
In the forests of the night

but rather a creature who moves gently through the night from east to west, reminding us that he, too, longs for all that we are looking forward to, "the time of the singing of birds," the time when "the winter is past."

Whether the peepers are in voice or not, the ascent of Leo tells us that spring has come. "Tell me," said Martial, "if you were to become a lion, what sort of lion would you be?" If I dared to answer, I should say, "I should like to be like the lion Leo, who speaks only of good things close at hand."

we drove the back roads

the tapping had begun

Sugar Camps

ON A SUNNY DAY IN SPRING, VERY EARLY SPRING, TOM and I were on our way to Somerset County, there to watch the magic rites of maple sugar making. In spite of the sun the air was cold, and the night before there had been a heavy frost, perfect weather for the rapid flow of sap. The tapping had begun, this year, in early February, after the first warm thaw. By the end of March the occult operation of making the best maple syrup in the world would be at an end.

We drove the back roads instead of the highways, so we could drive slowly, looking for signs of the new life that would soon be upon us. March, though, is a month of expectation rather than of fulfillment. We must wait for April to show us Thoreau's "natural resurrection."

As we drove along we did occasionally see clumps of skunk cabbage, sure signs for those with faith, and once Tom insisted he had seen a chipping sparrow. At Champion a bluebird streaked across the road, the redness of his breast more noticeable than the blueness of his wings. Near Indian Head we stopped to look at a tawny chipmunk sitting upright on a rail fence and enjoying the warmth of sunlight on his gray belly.

Spring was close at hand yet hard to locate—a sensation rather than a visible reality, a premonition of things about to happen, foretold less by the bluebird and the trickle of hillside water than by the blue sky flecked with summer clouds and by the smell of warming earth and of decaying things ready to bring forth life. Laurel Hill Creek, when we passed it, was turbulent with melted snow, but not so turbulent as to discourage two youthful anglers who apparently preferred sunlight and sucker fishing to chalk dust

9

the Somerset keeler, oaken and strong

10

steam rose from the eaves of the evaporating shed

and an eighth-grade reader. Suspicious and experienced, they moved under the bridge when they saw us.

"Playing hooky has its points," Tom said. "I used to do a little myself."

And indeed it does have its points, if its destination is a woodland stream instead of a corner drugstore. It is a bright day stolen from time and added unto the life span of the boy, a day of sunlight and adventure—since no experienced truant plays hooky in the rain—a day when the truant from the blackboard learns things that never can be told in books: the goodness of wet earth underfoot and the blackness of it under the fingernails and the tentative song of the sparrow trying to recall a summer melody and the discovery of a wet cocoon—could it be a swallowtail's?—on a twig of black birch and the smell of marshy places and the hope of catching a giant sucker with red fins under the roots of a willow clump.

We drove on, remembering other times and other willow clumps, drove on through the rolling mountains of Somerset County towards West Salisbury,

past the hillside meadows, the rail fences, the snow lingering in steep ravines, and cloud shadows racing down one mountain and up another. And then, suddenly, we came upon the first sugar grove. It lay to the right of us and stretched at least a half mile down the road. The great trees rose against the blue sky in a tangled pattern of branches, fifty, seventy-five, perhaps a hundred feet high.

Beneath the trees the ground was clear of underbrush and dark with fallen leaves except where snow still lingered along rail fences. And hanging from each tree, about two or three feet from the ground, was a wooden bucket—the Somerset keeler, oaken, strong, and perhaps a couple of generations old. Clearly this was a farm that clung to tradition, for in most farms the oaken keelers have long since been replaced, first by galvanized iron buckets and then by plastic bags.

We turned off the road into a lane that wound through the maple grove, stopping from time to time so that Tom could take pictures of sugar water dripping slowly from little spouts into the oaken buckets, sweet water that would soon be on its way to the

11

evaporating kettles. A short distance down the lane we met the proprietor, busily pouring the sap from buckets into a horse-drawn tank. Yes, he said, we could roam around as much as we wished. Just send him a picture or two when we could. And don't forget to visit the evaporating shanty. That always made a pretty picture. He pointed with his arm through the trees.

We left him pouring the precious liquid into the tank wagon while the horses waited patiently, and we walked through the grove over the sodden maple leaves. In a few minutes we came to the shanty, a small building with vertical slabs for siding and a slab roof curled with wetness and green with moss. Steam rose from the eaves, and from inside came the sound of voices, women's voices.

We stepped out of the bright sunlight and into the steamy darkness of the shanty. For a moment we could not see well, but in a brick fireplace a fire glowed under a huge iron kettle of boiling sap, and

a woman stirred the bubbling sweetness with a ladle. She smiled at us as if visitors were not uncommon and went on about her business of stirring, and lifting the ladle to watch the texture of the drippings, and stirring again and lifting.

"That kettle," I said, "looks like an old one."

She looked up and smiled again. "Four generations," she said, and she tapped the kettle gently with one end of the ladle.

In the dimness beyond her, a young girl, very pretty, was stirring a thicker liquid in a trough that had been hollowed out of log. She was making maple sugar from the syrup and was as engrossed in her task as if she were working with molten gold. We watched them for awhile, the older woman moving the ladle round and round the kettle and constantly inspecting the condition of the boiling sap, the younger girl, eager but less experienced, learning the old rites from one who had learned them long before.

hollowed out of log

pouring the sap

At last the proper moment came, and the older woman swung crane and kettle out over the wooden trough, into which she and the younger girl ladled the amber fluid, and steam rose from the trough and blurred their faces. So, in the shadows of the sugar shanty, the mysteries of maple syrup production in Somerset County are passed on, generation after generation, from the older women to the younger; and so, too, the people of Penn's Woods West, sitting down at the breakfast table on an April morning, can count among their blessings a fresh supply of the best maple syrup in the world—not excepting that delectable but less ambrosial liquid produced in the state of Vermont.

Out again in the bright sunlight, we walked back to the car. The air smelled sweet and smoky. Far down the lane were the horses and the tank wagon and the farmer emptying the keelers. When I touched the horn of the automobile, the farmer turned towards us and waved good-by.

All the rest of the day we wandered in and out of sugar camps, large and small, young and old. The maple grove of the Wagner family was probably producing sugar in 1800. Now it is managed by Leona and Dorothy Wagner much as it was managed by their great grandmother. At five o'clock in the morning they light the fires, and they are busy at the camp until late at night. After the rush of syrup making is over, they begin their work on other maple products—maple creams and maple butter and sugar cakes made in wooden molds.

Then there is the Compton Camp. With little enthusiasm the Comptons have acknowledged the presence of the twentieth century by replacing the kettle with a modern evaporating system, but that has been their only concession to the atomic age. Respecting tradition, they empty their keelers into a sugar water wagon, and when they prepare sugar for their own table, they use the trough and kettle method of their fathers.

13

Of all the camps, the largest and most modern is George Keim's—with 1,000 acres, 4,000 trees, 8,000 plastic keelers, and pipelines to bring in the sugar water. The Keim camp produces 3,000 gallons of pure syrup every spring. But even here tradition dies hard. As we talked to Mr. Keim we noticed a team of horses drawing a wagon through the grove.

"My grandson," Mr. Keim explained. "He's old-fashioned. He doesn't like the pipelines and he doesn't like the tractor. He likes a good team and a sugar water wagon."

Under the gray trees we stood awhile, talking with Mr. Keim, watching the clouds through twisted branches, and listening to the chickadees—"sugar birds" in Somerset County—as they expressed approval of the maple grove. Then we said good-by and drove back to the highway. As we turned west towards Mt. Davis, I kept thinking of the young man whom we knew by a single sentence. "Mr. Keim's grandson," I said to Tom, "sounds like a true native of Somerset County."

Tom was polishing the lens of his camera. "We should have stayed," he said, "until we met him."

   ✻   ✻   ✻

And we should have, for he and his kind are part of the quality of Somerset County. That quality is hard to define. It is woodsmoke, sweet and heavy in the spring, hollyhocks and old-fashioned gardens and freshly-painted picket fences in the summer, the flaming reds and the maple yellows of the groves in autumn, and the tinkle of sleigh bells on lonely roads in winter. It is an old woman in a sunbonnet working in her garden, an old man with a full beard and a flat hat driving to an Amish church in a buggy, a young girl by the roadside, her complexion as clear as the skin of a winesap apple, and a young man who, in spite of pipelines and tractors, still likes "a good team and a sugar water wagon."

an Amish church

it flows slowly, as a meadow stream should

Thorn Creek

IN THE COURSE OF A YEAR THERE ARE MANY GOOD DAYS for back-road driving, but the perfect day is not common. It should follow a night of gentle rain, enough to settle the dust but not fill the road with puddles or the valley stream with silt. There should be a bright sun and a blue sky with a few, a very few, cumulus clouds. Some of the songbirds should be back—particularly the Maryland yellowthroats— so that even when you are driving you can see them flash along the roadside and hear brief excerpts from their songs. And a few of the wildflowers that come "before the swallow dares" should be in lusty bloom —if not the skunk cabbage, then hepatica or yellow adder's-tongue. Such days are rare and should be accepted whenever offered.

That was why, after we had crossed the bridge over Thorn Creek, we had left Route 8 and its smell of burned gasoline and had taken the first back road to the right and then, a little farther on, another road to the right.

"Maybe this is the way to the creek," Tom said. "It goes down into the valley."

"Let's try it," I said, for wherever it led us, the way looked good—a rugged, twisting dirt road, on its left a green valley in the sunshine, on its right a steep hill in shadow. Down we went, slowly enough to see along the edges of the road the white tufts of colts-foot blossoms gone to seed and clusters of bluets beside the fence, slowly enough to hear a treble "witchety, witchety, witch" from the valley and the tenor trumpet of a robin somewhere up the hill.

It was, indeed, a perfect day, with birds singing and flowers blooming and sunlight and shadows on the road, and at the bottom of the hill, as Tom had surmised, the blue of Thorn Creek shimmered among the willows. We parked the car then and walked across the wet grass to the stream. It flows slowly, as a meadow stream should, its long pools separated by sparkling riffles, its undercut banks the home of many a leader-breaking trout—for Thorn Creek,

15

though only thirty miles from Pittsburgh, is a good trout stream to those who know its ways.

We looked for rises but, seeing none, started walking up the stream. In sunny places the bluets had spread their colored lace across the pastures, and in shady places violets bloomed in velvet luxury—white and blue and yellow. Dandelions and orange ragwort brought sunrise colors down to earth, and every thicket was a gathering place for trillium, their blossoms white as summer clouds.

There is something special about spring flowers that sets them apart from the flowers of any other season. Perhaps it is the diffused sunlight of April and early May that accounts for their special loveliness or the dampness of earth and air or the coolness; or perhaps it is the courage of the fragile pioneers or their secrecy in coming unannounced or their reassurance that winter is but one of the four seasons. But on that perfect day for back-road driving, when we come upon them suddenly in spotted thicket or in sunny meadow, we do not care for reasons. It is enough that we see them and are glad. "I regard them," said Izaak Walton, "as Charles the Emperor did Florence, that they are too pleasant to be looked upon except on holidays."

We went back to the car and drove upstream another mile or two. Where the shore of the stream was sandy, two fishermen in white shirts were idly fishing a blue pool. We stopped and talked. They had not had much luck. But the day was good, one asserted, and the sun was warm, and they were having an excellent time. Another mile or two along the road and we came to an iron bridge across the stream. Above the bridge were two more fishermen. They had been more fortunate than the two downstream—six trout, they said, and they had been fishing only a couple of hours. They were good worm fishermen, deftly drifting their baits along the bottom of the pool.

While we watched, the younger man had a solid strike, and Tom began to focus his camera. There were two or three sturdy rushes across the creek and up, deep rushes towards the bottom, but after a time it looked as though the trout had weakened. A black fin cut the surface of the water in a heavy swirl, the leader rose, desperately taut, and I heard Tom's camera click. Then the line went limp.

"I told you," the older fisherman muttered. "I told you to use a heavy leader."

The younger man laughed. "He *was* a good one, wasn't he? Never mind, there's a bigger one than that in this pool. I know. I lost him, too. Yesterday." He laughed again.

"I told you," the older fisherman answered. "There's some big ones in here. You ought to use a heavier leader."

a gathering place for trillium

16

We chatted awhile with the two anglers, one eager, one content, and then we got into the car and drove on. The road took us away from the stream, but we did not care, for we knew we could circle around to it again or turn back. Off to our left a white barn shone in the sunlight. Cows grazed in the pasture that stretched between us and the barn, a green pasture flecked with blue.

At the next crossroads an old man in a country store supplied us with a lunch of milk and crackers and with conversation about the weather, the President, and the state of the local Grange. We left then and selected the road to the right because it led downhill and because, not far away, a rail fence took our fancy. All afternoon we drove and stopped and walked, admired the dogwood blossoms and the misty shadbush, found hepatica among the shadows, wild phlox along the roadside, and the broad leaves of the skunk cabbage where the ground was low and moist. The birds were still pleased with the day and themselves, and we with both.

Surely there is no driving pleasure that can equal the unexpected curves and dips and rises of a country road. We passed half-hidden farms on blossoming hillsides, and white barns with rolling foregrounds of green and yellow ochre, and every now and then Thorn Creek appeared to our right or left, catching the warm blue of the sky and the pale green of willow clumps. Most of the time we were lost, but to be lost on a country road is pleasant rather than annoying. There is the mild thrill of the unexpected turn or the sudden view of valley and moulded hills or the sound of a farmer's axe from the darkness of a wood lot. And mingling with the unexpected are things known and good—snatches of familiar bird songs, a farmer leaning on his pitchfork, blue sky above us, and all around, in woods and fields, by roadside and streamside, the abundant wildflowers of Thorn Creek's gently sloping valley.

Late in the afternoon, without warning, our dirt road came to a concrete highway. Cars sped up and down the three lanes, their drivers looking straight ahead. They were not lost. They knew where they were going.

But perhaps we, also, had known where we were going. Perhaps we had not been lost at all. The roads that lead from city to city are straight and wide. But if there are roads from earth to heaven, I think they must be back roads, narrow and twisting, uphill and down, shadowy and sunny, and bordered now and then by trillium and dandelions.

colored lace across the pasture

We turned left on Route 8, got into line, pushed the speedometer up to fifty, and, like a thousand other motorists, kept our eyes straight ahead on the concrete highway.

Kooser Lake

IN THE EVENING SUNLIGHT OUR CABIN AT KOOSER looked bright and comfortable. We unloaded duffle as quickly as possible and, agreeing to return by nine o'clock, departed for the ways of our choice— Tom with his camera for the woods that surrounded the cabin, Ray and I with our rods for the lake about a quarter of a mile away.

The walk to the lake was pleasant. Catbirds were in full, imitative voice; high in a maple tree a thrasher was talking to the sun; and all along the road the trillium and wild phlox bloomed. Beside a trail that led from road to lake, rhododendron grew in dense thickets, and I tried to imagine how it would look in late June or early July, the pale pink blossoms and the burnished leaves mingling with the

from road to lake

shadows of pine and hemlock. In all of Penn's Woods West there could hardly be a lovelier sight than the rhododendrons of Kooser in bloom along this narrow path.

Ahead, we saw the lake, golden in the sunlight, and the white beach and three mallards that moved steadily away from us across the water, leaving twin V's behind them. We followed the path a little farther and then left it and sat down on a sunny boulder at the edge of the water. "This is nice," Ray said. "I like to fish from a rock."

He reached into his pocket and brought out a cardboard box with three worms in it. "Found them under the woodpile," he said. He threaded one on his hook and swung it into the water.

The ducks had changed their course now and were swimming towards the marshy inlet. Across the lake a few fishermen sat along the bank, occasionally drawing in their lines and casting them out again. That side of the lake was already in shadow. On our side, a few feet from the rock, a flotilla of water-beetles patrolled a patch of foam.

After awhile I put a hook on my leader, appropriated one of Ray's worms, and dropped the line into the water. The ducks were undecided about entering the inlet. Tails up and heads under water, they searched for food among the weeds. In the sky to the south a solitary cloud, catching the last of the sunlight, floated like pink fluff.

Ray lay back on the boulder. "Rock's still warm," he said.

I watched the shadows deepening about the fishermen on the other side of the lake. Against the horizon the trees were black and stiff, like cut-outs pasted on a kindergarten window of long ago. The half-remembered images of half-forgotten things are part of the pleasure of "fysshinge with an angle." Sitting on a rock we look down at a thin line that wavers in the water. The bright ripples move in upon us, and we watch them and lose them, and the line seems to cut into the flecks of sunlight but does not really move, and after a time, weary of deception and of faulty recognition, we give in to the mild hypnosis of dots of brightness hovering around a black point where line and water meet.

Then we look away and let the mind blur and rest and relax, and we let the quietly insistent images rise like bubbles from a pond, filtering upward from the dark—the dimly remembered boys with buckets

18

three mallards moved steadily away from us

picking wild strawberries from a sunny bank of no location; the friendly toad who lived under the front porch of a house not thought of for years; the foam of elder blossoms on a still pool where sunfish built their nests—Mill Run? Tub Run? or Shawnee Creek when Dr. Bowman lived there?; somewhere on a country road, the handful of bright cherries offered by a little girl who cried but could not talk; pasture roses, an almost forgotten haymow, and a rusted tin cup that hung from a pump with a wooden handle; the thud of a stricken owl as it hit the ground and a gentle voice saying, "Why did you do it?"; and a day of unremembered time and place when in the woods a thrush sang of things that no man understands.

There is much to be said for this kind of fishing, especially if the trout are in some other part of the

faulty recognition

19

stream or lake. Then the angler need not even trouble himself to attend his rod and line but can give himself over wholly to idleness, the dissolution of time, and the recollections that flutter aimlessly like butterflies along a dusty road.

The other side of the lake was in complete darkness now, and the horizon was a thin band of saffron behind the trees. Fireflies glowed along the shore, and from behind us whippoorwills were chanting. There was a smell of woodsmoke in the air.

Ray had been lying down. Now he sat up and lifted his rod. In the dimness he examined his hook.

"Worm's gone," he announced. He made no effort to put on the last worm.

"Quitting?" I asked.

"I guess," he said.

I raised my own rod and looked. "Mine, too," I said.

For half an hour we sat on the rock and looked out over the lake. A light wind had come up, and ripples swept quietly towards us and broke with little splashes against the rock. There was no sound from the fishermen across the lake, if indeed they were

still there. After awhile the saffron faded from the horizon and we could no longer see the trees.

We got up then and walked back along the trail and the road to the cabin. It had been a good evening for "fysshinge with an angle."

Tom was sitting on the front porch. "Any luck?" he asked, and before we could answer, "Beautiful woods back there."

"No luck," Ray said.

Here, too, whippoorwills sang, and fireflies danced, and inside the cabin a fire glowed in the fireplace. Above us the wind moved quietly among the treetops. "No luck," Ray said again, but it had been a long time since I had seen the rusted tin cup, the little girl, the front porch lost among the years, and the yellow mixing bowl filled with violets.

"I was thinking about tomorrow," Tom said. "Maybe we could drive over to Mt. Davis for a couple of hours. That's the highest point in the State."

We agreed that it was the highest point in the State and that we should go there.

Tom leaned back against the porch post. "Gosh," he said, "it was pretty back there."

cabin at Kooser

20

sails above a lake

Mt. Davis

"I AM IN LOVE," HE HAD SAID, "WITH HIGH, FAR-SEEING places." I remembered Ficke's words as Tom and Ray and I stood on the fire tower of Mt. Davis. Ficke would have liked it here, for of all the hills and mountains in Pennsylvania, Mt. Davis is closest to the sky. From its height of 3,213 feet we could see much of earth and much of heaven. Ridge after rocky ridge streaked away towards the horizons, gray ridges where even the wind-blown pines had trouble keeping their balance. And directly below us were acres of gray boulders and stunted trees not yet in leaf and pines twisted into grotesque shapes from winter winds and ice storms. On the tower we stood so high that the earth seemed to slip away from us and to tumble downward, gray and green, towards the sky beneath.

How much earth there was as we looked down, but then as we looked up, how much sky!

We had our choice of "green calm below, blue quietness above." But since we had climbed the rocky road and the steep stairs to get as close to the sky as possible, it seemed a shame to spend our time looking at the earth.

Some of the best scenery of Penn's Woods West is in its sky. The view is best not when the sky is a calm and monotonous blue, but when the blue is merely a backdrop for those airy vagrants that drift above the earth. Time after time they change. Some stretch flatly across the sky like ripples on the sand at Presque Isle; others rise mysteriously like mountains being born. Some travel in the select company of their peers; others move in isolation and solitary grandeur. Some are so high and tenuous that they seem to have no relation to mortality; others are so down-to-earth that we can walk with them in the green valleys. And the Latin names they go by may whisper like the riffles of a trout stream in the morning or may rumble like the incantations of a waterfall in darkness.

Cirrus clouds are high and are as delicate as the

21

like ripples on the sand

airy vagrants

"lock of hair" which names them. Drifting in thin air as high as seven miles up, they are so filmy that when they cross the sun they do not even blur it and they cast no shadow on the earth. When they alone are in the sky, the day is fair and so is the promise for the next day. There are times when this forecast from cirrus seems strange. As we stand on a hill in summer, with heat waves shimmering in the valley below, it is hard to believe that the promise of tomorrow's sun and warmth is coming from a cloud composed entirely of ice crystals. Up there, the temperature is seventy degrees below zero.

High winds sweep cirrus into varied forms. Sometimes they fan out like the leaves of a maidenhair fern or like the wing feathers of a duck in flight or like the familiar "mares' tails," by which they are often called, that stream after the invisible weather-horses of the sky.

Also high in the blue are the icy sisters of cirrus: *cirrostratus* and *cirrocumulus*. The fine white veil of cirrostratus sometimes covers the sky for tens of thousands of square miles. This is the cloud whose frozen crystals throw a halo around the sun or moon. Though it is too frail to dim the light of day, its ring around the moon or sun often forecasts the approach of bad weather.

As cold and frail as cirrostratus is cirrocumulus. Frequently cirrocumulus takes the form of a "mackerel sky"—small, rounded clouds arranged in bands like the scales of a fish or like the ripples of sand on a beach and promising, like its sister, bad weather in the morning. An old weather rhyme tells us that

> Mackerel scales and mares' tails
> Make lofty ships carry low sails.

though another informs us with equal assurance

> If woolly fleeces spread the heavenly way,
> No rain, be sure, disturbs the summer's day.

And so we take our choice between rain and sun and, at the same time, between pessimism and optimism.

ring around the sun

The middle clouds, too, may promise fair or foul, but like cirrus they remain aloof in the troposphere of weather. At 20,000 feet *altocumulus,* the "billow cloud," rolls wave after airy wave across the ocean of the sky, but none of its moisture reaches the earth. *Altostratus* snows across acres of blue, but none of its crystals reach field or forest or city street. For the moisture in the high clouds remains forever frozen, and the moisture from the middle clouds evaporates before it touches the earth.

It is the lower clouds of the sky that wrap the earth in a gray mist, that pelt the ground with rain or hail, that fill a wood with whiteness. The *stratus* cloud is closest to man, often within touch as well as sight. On clear nights in spring or fall or on chilly mornings before the sun has warmed the ground, stratus fills the valleys with fog and wraps mankind, walking early or very late, in primordial mist—for so

the fog covered the face of the earth in the days of the giant ferns. In summer, stratus spreads a gray ceiling across the sky, and the sun then rides above the ceiling like a pale ghost of no substance, unreal, indifferent, and remote.

Cumulonimbus is the threatening one, the thunderhead. Moulded of misty ebony and ivory, it rises like disaster in the sky, rolling thunder in its convolutions and cracking whips of lightning. It is then that the wise camper, having seen the vision, repairs discreetly to his tent, tying the flap behind him, there to ruminate upon the vagaries of the thunderbird but meanwhile holding down the center pole.

But of all the clouds at whatever level, not even excepting the dramatic cumulonimbus, none is so impressive in its ability to build memorable images as the fair-weather *cumulus.* It is cumulus that moves in a fleet of puffing sails above a lake, like the seeds

in primordial mist

time after time they change

of a dandelion blown all at once into a slow current of air. It is cumulus that towers into the sky like a solitary iceberg, that forms in a great snowbank on the crest of a hill, or that mushrooms ponderously miles high as if determined to occupy all space.

It was cumulus that Shakespeare remembered as "a towered citadel" and Tennyson as "a looming bastion fringed with fire," cumulus that Wordsworth saw on the day of daffodils when he wandered "lonely as a cloud," and that John Keats saw on a starry night when death seemed near—"huge cloudy symbols of a high romance."

Whatever the day, whatever the hour and the cloud, we miss half of nature's scenery if we keep our eyes upon the earth. We know that there is a world above men's heads, and we want to see it. And so, to get from a day spent out of doors all that the day can offer, we let our eyes slip impartially from earth to heaven, and from heaven to earth. In cloud-gazing as in stargazing, there is a danger one may lose his footing and his balance. For perfect equilibrium, physical and mental, man needs the ground as well as the sky, and so we came down from the fire tower to the earth, remembering with comfort that the rest of the day was not lost and that, though the heavens declare the glory of God, it is the firmament that showeth his handiwork.

      ❖   ❖   ❖

As we started back for Kooser Lake, Tom said, "Maybe tomorrow we could run down to Ohiopyle. That isn't far from here." He looked at us hopefully. The look and the plaintive note in his voice settled the matter. In the morning we would "run down to Ohiopyle," the great falls of the Youghiogheny.

25

from precipice to precipice

Ohiopyle

IN THE MORNING KOOSER PARK WAS SO ATTRACTIVE IT was hard to leave. Sunlight came through the trees in scattered splotches and shone brightly on leaves still wet with dew. Near the cabin the trillium looked fresher than they had the day before, and all around us, birds were singing as if there would never be another time for song.

Nevertheless we departed for Ohiopyle, taking a route sufficiently indirect to give us for another hour or two the pleasures of an April morning in the woods. A few minutes after leaving Kooser, we were driving slowly through Laurel Hill State Park with its clear streams and its four thousand acres of wooded peacefulness. We walked a mile or two along one of the trails, looked for wildflowers, listened to the murmur of Laurel Hill Creek as it flowed through the shadows. In the car again we took a dirt road that crossed Indian Creek and brought us to Route 381. There we turned south and in a short time arrived at the little village of Mill Run, where the few houses hid behind pines and rhododendrons. Then came the long grade down the mountain to Ohiopyle.

Even before we entered the town itself we could hear below us the roar of the falls, for the village of Ohiopyle is located on a narrow neck of land around which, for nearly two miles, the Youghiogheny River rushes in a narrow U. The neck of land is an extension of the mountain where the rapids and falls begin. By the time they have ended, they have dropped a distance of ninety to a hundred feet, forty of them in a single plunge. Nowhere else in Penn's Woods West is there such a display of falling water, its power, its fury, its thundering white roar.

More than two hundred years ago George Washington left Virginia and explored the upper reaches of the Youghiogheny in the hope of finding a water passage from his Great Meadows camp to the forks of the Ohio. At first, he found that the river was "narrow, has many currents, is full of rocks and rapid," but concluded that it would "not be difficult to cross it with canoes." Then he came to Ohiopyle. There, as he surveyed the tremendous falls of the Youghiogheny, he changed his mind about the advantages of the river route, and because he changed his mind, the armies of Washington and of Braddock eventually took the difficult mountain route towards Fort Duquesne and bitter defeat. What would have happened, one wonders, if Washington, standing on the brink of the falls, had elected to make the hazardous portage and to continue on the river route.

For hours we wandered around on the peninsula and looked at the falls from different vantage points. We looked for trees and shrubs and wildflowers not known to the regions north of Ohiopyle, for here many plants of the south reach their northern limits. And we walked about the town among the white houses with laurel and rhododendron and pawpaw trees on the front lawns. Wherever we went, the roar of the falls was with us, millions of gallons of water tumbling from precipice to precipice and boiling at the base of each in mist and white foam.

Back at the car we took our last look and then began the long climb up Laurel Ridge towards Kooser. But somehow the sound of roaring water stayed with us long after we had left it.

on the brink

little waterfalls and quiet pools

Rolling Rock

THE NEXT EVENING I LEFT TOM AND RAY AND DROVE over to Rolling Rock Club, there to have dinner with Leland Hazard and with Ted Weeks, the great and amiable editor of *The Atlantic Monthly*. Rolling Rock is an excellent illustration of what private enterprise can do to preserve for future generations the green and productive land of Penn's Woods West.

Before the white man penetrated the wilderness, the land that is now Rolling Rock Farms was a great forest of mixed hardwoods, and the town that is now Ligonier was an Indian village called Loyalhanna Indian Town. Shawnee and Delaware roamed the forests of Chestnut Ridge and Laurel Mountain and the trails along the Loyalhanna. Guyasuta, the Mingo chief, knew the mountains and the great valley between, and not far away had lived Kickenapaulin, the Delaware.

Then through the deep shadows of the woods came the white man and his rifle. By 1758 the Indian town of Loyalhanna had disappeared and in its place stood Fort Ligonier, the chief supply base between Fort Bedford and Fort Pitt. In that year Christian Frederick Post wrote, "We went the path that leads along *Loyal-hanning* Creek, where there is a rich fine Bottom, Land well timbered, good Springs and small Creeks. . . ." It was the kind of path that settlers had traveled thousands of miles to walk upon, the kind of land they dreamed of as they walked the dark trails westward. In 1772 David McClure wrote that "the settlement in the valley of Ligonier consisted of about 100 families, principally Scotch & Irish."

One hundred families needed land that was clear of trees, and so some of the great forest went down,

28

bordered with rhododendron

and the rifles that had fought off Chief Pontiac were laid aside, and the plow took over. The farms prospered in the rich valley, and the white men grew in numbers. A century later a busy country needed as much lumber as it could get—for houses, bridges, plank roads, railroad ties—and so most of the remaining timber went crashing down. Within a few years the green hillsides had become gray and barren. In the spring the small creeks and the Loyalhanna flooded and carried away the rich topsoil, and in the summer they settled into trickles of water in mud-caked stream beds.

As always, nature did its best to repair the damage. Very slowly, weeds and grasses and briars took foothold where the forest had once towered. After a time, when the soil had been adequately prepared by the low growth, trees began to fight for the land that had once been theirs. The streams still flooded in the spring but less violently. Barring another catas-

trophe, with neither help nor hindrance from man, nature would be able to complete the job of restoration within a few hundred years.

But presently nature received help in its effort to restore the land and streams to productivity. The Richard Beatty Mellon family organized Rolling Rock Club, and immediately thousands of acres of mountain side and valley came under the intelligent supervision and cooperation of man. Where nature had not been able to seed the mountain sides, man did the planting. Where erosion gullies were cutting deep, man placed impediments of rocks and brush, and the gullies began to fill. Where streams were silted and sluggish, man speeded up the flow of water with deflectors and little waterfalls.

Nature responded with renewed vigor. Birds came back to help with the replanting. Because of the vegetation and the water, insects came back and fed the birds. Because of the insects and the trees and

29

the cooler water, fish began to populate the creeks. Springs that had gone dry began to flow again, and ducks and herons returned to the creeks and deer and bear to the mountains.

Slowly, in the evening, I drove through the valley. The fields and pastures were green. Second-growth timber threw long shadows across the road. Along the edges of the creeks and under the shade of hemlocks, rhododendrons grew luxuriantly, and birds were singing everywhere. Two hundred years had made a difference, but much of the wonder of trees and singing streams had returned to the valley of Ligonier. Christian Post, were he granted the ghostly privilege of revisiting the valley, might still recognize "the path that leads along the *Loyal-hanning* Creek, where there is a rich fine Bottom, Land well timbered, good Springs and small Creeks. . . ." And he would find more deer, trout, and wild turkey than were there in 1758.

Leland's home looks out over the valley and up to the mountain range known as Laurel Mountain. Be-

fore dinner we sat for awhile on the patio and watched the storm clouds coming in from the mountain, dark clouds tinged with red and ominous purple. Then a wild wind took over the valley and tossed trees and shrubbery and hurtled leaves through the air and brought the heavy roll of thunder. With the first few drops of rain we went into the house and sat down to one of Mrs. Hazard's fine dinners. There was talk during dinner and after of books and trout fishing, of music and of plays, of paper mills and Boston and Thoreau and Hemingway, and of a new city growing up where the Allegheny and Monongahela meet. By midnight the storm had passed over and we were on our way to the Club. Leland was taking a late train to New York. Ted and I were to sleep at the Club and to have breakfast there before the trout began to rise on Rolling Rock Creek.

Shortly after sunrise Pete Woods and his Jeep met us at the Club and took us a winding mile down to Rolling Rock Creek—a small stream bordered with hemlock and rhododendron, beautiful in the morn-

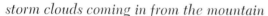

storm clouds coming in from the mountain

30

ing sunlight. There we parted, as trout fishermen should, and agreed to meet at an appointed place where Mrs. Woods would have lunch prepared for us.

After the sound of the Jeep had faded up the valley, I assembled my rod and greased my line and sat down on a rock to look at the stream for a few minutes before starting to fish. The creek had risen a little from the rain of the night before, but the water was clear. Directly in front of me it sparkled over the riffles and then swept into a shadowy slick under a mass of rhododendrons. Upstream, it spilled over a little dam at the foot of a long, dark pool. If there were any hatches on the creek, I could not see them, but as I left the rock and moved closer to the pool, a trout broke the quiet water under an overhanging hemlock bough.

I walked quietly up to the dam and then hobbled a few yards farther on my knees. A catbird lighted on the hemlock bough and sent a shower of drops to the stream. I waited a minute or two longer and then sent a Quill Gordon into the air above the hemlock. It dropped gently. Fly and leader drifted downstream without drag, and then, just as the Quill Gordon moved into the shadow, there was a sudden swirl, the flicker of a dorsal fin, and a tension on the line that made the lifting of the rod tip all that was necessary to set the hook.

He was a sturdy trout. Twice he took the direct route towards the head of the pool, and once he made a rainbow leap at the end of his run, but after two or three minutes he came to net and to release, thirteen or fourteen inches of golden, spotted trout.

So the morning went, with the trout rising vigorously in fast water or slow, and olive warblers darting among the trees and rhododendron leaves glimmering like burnished metal and in a grassy spot a fawn with lowered head and then the shadows of the rhododendron thickets again and the hemlocks that leaned over the water.

Late in the morning I saw Ted coming down the stream, and I stepped out and circled round him so that I could watch the master angler at work. He was fishing fast water with either wet flies or nymphs. I watched him send the fly across the stream and then, with rod tip low, search out every pocket and drift within his quarter circle. On the second cast, almost at the end of the drift, the rod tip bent, the line rose from the water, and a brownie leaped into the air. For a moment I thought he had shaken the hook or broken the leader, for the line slackened, but in an instant it was tight again as Ted

in a grassy spot

raised the light rod and stripped in line. Stubbornly the trout lunged upstream, tiring himself against the rush of white water. After a time he turned on his side and drifted back, head first, into the net—not all of him, though, for the great tail splashed the water outside the net.

Stooping, Ted released the noble fellow from hook and net. A moment later, in the pool below the riffle, a great V streaked across the surface as the defeated warrior returned to his lair among the rhododendron roots.

"That was a beauty," I said.

Startled, Ted looked up. Then his face relaxed. "It *was* a beauty, wasn't it?" He looked down towards the pool below the riffles, and I knew what he was thinking—that it was *still* a beauty, still the royal ruler of its green pool.

He came out of the creek, and we walked the quarter-mile upstream to the luncheon spot. Pete and Mrs. Woods were already there, as gracious among the pines as in their home. A fire crackled in the fireplace, the table was set, and on the table was an empty frying pan. "The trout?" Mrs. Woods inquired.

"I didn't keep any," Pete explained. "I thought you and Ted . . ."

The three of us looked towards the stream. "We'll be back in ten minutes," Pete said.

Ted took the riffle downstream, Pete the riffle upstream, and I the pool between. In ten minutes we were back with five brownies, cleaned ready to fry.

And in half an hour we were enjoying in retrospect as fine a luncheon as was ever served in any woods by any shadowed trout stream. Above us the birds talked quietly of things we did not understand, and we, ourselves, talked of things they did not comment on—of books and wines and Edith Sitwell, of

with neither strike nor rise

into the air

English chalk streams, New England lakes, and Pennsylvania rivers.

In the afternoon we drove down to the bridge that crossed the Loyalhanna, not so much in the hope of catching one of the monstrous brown trout that inhabit the stream as in the hope of finding the little river as beautiful as it is said to be. Under a broiling sun we fished the deeply moving pools and the wide riffles with wet flies, nymphs, and streamers. We drifted dry flies under the willows and beside half-sunken logs. But the big browns were wiser and more patient than we were. They would wait for dusk and big moths and foolish frogs and minnows in the shallows. For two hours we fished with neither strike nor rise. At five o'clock we clambered out of the stream and "went the path that leads along the *Loyalhanning* Creek" until we reached the bridge and the Jeep. Looking back, we agreed that though we had caught no trout, the Loyalhanna was not to blame. It is one of the loveliest little trout rivers in all of Penn's Woods West, one to remember on lonely winter evenings when the snow piles heavily along the window sill, one to return to on a May dusk when the shadflies dance above the water.

Back at the Club we shook hands and parted. Ted and the Woods were to spend the evening together, and I had promised to return in time to have a late dinner with Tom and Ray. Storm clouds were already gathering in the west as they had gathered the night before, dark, purple, and crimson. But as I drove back I knew that Rolling Rock Creek and the Loyalhanna would not flood unless a cloudburst struck them. Lush grasses and young forests cover their watersheds; the topsoil is spongy with humus; even the subsoil is honeycombed with roots. Much of the rainfall of two stormy nights will be stored away in a natural reservoir against the dry days of another month. Because a few men could not quite forget the woods and streams and mountains of their boyhood, thousands of convalescent acres of Westmoreland County have been restored to health in Penn's Woods West.

Ghost Plant

THIS EVENING AS I WALK ALONG A TRAIL THROUGH THE dim woods, I come upon a ghost flower, almost luminous among the shadows. Yesterday morning I walked this same trail and went past this same place, and I could almost swear that then no ghost flower bloomed under the great oak. Yet this evening he stands there, white, naked, and unnaturally beautiful, a vagrant from some nether world of phantoms and lost hopes.

For him, though, his shape and his pallor are entirely natural; he does, indeed, live upon death. He is a *saprophyte*. Devoid of chlorophyll and unable to manufacture his own carbohydrates, the ghost flower depends for life upon a fungus living with its roots, a fungus that in turn is saprophytic or parasitic and that feeds upon decaying matter, the humus of the woods.

Erect and naked, as waxy white as the hands of the dead except for a faint flesh pink in the cup of the blossom, the ghost flower rises from decay, extracts from death the essence of existence, and at last turns black before it, too, enters the land of the dead—which is the earth on which we live. For this, we have called him a *saprophyte*. The name is accurate enough, I suppose, but illogically discriminatory.

The violet and the daisy, too, live on the dead in the land of the dead, and so do the grasses and grains, and the rabbits and grasshoppers and quail, and the beef cattle that feed on the grasses and grains that feed on the dead. I kneel down before the ghost flower—only that I may see it more clearly in the dimness that is almost night. Like Edgar in the storm, he acknowledges what he is, life in its primal nakedness living on post-primal death. He is my sometimes forgotten brother. We come from the same parents, we *saprophytes*.

I get up and walk on towards the tent. The trail is soft and spongy. There is a faint, mephitic odor in the air. I walk among the living and the dead, and I am part of both.

33

across the footbridge to the Youth Hostel

Hostel

IT WAS DARK WHEN WE PULLED UP BESIDE THE CABIN in the woods. Ray and I had just driven the seventy miles from Pittsburgh to Ebensburg. Four other cars had preceded us. One after another, they had turned in from Route 219 and, taillights flashing, had bobbed along a dirt road to this space among the trees.

Two of the cars carried bicycle trailers. Back in Pittsburgh we had helped load them at the American Youth Hostel headquarters. By the time we got out of the car, the early hostelers were already wheeling their bicycles to the porch of the cabin. Over at the trailer we took the ones assigned to us and in the darkness started along the path with them. Once again I was surprised by the lightness of the English bicycle.

The path led across a footbridge, at the other end of which a group of shadowy hostelers, boys and girls, men and women, waited for a chance to get back to the cars for a second trip. As we passed them, the outside light of the cabin came on, bright enough to be blinding.

"Ken's got the cabin open," someone said.

From the bridge another voice called through the darkness. "How long till coffee?"

When we got inside the cabin, Ken was shaking the grate of the coal stove. He is a research chemist with cycling and hosteling as hobbies. Other people came in. John and Stewart and David are chemists, too. Dianne is an artist. Betty is a grade school principal. Gil and George are teachers. Susie is a junior in high school. Joan and Fran had just returned from a cycling tour of Europe. And so it went. There were seventeen hostelers of different ages and sizes and occupations but with one thing in common—all enjoyed looking at the earth from the seat of a moving bicycle.

For an hour or so, as we sat around the coal stove, there was talk about hikes along the Baker Trail and the Appalachian Trail, about cycling tours, about mountain climbing, and about canoe trips down the Allegheny or among Canadian lakes. It was the talk of people who moved through the country slowly enough to become familiar with it and to know and love it. As I listened I could understand why the hostel movement is popular. It is good for the older man who listens secretly to his heartbeats, since the hosteler may walk or cycle as slowly as he chooses and still reach the evening destination in time. For the adolescent it is the largest of recreation centers, bounded only by the earth and sky, where in the company of people of different ages he can make friends without the need of hovering host and hostess.

After a time the group began to thin out. Ray and I were among the first to go. We climbed the stairs to the loft, where there was a room for the men to sleep in and another room for the women. On the floor were mattresses. We found two near a window and unrolled our sleeping bags. The room was cool and musty smelling. Downstairs there was the quiet hum of talk, and through the opened window I could see the sky, bright with stars.

"A sleeping bag," Ray murmured, "makes you feel like a cocoon."

"Would you like to be one?" I asked.

"I don't know," he said. "I'll think it over."

Now there were many footsteps on the stairs, and shadows began moving quietly around the loft looking for places to sleep. Presently the shadows settled down, and there were sounds of sleeping bags being zipped shut. The air was getting colder, and the smell of must had almost left the room. The stars seemed brighter than before. From the sound of his breathing I could tell that Ray was already asleep, and then, after awhile, downstairs, as final as the winding of a clock, someone shut the stove damper.

In the morning when I woke up, the window was an oblong of dim light. Someone was shaking the ashes from the coal grate, and there was the sound of pots and pans being bounced around. In a few minutes we were downstairs helping seventeen other people to prepare breakfast and to pack lunches. An hour later, breakfasts eaten, lunches packed, and cabin door locked, we stood outside under the hemlocks in the cool morning air.

with John in the lead

Everything was wet with dew. The cyclists who were first mounted wheeled in figure-eights around the trees to keep warm while they waited for the others. Then one by one we coasted or walked across the footbridge and pedaled along the dirt road to the highway and the open sun. How warm the sunlight felt after the coolness of the hemlock grove! Strung out in a long line with John in the lead, we started up our first hill on a trip that would take us on a thirty-mile circle back to the cabin.

Oscar Wilde once said that America had produced Walt Whitman and the Rocky Mountains and should rest content. Well, as we started up that first long hill towards Carrolltown, I felt that England had produced Shakespeare and the English bicycle and should also rest content.

One after another the bikes click-clicked into low gear. Everyone pedaled at the same speed, the slow circle of the pedals barely keeping the wheels moving. Perched high on the seats, the weight of our bodies comfortably forward on the handle bars, legs moving up and down, we crept steadily up the hill.

I thought of the bicycle of my boyhood, the heaviness, the frenzied speed down the hill so that we could get partly up the next one, the sweat burning into our eyes, the last, desperate, full body-weight on the pedal as the front wheel began to wobble,

there was a road for us

36

and then the inevitable dismounting and the long push. Now I watched a frail girl ahead of me keeping pace with the men, and I realized that even with my unaccustomed legs, I should have no trouble going along with the pack.

At the top of the hill we stopped. It was a day of blue sky and drifting clouds. Beneath them the broad valley was banked by rolling hills. There were clusters of houses in the valley and a stream that sparkled and pastures where cattle grazed.

"Look," Ray said and pointed to the sky.

Against the blue, higher even than the hill we rested on, a hawk drifted down the valley in undulating flight. He was not, I think, on a hunting expedition. He seemed merely to be enjoying his flight along the airway, the warm sunshine, the vision of green, the effortless coasting down an unseen, airy road. We watched him until he was a wavering dot.

Again I looked down into the valley. There was a road for us, too, a coasting road as easy as the way of the hawk. Ken started off, and soon all of us were in motion. For awhile I kept my fingers on the hand brakes, watched the green of the hillside rushing past me, smelled the clean, fresh air, looked down at the berm of the road slipping by with blurry speed. At the top of the hill I had taken off my jacket, and now I could feel the wind tugging at my shirt, making it billow out behind me. As I gained confidence, I released my grip on the hand brakes and let the wheels spin as they would.

The floor of the valley moved towards us, white houses, barns, wide fields. If once I envied the hawk, I did so no longer. This was not cycling, this was flying. The road was too smooth to be real. It was a cushion of emptiness. The sun drenched us and the wind swept by, and there was a feeling of strength, of flight from the earth, of a journey that could not end until it had taken us to some unreal world of clouds and sunrise.

But after awhile the hill began to level off, as hills do. Our speed slackened. The wind was only wind now and not a flyway. Ahead was a flat road, a stand-

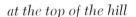

at the top of the hill

37

beside mountain streams

bright patches of dandelions

ard road made not of air but of ordinary macadam. Heaven over, I began to push the pedals, and the earth came closer—golden patches of dandelions along the roadside, a hillside, pink with scattered clumps of spring beauties, the sound of a flicker in a locust grove, a groundhog lumbering towards a log as we passed, once, the smell of unseen wood-smoke for a hundred yards or so, and often clouds of forget-me-nots that made the pastures seem more blue than green.

At a churchyard along the road we stopped for our first rest. There we talked of what we had seen, drank long drinks of water, stretched out on the cool grass and looked up at the sky. On our way again, we climbed the next hill and stood for a time looking down into a great basin among the hills. Below us, bright in the sunshine, lay Spangler, Barnesboro, Hastings, and Patton, the towns we would cycle through before we got back to Carrolltown, and be-tween them were fields of green and brown and winding dirt roads and orchards in full blossom.

Ken started down the hill first. We followed him, as we followed him all the rest of the day—downhill and up, along pastures where the wild mustard bloomed, past wooded plots where dogwood and shadbush flowered above rail fences, and beside mountain streams where trout fishermen waved to us as we passed. Though a member of the group, each of us, throughout the day, was alone with the wind and the sun and the road in that special kind of solitude that belongs, I think, only to the cyclist on a country road.

Early in the afternoon we ate our lunch at the edge of an orchard near Hastings. It was a beautiful spot except that someone before us had littered the ground with picnic plates and paper napkins. Betty gathered them into a little pile and burned them.

After lunch Ray wandered around taking pictures of blossoms and of friendly steers across the road.

When we were ready to leave, I looked around. Not a single piece of paper had been left at the luncheon site. Hostel people are good campers.

By the time we reached Patton, the shadows were growing longer and the valleys cooler. At Carrolltown women and old men were sitting on their porches, enjoying the last of the afternoon sunlight. Lilacs bloomed near the porches and filled the roadside air with their fragrance. Three boys and a girl were playing hopscotch on the sidewalk while an old airedale looked on without enthusiasm.

From the top of the long hill out of Carrolltown we looked down to the cabin road below. This time Ken did not stop at the crest of the hill. Behind him,

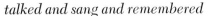

talked and sang and remembered

we hesitated a moment and then sped down the slope, the wind whistling in our ears, tree shadows flicking dizzily across the road, the cabin road coming closer and closer. In a few minutes we were wheeling our bicycles across the footbridge and up to the porch of the cabin.

That night, after dinner, we sat around a campfire, and talked and sang and remembered the day and its fullness—the hawk above the valley, the fog of bluets, the windy speed of the flight downhill, goldfinches and dandelions, the fisherman who waved, the smell of lilac blossoms, and a little girl in yellow pigtails who smiled at us as we passed through Barnesboro—a montage of details that would grow in meaning with the months and the years, that would become part of those who had seen and heard and felt, that would make nineteen people a little richer for the experience of thirty miles of cycling.

Ken and John were playing their harmonicas, Stewart was plucking at his banjo, and almost everyone else was fumbling with the half-forgotten words to a familiar tune. Dianne seemed to remember them best.

> *They hunt no more for the 'possum and the coon*
> *On the meadow, the hill, and the shore;*
> *They sing no more by the glimmer of the moon*
> *On the bench by the old cabin door.*

Knees up, I lay back on the wet grass. Above, lit by the fire, the gray branches of hemlocks quivered in currents of warm air. Through an open space among the branches I could see, even with fire-blinded eyes, the bowl of the Great Dipper. Both earth and sky were near, and between them was the lonely melody.

> *The day goes by like a shadow o'er the heart*
> *With sorrow, where all was delight.*

But for us there had been no "shadow o'er the heart;" for us, the birds had made "music all the day." There had been warmth of the sun, freshness of wind, and in our hearts, communion with other living things that share the earth with us—hemlocks and flickers, airedales and forget-me-nots, a girl with yellow pigtails, a hawk, an old man sitting on his porch.

Those who belong to a hostel group see much in the day and remember much in the evening. They are close to the ground and the sky. They use the sixth day and the seventh for a return to health and sanity. At night they sleep well. In the morning their faces are not drawn. They live longer and more richly, I think, than those who see the earth through a windshield.

the shadbush

40

dogwood in the valley

Strip Mines and Raccoon Park

IT WAS EVENING, AND WE WERE SITTING BESIDE OUR campfire at Raccoon State Park. The air was cool. Down in the valley the spring peepers were telling one another about their satisfaction with the evening, and in the faint moonlight we could still see the cloudy white of dogwood blossoms at the edge of the clearing.

All day we had wandered up and down the steep trails and along the narrow roads bordered with orange ragwort. Now, before the campfire, we remembered the bluebells and spring beauties and hepatica, the forested hills, the indigo buntings and warblers and the Baltimore oriole near the water pump, the lake and the fishermen along its shores and the white clouds reflected on its surface. Though only thirty miles from Pittsburgh, we saw no red glow in the sky and heard no shuffling feet or whining automobiles.

The moon was a slim crescent that did not blur the stars. Wind murmured in the treetops; down in the valley whippoorwills sang; and all around us were the indistinguishable sounds of the night—the rustle of dead leaves, little, scratching sounds, the snap of a twig broken perhaps by the paw of a raccoon, the throaty complaint of a bird distressed by unusual fireshine. When one sits by a campfire at night, he does not listen to the sounds around him: he absorbs them, becomes part of them, drifts gently into the spirit that brings them into being. In the heat of the fire the muscles of his face and legs relax; in the dimness of the night, the tensions of his mind are soothed into simple consciousness and a fluttering shadow from the fire is more real and more important than a half-forgotten decision of the day.

Thirty miles from the city, yet the world was so quiet that we heard the scrabbling of a wood mouse among the dry leaves of his home, the liquid snort of a deer unaccustomed to the smell of woodsmoke and of fellow creatures with two legs, and the faint trickle of water oozing from an unseen spring. We were content with quietness and with the sounds that make it clear. The peace of the woods, the calm of

41

up and down steep trails

the shadowy hills, and the depth of a night sky had settled over six thousand acres of land and over us who sat beside the pulsing embers of a campfire.

In the city, we knew, the streets were still bright. Driven by habit or compulsion, people moved rapidly from place to place in cars or on foot. There was something that had to be done—an appointment must be kept, a purchase must be made, a late meal must be eaten from table or counter. Among the countless musts, stunted newsboys shouted into a night of no moon or stars or shadowy hills, and men and women with drawn faces looked for the things all faces search for, half-forgotten but still remembered, hidden by a confusion of musts.

"Eight-thirty," Tom said. "I'm wonderfully sleepy. I think I'll go to bed." He got up and walked into the tent, his shadow grotesque against the drooping walls.

"I won't be long," I called after him.

All men, I think, should spend one week out of fifty-two in a tent among the trees or in a cabin near a talking stream. A vacation so spent has a psychological and therapeutic effect on the camper which he begins to feel within twenty-four hours of treatment. His world and his soul are no longer policed by *musts*. He may turn over after the first awaking and go to sleep again. He may get up and watch the sunrise or simply throw the flap of the tent back and watch the sight from his elbow in bed. He may take a walk before breakfast or go fishing, but he does not have to take a walk or go fishing. He might prefer to look for fungi growing on tree trunks or to watch a red squirrel leaping from branch to branch or to follow a mother 'possum on a conducted tour of the trails.

If he wants to eat three meals before dark, he does, but there is no social custom in the woods that says he must. If he wants dinner at four instead of seven, he has it at four—and then, if he wishes, he goes fishing until nine, or ten, or three, or he does not go fishing at all. He does not have to go to bed early because of an important conference the next day, nor does he have to stay up until the eleven o'clock newscast is over, and if he wants to go to bed at eight-thirty, he does not have to explain that he is not at all ill, that he is, as a matter of fact, in excellent health.

To be truthful, I like the eight-thirty retiring hour. It is then that the night sounds are at their best, and I have a longer time to enjoy them before everything fades into peaceful sleep, peaceful because the next day holds no deadline. Like too much medicine, too

a conducted tour

Washington County was a land of plenty

much of this freedom from responsibility might be enervating, might lead a man into downright, blessed laziness or serenity.

At about nine o'clock I put out the fire. The stars were bright. The young moon outlined the edges of a cloud passing over it, and the wind whispered among the trees of Penn's Woods West much as it did when Queen Alliquippa called the woods her home.

The next morning was chilly, a dew lay heavy on the grass. The sun promised a fair day, birds sang as if there might never be another morning quite so good, and a light wind shook drops of sparkling water from the trees. Down in the valley dogwood and shadbush fringed the woods with lacy whiteness.

We ate a leisurely breakfast while we warmed ourselves at the fire, and then, getting into the car, we set out for the land of desolation. In a few minutes we had left the wooded hills of Raccoon Park and had crossed by way of Route 18 into Washington County.

Long ago, Washington County was an area of green, rolling hills and fertile valleys through which flowed pleasant streams. Much of the land was in timber, but even in 1828 a quarter-million acres had been cleared and turned into rich pastures for the herds of Merino sheep that grazed in the valleys. In those days Washington County was a land of plenty. There were prosperous farms and good schools and stone churches and woolen mills. There was a college in Canonsburg and another at Washington. There were grist mills and distilleries and fields of wheat and rye and oats. In 1840 more than 220,000 head of sheep yielded more than a half-million pounds of wool.

And all the wealth of Washington County came from a few inches of topsoil that lay on the hills and on the valleys. It was the topsoil that made possible the oak groves, the fields of grain, the schools and churches, the grist mills and woolen mills, and, most important of all, though no one thought of it, the streams of pure water that flowed through the valleys.

There was, though, another source of wealth that lay only a few feet under much of that precious and life-giving topsoil—a rich vein of bituminous coal.

43

where strip miners dug out the coal and left unnatural gullies

Its presence had been known even to the pioneers of the eighteenth century, who saw it cropping out on the hillsides and who mined it in a desultory way.

As coal became more and more important in the life of industrial America, the relative value of the topsoil seemed to diminish. Farmers found an easy way to wealth. They could sell their land to the coal operator and then retire in financial security to a house in the village. Thousands of them did so. All over southwestern Pennsylvania, coal operators moved in to mine the coal that America needed. In those days no one realized that poverty and desolation might follow in the wake of the stripping machines, that towns and cities might perish, and that life might become impossible over large areas of Penn's Woods West.

The machines moved in, felled the trees, tossed aside the golden topsoil, dug out the coal, left un-natural gullies, and moved on. Now the forests and green pastures were sterile mudbanks and chasms. Even weeds had trouble getting their roots into the clay and shale. The deer, rabbits, quail, grouse, and songbirds left the devastated areas. Silt and sulphuric acid filled the streams, poisoned the fish, drove away the wildfowl. What had once been a land of plenty was a barren desert.

We did not talk much as we drove, for a great sense of depression had settled over us, as it settles over almost anyone who drives through this desolate country. Once we stopped the car and turned off the engine so that we could listen to the silence.

Silence is usually a monotony of sounds so familiar that we hardly notice them. At home, silence is made darkly audible by the hum of the refrigerator, the slow ticking of the clock, the rustle of the curtains before an open window. In the woods it comes to

44

life with the rustling of leaves, the cracking of twigs, the nearly inaudible sound of burrowing moles, growing grass, and whirring insect leaves, the high murmur of wind among the treetops. But here in the morning sunlight no sound made the silence dramatic. The topsoil was gone. There was no bird to sing, no leaf to rustle, no bee to thunder through the emptiness. The silence was absolute.

We drove on through the desert, sometimes passing abandoned farmhouses, sometimes crossing sulphurous streams. At Burgettstown we stopped for lunch and heard talk of impending disaster for the whole region. The Dinsmore Dam was being closed. Drainage from strip mines in the watershed had polluted the water supply of Burgettstown. There was a chance that the city could tap into a line from the West Penn Water Company, but the Company did not have enough surplus to supply more than about a third of the town's needs. The loss of trees and the spongy topsoil had been costly.

A great chemical company had already moved out of the area. New industries, desperately needed to preserve the life of Raccoon Valley, could not be induced to come to a land of desolation, shale, and dryness. Economic collapse seemed close for much of southwestern Pennsylvania.

Outside, on the streets, we heard men talking about State aid and Federal aid and about the $300 performance bond. It is the bond, of course, that holds the key to the future of the strip mining districts. At present only a $300 bond per acre is required by the coal operator to guarantee partial restoration of the topsoil by backfilling and tree planting. Many operators find that they can make a few dollars more by forfeiting the bond instead of obeying the law. And so the land is rendered dry, sterile, and dangerous for the generations that follow.

Thousands of square miles of Penn's Woods West will be saved for our agricultural and industrial development on the day the State Legislature doubles

Dinsmore Dam was being closed

45

the performance bond from $300 an acre to $600. The solution is as simple as that, they were saying. But unless it is reached quickly, much of the southwestern part of Penn's Woods West, for the next hundred years or longer, will be a barren wasteland unfit for either farm or factory, unfit for human life.

As desolate as the land itself, we left Burgettstown and drove towards the holdings of the Harmon Creek Coal Company. We had been told much about the model operations of this company, about its backfilling, grading, and contouring and about its experiments in reforesting. We had met Jim Hillman and knew him to be a conservationist as well as a coal operator. "Maybe we make a little less on a ton of coal," he had said, "but we can look back and not be ashamed. And in the long run, we'll be ahead." Nevertheless, as we pulled up at the office of the coal company, I was not hopeful.

Ned Davis greeted us. "Hop in," he said, pointing to his car. "I'll give you the grand tour."

A few minutes later we were on our way down the road. A left turn took us into the Harmon property.

There we bumped along a shale road and presently entered a deep canyon that had been gouged out by a mechanical monster that was working even then at the far end of the canyon. We drew close to it, watched it scoop out tons of rock at a time and pile them high at the rim of the ravine.

"It looks like all the rest of the land we've been through today," I said.

"There's a difference, though," Ned said. "After we take the coal out, this gulley will be filled in and graded and contoured. Then we'll plant the hillsides. I'll show you—now."

He turned the car around and we left the ravine. In a few minutes we were at the Harmon nurseries, where there were row after row of multiflora roses, pine seedlings, locust seedlings, and Russian olive seedlings.

"The Russian olives," Ned said, "are an experiment, but they're working out very well. Now let's look at some of the reclaimed area. You'll be surprised."

Again he turned the car around, and we drove into acres and acres of reclaimed land. The change was

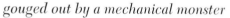

gouged out by a mechanical monster

46

where pines had taken hold

startling. Hillsides and terraces sloped quietly into valleys, and the hillsides were spotted with green where little pines had taken hold. There were no gullies, no gray cliffs. Sometimes whole hillsides were green where alfalfa and grasses had been carefully started, and among them stood pines three or four feet high.

"We like to get grasses and alfalfa started first," Ned explained, "to stop erosion. After that we plant the trees."

"This is wonderful," Tom said. "It's hard to believe."

"Oh, this is new stuff," Ned said. "Wait till we get to the established places."

"What about the expense of operations like this?" I asked. "Doesn't it eat into your profits?"

"A little, maybe," he said, "but not too much. It's surprising what you can do with very little—if you know how. And then," he added, "think of the value of the reclaimed real estate."

For half an hour we drove along the shale road, hardly believing what we saw, and then we came to the older parts of the restoration. Along the roadside, weeds and grasses grew, and in one place there was a clump of interrupted fern. Pines marched up the hillsides, and locusts, even taller, were just beginning to show green on the hilltops. Ned stopped the car for us to look. Off to our left a pheasant honked.

"We raise a lot of pheasants, too," Ned said. "The hunting's pretty good here."

A flock of goldfinches passed us in darting, black and yellow flight. "Look!" Tom shouted, pointing ahead. "A deer."

"We have a lot of deer," Ned said. "They like the alfalfa, and we try to contour the land so they have some waterholes." He started the car again. "The lake," he said. "I think you'd like to see that, too."

We drove on among the forested hills, bright in the sunshine. Sometimes the roadside notes of the Maryland yellowthroat flickered into the car, and we

"water's precious, almost as precious as the coal"

leaned back in our seats enjoying the green as it flowed past, knowing that near Burgettstown, Penn's Woods West was being born again.

And then we came to the lake. It was not a large lake, but with the reflections of clouds moving across its surface, it looked like a bit of sky come down to earth. Grass grew luxuriantly clear down to the water's edge, tall willows, already in leaf, cast restful, afternoon shadows along the shore, and out in the middle of the lake two mallards moved away from us in rippling V's.

"It's a good bass lake," Ned said. "The water's cool, and there's plenty of food. The ducks and deer like it, too."

We got out of the car and walked across the suspension bridge that crosses the upper part of the lake. In the shadow of the bridge bass moved about among the water weeds.

"How deep is it here?" Tom asked.

"Deeper than it looks," Ned said. "Four or five feet. The water's always clear even after a heavy rain. Around here," he added, as we walked back to the car, "water's precious, almost as precious as the coal. After while, we'll have more of these lakes."

Half an hour later we were back at the offices of the coal company and were saying good-by. Before

we left, Ned pointed to a green ridge in the distance. "The whole countryside could be like that," he said, "if . . ." He did not finish the sentence.

It was twilight when we got back to camp. We built a fire and cooked our dinner. After awhile Tom looked at his watch. "Nine o'clock," he said. "I think I'll turn in."

I sat by the fire a long time. Whippoorwills were singing in the valley. The edges of the woods were misty with blossoming dogwood and shadbush. The smells of spring were in the air—of damp earth, of blossoms and growing things, of leaf mould decaying into topsoil, that vital covering of the earth's surface that makes life possible for worm and robin and duck and deer and toad and for millions of city dwellers who walk on concrete but whose destinies are tied irrevocably to a thin layer of leaf mould on top of barren rock.

Life is as precarious for man as for the spider and the fox, and only a few inches of topsoil separate us all from death. Those few miraculous inches give us most of our food, our clothes, our houses, our cocktails and silverware and radios, and the books we read and the shoes we wear and the cool water we drink. Without topsoil and trees on the hillside there

without the shadbush, no lights in the city

could not long be factories in the valley. Without the dogwood and the shadbush that blossom here tonight there could not long be lights in the windows of the city.

trees on the hillside

49

a swallowtail

Bog

WE WERE WALKING DOWN THE LANE THAT LED TO THE cranberry bog—Tom, Dick Hartman, and I. Dick is a botanist who knows, I think, the name of every living thing that is green. Though the sun shone, the western edge of the sky was overcast—dark clouds rolling in with the assurance that rain would fall before the day was over.

Down the lane we clumped in our hip boots. The lane was rutted, and in the ruts lay stagnant water where thousands of tadpoles clung to the mucky bottom. When we came up to them, they scurried for shelter that did not exist and then settled again on the mud. They would have to grow up quickly, for their aquatic home was already a trap of death. They would have to hurry. What would happen, I wondered, when the sun evaporated the puddles, when the mud cracked and curled, when dry elderberry blossoms drifted in the ruts? We left the tadpoles to the whim of sun and rain and walked on towards the bog.

A bog is a botanist's heaven, but in botany as in life, the roads to heaven are not smooth. Pin cherry and viburnum grew on the lane, and fallen trees lay across it. In some places, the ruts were knee-deep. Blackberry shoots in faded blossom drooped over the ruts and clung to our shirts as we passed. Mosquitoes and black flies took up stubborn residence on neck and face and drew blood from the backs of our hands.

"Only about a half mile now," Dick said, pulling at his boots, and we plodded on through the steam and sunshine. Once, we stopped to look at the tracks of a raccoon, at another time to photograph a dignified toad who sat, unblinking, in the shade of a tuft

a toad, unblinking

valley trembled on their stems. We stepped into the dimness, and everywhere we looked, at the base of a pine tree or under a young hemlock, the orchids bloomed, pink and luminous and lonely.

"I've never seen so many," I said.

"No one knows they're here," Dick said. His voice sounded out of place in the quietness. "No one comes here except a few botanists."

loveliest of native orchids

of grass—a wrinkled, gentle old fellow who, if he were as wise as he looks, would be wiser than the prophets. For all his friendliness, his quick tongue meant the end of life to flies and insects that came too close to him. We wished him a full stomach and time for philosophic contemplation and walked on until the lane came to an end in a grove of quaking aspens. There we turned left over a barren tract of rising ground where lichens mingled with awakening pigeon-wheat.

For the pigeon-wheat, early June is a time of mossy love. The males stand tall and proudly yellow-tipped, ready to dispense their necessary blessings to the waiting females. And beneath both, in this month of intimacy among mosses, grow the lichens, gray and splotched with carmine.

"It's over there," Dick said in a low voice, as if we were intruders in a land where the voice of a human being was unwelcome. We plodded up the knoll, the dry pigeon-wheat crunching under our boots. Part way up the hill a giant swallowtail posed for his picture with bright, extended wings. He who had once been the boldest of the caterpillars, protected by scent organs against even the birds, was now air-borne and would henceforth live on nectar until the day of death and tattered wings.

Ahead, at the top of the knoll, was a sweeping curve of trees, very dark with the gray-green of the tamarack and the blue-green of the hemlock. "They mark the outer edge of the bog," Dick said. "That's where the bog began." Above the curve of trees, the storm clouds had risen higher into the blue of the sky.

At the edge of the trees we stopped and peered into the silent darkness. Lady-slippers, loveliest of native orchids, glowed pinkly among the shadows, and though there was no breeze, wild lilies-of-the-

51

in a patch of sunlight he kneeled to look

He led the way slowly among the trees, following most of the time what seemed to be a deer trail. Now and then he stopped to examine a leaf, a stem. Sometimes he took us in half circles to avoid tramping through groves of ferns, and once, in a patch of sunlight, he kneeled to look, almost tenderly, at something on the ground. "No one else knows," he had said. And because no one else knows, the orchids live and thrive. In nature, every living thing has its enemies, and the worst enemy of the orchid is biped man who, out of thoughtless love, destroys with trowel or scissors what he would possess.

In a few minutes Dick stopped and parted the bushes ahead of him. "Look," he said quietly. "There it is."

It lay before us, black and mysterious in the sunlight, rimmed by a great circle of trees. Between the trees and the open water, filling all the space between them, stretched a level mat of sphagnum moss, bright green and golden brown and dotted with the purple blooms of pitcher plants. And in the center of the circle of moss glimmered the black lake, unruffled, steaming, flecked with patches of green

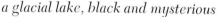

a glacial lake, black and mysterious

the abandoned beaver hut

scum. No leaf moved, no wind ruffled the still water, no sound came except the almost imperceptible whisper of swamp gas as it seeped through the sphagnum.

"It always looks the same," Dick said. "Even the abandoned beaver hut over there. And the deer trail that leads you in."

"How old *is* it?" Tom asked.

"Thousands of years. As old as the glacier. The glacier cut out the hollow, springs filled it with water, and the sphagnum began to grow along the edges. It's taken the sphagnum thousands of years to get that far into the lake. Back where it started, after it had laid down a thick mat, the trees began to grow, the larches and hemlocks. And then when the mat got thicker, new trees took hold and crept closer and closer to the lake. Look, you can see how they grew."

We looked. The trees formed a sloping amphitheater around the lake—old, towering trees at the outer edge of the circle, then shorter and younger trees, and finally, towards the inner rim of the encroaching sphagnum, little trees only two or three feet high, born to the task of extending the kingdom of the plants over the kingdom of a glacial lake. As we looked we saw the scars of ten thousand years of stubborn warfare and the battle not yet won. But the battle would be won, for nature was clearly on the side of the plants, and nature never loses.

"How long," I asked Dick, "before the whole lake goes?"

He shrugged. "Not long. A thousand years, maybe two."

For a few minutes we stood there in the midst of the silent, biologic warfare that had been going on for centuries. It would not be long before the end. Only a thousand years or two. But for nature a thousand years is only a lifting of the finger, a sigh, a moment between heartbeats.

"Shall we go out on the mat?" Dick said.

As we stepped on the sphagnum carpet, a quick sensation of dizziness came over me. I stopped, wondering what was wrong. Dick and Tom walked on ahead. Watching them, I saw what was happening. With every step they took, the mat of sphagnum swayed and tilted. A hundred yards away, little ripples showed that the shore of the lake was moving up and down, and there was a faint buzzing sound as the swamp gas filtered up through the wet moss.

53

the blossom of the pitcher plant

the leaves half-filled with water

I walked on after Dick and Tom. They had stopped at a pitcher plant, its blossom richly purple, and Dick was examining one of the bulbous leaves. The pitcher was half-filled with water, in which three beetles lay drowned. Hours before, in search of pleasant food, they had crawled into the neck of the leaf, where slippery bristles slanted downward, and had not been able to crawl back. Now they, themselves, were succulent dinner to this insect-eating plant that had lured them to destruction with the sweet smell of nectar glands. I thought of the toad that feasts on mosquitoes, of mosquitoes that feast on the blood of man, of man that feasts on the flesh of other animals. The pitcher plant was in reasonably good company.

For half an hour we walked around on the tilting bog and examined the vegetation characteristic of such a place—the leather leaf shrub, its leaves shiny gray above and leather brown underneath, the cranberry bushes whose delicate blossoms seemed too fragile to produce so luscious a fruit, the yellow spatterdock that had made a military coalition with the sphagnum to destroy the lake with green.

But of all the bog flowers none, I think, is quite so lovely as the sundew, for all its amoral conduct. It lies half-hidden on the sphagnum, the copper-gold of its leaves tipped with translucent, sparkling drops. Though the small white blossom is pretty in the flowery way of most blossoms, it is the leaf that is spectacular—a small disc, no bigger than a dime, covered with short scarlet hairs, on the ends of which tiny globules, wonderfully bright, glisten like drops of early morning dew.

The glistening drops, however, are neither dew nor rain. They are formed from a sticky substance exuded from small glands at the ends of the scarlet hairs, and their purpose is sinister. If a small insect comes in contact with the drops, it will never be able to free itself. Slowly, inexorably, the hairs curl over the victim, the leaf partially closes, and the sundew digests its prey as thoroughly as if it had fallen into the bulbous leaf of the pitcher plant or upon the darting tongue of the toad.

While I was stooping down to admire the beauty of these miniature suns, the first of two strange things happened. A dragonfly with light blue body swooped down upon the clump of sundew as if to attack it. What prompted the attack I shall never know. Perhaps the dragonfly was merely clumsy; perhaps it saw an insect entangled in the sundew's scarlet hairs and meant to capture it. Whatever the reason, the dragonfly struck one of the golden discs with violence. He flew no farther. His flight ended as abruptly as if he had struck stone. Though his wings beat in a frenzy and though his slender body writhed and twisted, the moment he struck the diamond drops he became a helpless captive. I watched the struggle, fascinated and somewhat horrified, and then I remembered Tom. I stood up and started to call him, but did not do so. Death is a lonely event for man or dragonfly, and yet . . . Again I started to call, again stopped.

the sundew

the lane was rutted

When I next looked down, the second strange thing had already happened, but because I had had my eyes on Tom I had not seen it occur. In some ways I am just as glad. Crossed against each other at right angles, two dragonflies now struggled to escape from the sparkling drops and closing tentacles. By this time, the wings of the first dragonfly were hardly moving, the body hardly twisting, but the second victim still clung piteously to hope. For awhile there was a frantic whir of wings, and then the whirring slowly subsided and the writhing of the body almost ceased. After a time both dragonflies were perfectly still, forming in death a sky-blue cross.

Suddenly I realized that Dick was shouting from the edge of the bog. "That storm's going to break soon," he called. "Maybe we better get started."

As I started out of the bog, lightning flashed and a clap of thunder made the earth tremble. I caught up to Tom. "Better hurry," he said. "This place gives me the creeps anyway."

At the edge of the woods I looked back. The sky was purple behind the tamaracks, and steam, like a witch's brew rose heavily from the lake. Then a wave of rain rushed towards us, washing out trees and lake and sky.

In the darkness the three of us stumbled through the woods and reached the lane. The storm still whistled around us. Behind me I heard Tom say, "At least the tadpoles get a break."

That night, after the storm was over and we were dry and sitting in front of the campfire, I thought again of tadpoles, toads, and frogs, of the pigeon-wheat and the lichens, of pitcher plants, sundews, and dragonflies. The bog and its inhabitants had raised a few questions.

Perhaps they were not important questions, but at night, between campfire and tent, there is little to do except enjoy the darkness and remember the day and wonder a little about both. And so with nothing better to do I reminded myself that I am not so far removed from moth and toad and sundew as I sometimes think. A few billion years ago the cosmic miracle of photosynthesis, by which the sun was induced

for a mouse

to cooperate in forming the first green leaf, brought into being the alga and the lichen, as a little later and by devious routes it had a part in the development of pitcher plant, tadpole, frog, fox, and man. Now we share the earth together, and we are governed by much the same laws of life and death.

Should I feel a prick of regret at the almost certain death that nature had prepared for the tadpoles? Should I think the toad and frog less gentle because they bring destruction to the moth and May fly? or the lichens and the pigeon-wheat more desirable citizens of the earth because they seem to live in harmony? or the pitcher plant and sundew less desirable because they trap and then destroy the dragonfly? Should I have tried, as a civilized person with a conscience, to release the dragonflies from their captor?

For millions of years nature has governed her myriad forms of life with an efficiency unequaled by men. With checks and counterchecks she gives life and takes it away. She is the perfect proportion, the great efficiency, the judicial equalizer. She is the combined instincts of all living things and so surpasses in many ways the single intelligence of man.

In general I would do well to let her alone lest I disturb a balance too delicate and too complex for me to understand and lest I bring upon myself and my kind some measure of disaster. Life preys on life not from cruelty but from necessity, not from pleasure but for food—with man and his house cat as notable exceptions. I would do well to mind my own business and to let such innocents as toad and tadpole, moth and pitcher plant alone. Nor, if I am sensible, should I interfere with the not wholly pleasant behaviour of hawk and weasel, cowbird, owl, and snake. Nature has ways of balancing accounts—wiser ways, I think, than man's. And as for the sundew and the dragonflies—if my impulse of that moment had been morally sound, then to be consistent, I should have to spend much time each spring in snatching worms from robins.

I put out the fire and went to bed. Down in the valley the whippoorwills were singing as they swept the night for moths and fireflies. Somewhere in the woods behind us the owl was looking for a mouse, the weasel for a rabbit, the raccoon for a polliwog. Loveliest of bog plants, the sundew was merely competing for existence, and yet, in the darkness of the tent, I could still remember the frantic whir of wings and the twisting of the sky-blue, slender bodies against death.

ahead lay the lake

Allegheny National Forest

in desultory fashion

EARLY IN THE AFTERNOON WE PITCHED OUR TENT UNDER the black cherry trees at Twin Lakes, and while we worked, the cedar waxwings looked on. If they disapproved of our presence, they gave no sign of their displeasure, nor did the chipmunk who supervised our labor from his station on the stone fireplace.

While I finished making camp, Tom walked over to the pump for a bucket of water. He was gone a long time. When he came back he said, "Two deer over there by the pump. They let me get within thirty feet of them." I was not surprised. Deer are plentiful, far too plentiful, in the Allegheny National Forest.

We cooled ourselves with long drinks of the icy pump water, watched the cedar waxwings for awhile, and then took the path that led through the grove towards the lake. In a few minutes we came to a footbridge crossing the inlet to the lake. There two youngsters fished in desultory fashion for the speckled trout that lie in the shadow of the bridge.

Ahead lay the lake, the thin band of beach, and the broad lawn where bathers sprawled, enjoying the turf, it seemed, more than the cold water. As we learned later, the lake is better adapted to brook trout than to man until about the end of June. A few

57

a woodsy path bordered the lake

among the ferns

hardy souls, to be sure, challenged the trout but returned quickly to lie in the pale sunlight on the lawn.

We passed among the bathers and took a woodsy path that bordered the lake. For awhile a scarlet tanager led us along the path, but shortly he took his black and scarlet way across the lake. We walked on under the tall cherry trees and maples and among the ferns and wood sorrel that crept in upon the trail. After a time we came to the bridge across the spillway, where we stopped to listen to the roar of the overflow, to see an angler bringing in a nine- or ten-inch brookie, and to look at two young ladies who took pleasure in nothing more important than sunlight and the sound of tumbling water. On the bank of the spillway we picked a handful of wild strawberries and then went on through the woods until we came back to the beach and the pavilion.

"It's hard to believe," Tom said. "Waxwings and wild strawberries and trees and deer, and right in the middle of everything a place to go swimming. I wasn't born in the right place."

At the pavilion we chatted for a time with Carl and Jane Peterson, who are in charge of the Twin Lakes area from early in June until Labor Day. Carl is a college professor who likes the outdoors and who

the pavilion at Twin Lakes

insists upon courteous behaviour from his campers. He gets it. There is no finer place in Pennsylvania for family camping.

Late in the afternoon we followed the inlet up the valley, stopping long enough to watch the brook trout rising in small pools overhung by heavy cover and in the abandoned beaver dam a half mile up the stream. The dam was a beautifully desolate place of darkness and ferns and laurel and of trees rising naked and black from the water. Hemlocks on the western shore cut off the sunlight and dropped heavy shadows to the opposite shore. Neither leaf nor bird was in motion, and the only sound was of water trickling through the brush of the dam. We stood there quietly for several minutes, caught up in the spell of timelessness and desolation, of death rising from the black water. Then I heard Tom say, "Look! Quick!"

I looked upward. Against the reflected light of the sky the great creature swept towards us, like a bird from the prehistoric past, its tremendous wings outspread and slowly flapping. Almost directly over us and perhaps a hundred feet high in the air, the bird hesitated and folded its great wings against its sides. Then it plummeted downward like a dead thing

59

among the dead trees

stricken in mid-air. Forty feet away from us it hit the water with a tremendous splash and in almost the same instant was rising from the spray with a fish— no doubt a trout—clutched in its talons. Almost over our heads the bird wheeled. For just a moment as it passed overhead I saw, or imagined I saw, the bright fish curving against the talons. Then with slowly flapping wings the huge creature turned and settled in its great nest among the dead trees a short distance upstream.

"An osprey," Tom said. "I never saw one so close."

I was still too startled to answer.

We left the beaver dam, then, and the black water and dead trees, and walked quietly back to camp. On the dirt road we passed a group of girls singing.

After dinner, while Tom wandered off in search of deer, I spread out our map of the Allegheny National Forest on the picnic table. It is a huge tract of land, thirty-seven miles long by forty-three miles wide, bordered on the north by New York State and on the west by the Allegheny River down to Tionesta. Within its boundaries lie large portions of Warren, McKean, Elk, and Forest counties.

To the trout fisherman the forest offers more than five hundred miles of unspoiled streams, including famous Kinzua Creek and Tionesta Creek and its tributaries. To the bass fisherman it offers the Allegheny River and the lower reaches of Tionesta Creek and Spring Creek. The 50,000 hunters who enter the forest annually are rewarded with excellent bear, grouse, and small game hunting and with one of the largest deer herds in America. Those who prefer walking to fishing or hunting will find near Ludlow thousands of acres of virgin hemlock and hardwood timber, the largest stand in the State, and at Heart's Content a smaller tract of virgin hemlock and white pine. For the camper there are pleasant places to pitch his tent at Twin Lakes (seven miles south of Kane), at Loleta (six miles south of Marienville), at Heart's Content (fourteen miles south of Warren), at Kelley Pines (six miles east of Marienville), and at Allegheny (on Route 59 between Warren and Kinzua). Moreover, tables, fire grates, toilets, storm shelters, drinking water, and firewood cost the camper either little or nothing.

Before me on the table was a simple map that showed a half million acres belonging to the people, maintained for their profit and their pleasure. I folded the map, for the light had gone from the grove, and touched a match to the fire we had pre-

twin fawns in May

pared earlier in the day. In a few minutes Tom arrived. "Four," he said. "Three small does and a fawn. There must be as many deer up here as there are people."

We sat by the fire for an hour or two, listening to the night sounds and watching the firelight play on the underside of the cherry leaves far above us. Then Tom went to bed. I sat by the fire a little longer. I was thinking of three small does and a fawn. There was something wrong, terribly wrong, with those numbers. Why were there not three fawns, or six? Why only one? And why were the does small?

Two hundred years ago, when tremendous pine forests covered most of Penn's Woods West, there were not so many deer as people think. The deer population was held in check by its enemies the wolf and the mountain lion, but it was held in check even more closely by the lack of food. In the shade of those great forests there was little undergrowth for deer to feed on.

Nature struck a balance, though, as it always does, and the deer were large and healthy. In May, twin fawns or triplets were born. In the winter, if food became scarce and the deer sick, the wolf and the mountain lion weeded out the weakest, leaving the strongest to preserve the herd. Nature is wise, and she managed her herd so that the deer were larger, healthier, and more productive than the deer we know today.

Then the white man came with ax and rifle. The trees fell before his ax, and the deer before his rifle. With every year the herds grew smaller and smaller. There was plenty of food now, with second growth and underbrush replacing the forests, but the white man's rifle and rapacity and his dogs and his knowledge of salt licks were too much even for the wary whitetail. By the end of the nineteenth century the deer herd had been nearly exterminated.

Most people thought it was too late to do anything about the situation. The deer would go, just as the elk and buffalo had gone. Civilization and wildlife could not get along together. But the Game Commission thought differently. There was still a chance that the deer could come back. In 1897 laws were passed that forbade the killing of deer for market, the hunting of deer with dogs, and the shooting of deer at salt licks. In 1905 game refuges were established. In 1906 the Commission began releasing a few deer annually in remote, mountainous regions. And in 1907 an unusual law was passed that pro-

61

deer were diminishing in size

hibited the shooting of antlerless deer. The sportsmen fought bitterly against the law, but the Game Commission won the fight. Since then, it has had cause to lament its victory, but those were desperate days when the deer were vanishing, and desperate measures were needed to check the trend.

What happened after 1907 is, of course, a matter of record. In that year, it is estimated, only 200 deer were killed in the entire state of Pennsylvania, but in 1915, hunters took more than 1,200 deer—an increase of 600 per cent! The hunters and the Game Commission were happy. The deer were coming back. Five years later they were even happier. In that year more than 3,000 deer were taken, an increase of 250 per cent. Again in 1925 the take of deer more than doubled, reaching the astonishing figure of 8,300.

By this time, although the sportsmen could find no fault with their heaven, the more astute members of the Game Commission were beginning to worry. How long would this astronomical increase continue? How long would the food hold out? Their doubts were not allayed in 1930 when they discovered that the take of deer had increased from 8,300—five years before—to 26,000! Nor did 1935 bring any relief to the fear of informed observers that the deer population was running so wild that it might destroy itself, for in 1935 the deer kill again more than doubled and reached the incredible figure of 70,000!

By now the Game Commission was involved in almost open warfare with the sportsmen. The sportsmen were having Roman holidays. The Game Commission was remembering, "When falls the Coliseum, Rome shall fall," and the Coliseum was food. Things had got out of hand.

Looking back, informed people knew that the cause of the trouble lay in the Buck Law of 1907, an unnatural law that may have served its purpose then but that was biologically unsound in 1935. True, there had been open seasons on does from time to time. But an odd chivalry had been built up among hunters, who now felt that it was impolite or downright wicked to molest a female deer—the same group that had vigorously protested when the killing of does was prohibited in 1907.

Came the year 1940. Five years before, 70,000 deer had been taken, a figure that old-timers had trouble believing. What would be the tabulation now? The 1940 figure shocked even the hunters. Again the kill had more than doubled. A total of 186,000 deer had been taken! Thirty-three years before, the kill had been a meager 200.

Meanwhile, many things had happened, most of them bad. We had tampered with nature, had disturbed a delicate balance, and as usual we had lost. Deer were diminishing in size. Spikes had taken the place of the massive racks of another race of deer. The does were giving birth to one fawn or none instead of to two or three. Thousands of deer were dying of starvation every winter, their bodies lying in secluded valleys where early trout fishermen found them in April.

On the overbrowsed ranges, the cottontail had almost disappeared for lack of food. Squirrels could no longer find mast crops. Ruffled grouse and wild turkeys were dying out, unable to compete with the starving deer herd. Worst of all, perhaps, was the inability of young second-growth timber to reach maturity and to grow to forest size. Hordes of ravenous deer destroyed saplings as fast as they appeared, and the resulting deforested areas meant erosion and muddy water and poor fishing and, in faraway cities, diminishing water supplies. All because a deer herd had been unnaturally protected.

Today, conditions are little better than they were in 1940. At any time, disease may strike the undernourished herd and wipe it out. Fortunately, there is a ready solution to the problem—if sportsmen can be taught the biological facts of life. The solution was given in 1948 by a lovable man who was one of the greatest wildlife technologists in the world—Aldo Leopold, professor of Wildlife Management at the University of Wisconsin. His advice to Pennsylvania is worth repeating and worth thinking about until the thinking hurts.

In 1931 the Pennsylvania deer herd was estimated at 800,000 and the carrying capacity of the range at 250,000. The several doe seasons prevented a serious die-off, but not before thousands and thousands of acres of good range was spoiled.

Starvation occurs because these overcrowded deer kill their natural food plants by overbrowsing. These plants are then replaced by plants of little or no food value.

Reduction of the herd is the only way to prevent a tragic shrinkage of both the herd and its range. The only satisfactory way to accomplish a reduction is to shoot female deer.

Not entirely happy, I doused the fire with a bucket of water and watched the steam swirl up among the branches of the cherry trees. Still thinking of three little does and a fawn, I went to bed.

       ✿   ✿   ✿

The road to Heart's Content, one would think, should be paved with gold. Instead it is a dirt road that winds through miles of fine young timber, as carefully managed as a farmer's crop of corn. Ferns

the road to Heart's Content

land of the Senecas

grow along the roadside, and laurel and rhododendron, and sometimes, in a sunny spot, patches of wild strawberry plants are speckled with red.

Once, this land was covered with virgin timber. By day and by night, healthy deer wandered through the shadows of the great forest. Large does were followed by twin fawns, and young bucks, the first time they produced antlers, carried magnificent racks of eight or ten points. Then, the land belonged to the Senecas, who fished its many streams and who hunted for deer and elk and bear and buffalo.

Not far from Heart's Content, the Senecas still own a pitiful remnant granted to them, tax free forever, by the Commonwealth of Pennsylvania. When in 1822 the commissioners of Warren County tried to tax the property, the Senecas objected, as they had objected to two other innovations of the white man, whiskey and rape. An honest Legislature annulled the tax and sent two emissaries to apologize. At Warren they were met by Chief Cornplanter, an honorable man with a gift of language and of satire. In accepting the apology, Chief Cornplanter made a short speech. What he said then may indicate why

the Senecas, a short time ago, were reluctant to sell the last of their homeland so that a white man's dam could be built above Warren.

Brothers: The talk which the Governor sent us pleased us very much. I think the Great Spirit is very much pleased. . . .

The Great Spirit first made the World, and next the flying animals. . . . Then He made different kinds of trees, and weeds of all sorts, and people of every kind. . . . But stills to make whiskey to be given to Indians He did not make. . . .

The Great Spirit looked back on all that He had made. The different kinds He made to be separate and not mix with and disturb each other. But the white people have broken his command by mixing their color with the Indians. The Indians have done better by not doing so. . . .

He next told us that there were three things for our people to attend to. First, we ought to take care of our wives and children. Second, the white people ought to attend to their farms and cattle. Thirdly, the Great Spirit has given the bears and deers to the Indians. He is the cause of all things that exist, and it is very wicked to go against His will.

64

The Great Spirit wishes me to inform the people that they should quit drinking intoxicating drink, as being the cause of disease and death.

He told us not to sell any more of our lands, for He never sold lands to anyone.

Some of us now keep the seventh day; but I wish to quit it, for the Great Spirit made it for others but not for the Indians, who ought every day to attend to their business.

This is all I have at present to say.

We drove slowly along the road, for there was much to see. Throughout the forest, a quarter of a million acres of second-growth timber are being given the best silvicultural management. From this large acreage comes an annual harvest of about seven million board feet of saw timber and about 125,000 cords of wood. The cutting is done selectively, so that only mature trees are removed from the forest. Such removal of the mature trees speeds the rate of development of the remaining trees about 25 per cent. The result is a forest of continuous growth, one not only beautiful but also profitable.

Presently we came to a roadside marker that told us we were opposite Heart's Content—an area of a little more than a hundred acres of virgin hemlock and white pine. We parked the car and walked down the path into the woods. As we entered the forest, the bright light of day began to fade into a woodsy dimness. A hundred and fifty feet overhead, the crowns of the tremendous trees blacked out the sky, and all around us, as we went deeper into the woods, was that strange stillness of the forest, like the stillness of fog at night, so quiet that the chittering of a red squirrel seemed raucous and irreverent.

The ground was soft underfoot. Our heels made no sound. Some of these trees, we are told, were tall before the Mayflower set sail from England. To stand beneath them in perfect silence, to be willingly dwarfed, to sense rather than to see their grandeur is a chastening experience. Among these ancient inhabitants of the earth, our mortal pretensions are so out of place that we forget them. They dissolve into the silence and the twilight, and we stand alone and honest and humble among those that take their sustenance from earth and sky.

For an hour or two, saying very little, we walked among the great ones. Not until we were back at the car, I think, did we speak naturally. Then Tom said, "It isn't far from here to Ludlow." He looked at his watch.

Heart's Content—virgin hemlock and white pine

"Let's try it," I said. He did not know that I had a special reason for wanting to see the Tionesta Forest.

About ten miles of dirt road brought us to Sheffield; about five miles on Route 6 took us to Ludlow; and then we began the stony road into the largest tract of virgin timber in Penn's Woods West—a mixed stand of hemlock and hardwoods. Twenty minutes after leaving Ludlow we again stood among the giants.

Not far from where we parked the car an obscure trail led down the hillside into the darkness of the forest. We followed the trail for a few hundred yards until it separated into two trails.

"You try one, and I'll try one?" Tom suggested.

"Let's take an hour," I said, "and meet here."

I watched him go down the mountain towards the east. When he was almost out of sight, I started towards the west. Being alone made a difference, as Tom had guessed. It made the trees taller, the forest larger, the silence deeper. Here were not a hundred acres as at Heart's Content but thousands of acres, shaded by the same trees that had lived here before the frontier fort was erected at the forks of the Ohio, trees that were old before a white man ever saw them, trees that will be here long after all men now living are dead. No wind moved among their distant branches, and no birds sang. If deer, turkey, or squirrels were in the woods, they made no sound.

For a mile or more I walked down the dim trail, looking back from time to time to keep my bearings. There was little undergrowth—an occasional small hemlock, or a beech sapling courageously trying to find its way to the light. A few ferns showed green against the dark floor. When I stopped walking and sat down on a great log, the silence was more intense than ever, for my clumsy feet had been making a dreadful ruckus among the leaves. It was not an oppressive silence but so expansive, so pervasive, that it seemed to cover the whole earth.

A few hundred years ago the trees and the silence had, indeed, covered the earth from far west of here to the coast of the Atlantic Ocean. They stretched away, said Dr. Jennings, "for a thousand miles, a forest wilderness—a forest that, in area, in its variety of trees, its manifold utility, and its magnificence of autumn coloration, was unequaled in all the world— and the like of which will never again be seen by man."

From where I sat, my eyes caught a straight line of seven magnificent hemlocks, twenty or thirty feet

the stony road into virgin timber

apart. They were in a straight line because, about two centuries before, a great tree had come tumbling to the earth, had slowly crumbled into humus, and had become a nursery for hemlock seedlings. Now the seedlings, nurtured on the decaying humus, were themselves old trees, markers of the long grave of their patriarch, and the dead and the living were in close communion.

Sitting there, I thought of another time long ago, and I wished that every boy in Penn's Woods West could spend at least one hour of his life in Tionesta Forest. He might not be deeply impressed at the time, but he would remember the experience, I think, forever, just as I was remembering, even then, my first sight of these trees.

My father took me to see them when I was a boy. Before we went, he told me many things about the forest. Some of the trees were hundreds of years old.

67

They were virgin trees, he said. I did not know exactly what he meant, but I had a maiden aunt who often came to visit us, and I hoped the trees were not like her. He told me about the elk and deer and bison that used to roam the woods and about the Indians who hunted there. They were all gone now, he said, except for a few deer and the trees.

The next day, when we got to the forest and started along the trail, I was disappointed. The trees were tall, of course, and their trunks were big, but they looked much like the big trees in the hollow behind our house. The trees in our hollow were oak trees, though, and maybe that made the difference.

Although my father was ordinarily a fast walker, we went down the trail slowly. Sometimes he would stop beneath one of the big trees and, with his eyes, follow its trunk up to the branches at the top and the bit of blue sky beyond. I did, too. They *were* big trees. I talked a good deal while we walked, but my father hardly talked at all. Once he put the palm of his hand gently on a tree and kept it there a long time. He was just looking at his hand on the tree trunk.

to sense rather than see

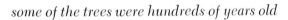

some of the trees were hundreds of years old

It was dark and shadowy and quiet in the woods, and the spell of it all began to seep into me. In spots, sunlight found its way through the branches and made bright brown splotches on the fallen needles. From down in the valley a sound came up, a sound like thunder.

"What's that?" I said.

My father looked down at me. "It's a grouse," he said, "a grouse drumming." Then he walked on, slowly, among the trees.

I had never heard a grouse drumming before, and I wanted to ask him about it, but this was not the right time. To me it sounded more like buffaloes. I had never heard a buffalo, either, but I had read about them and about how, when the herd was moving, it made a sound like thunder.

Maybe my father was wrong. Maybe a few buffaloes had escaped the white man's notice and the Indian's and were still living there.

Ahead of me, my father did not look so tall as usual. I saw him stoop down, looking at something on the ground. When I came up to him, he was selecting little hemlock cones and putting them in his white handkerchief.

"What do you want them for?" I said.

68

"I just want them," he said. "Maybe I'll plant them in the back yard. I just—want them." He put the handkerchief carefully into his coat pocket. "Remind me to take them out of my pocket when we get to the car," he said. "I don't want to crush them."

As we went on, I kept thinking about the buffaloes and the elk and about the Indians, too. I asked my father about the Indians.

"It isn't very likely," he said. "They're gone now, along with a lot of other things. I wish I could have seen them then, the trees. You couldn't get your arms around them, no, not two of you. They're gone now," he said, "except for just a few, like these."

I was still thinking about the elk and the buffalo.

"Here," he said, "try to put your arms around this one."

I tried, just to please him, but I knew I couldn't do it. My arms seemed shorter than usual, and the bark hurt my face. He was pleased, though, that I had tried, for when I turned around he was smiling— a strange smile that seemed to come in some mysterious way partly from him and partly from someone else.

"But it's a nice idea," I heard him say, still smiling, "about maybe the Indians still being here."

Where the trail turned uphill, the forest was not so dark. He talked a lot as we were going uphill, but I was thinking of too many things to hear all that he said. When we got back to the road, I turned around to look at the trees again.

Now that I knew them, they looked different. They were the biggest, the greatest, trees I had ever seen. I could still feel the bark under my fingers and the hurt of the bark on my face, and I could see the branches, black and high in the sky. I hoped that they would live forever, that my father would live forever, that nothing would ever die, not trees nor Indians nor buffalo. I was exalted and sad at the same time.

My father reached into his coat pocket and said, "Here, boy, have an apple." He had another one in his pocket for himself. Together, we rubbed them on our pants to make them shiny, and then we ate them on the way back to the car.

Now, forty years later, I stood in the same forest, remembering an important boyhood experience compounded of tall trees and quietness and the drumming of a grouse. Little had changed except for the absence of the tall man. Even the exaltation and the sadness were the same, though older and a little wearier.

69

SUMMER

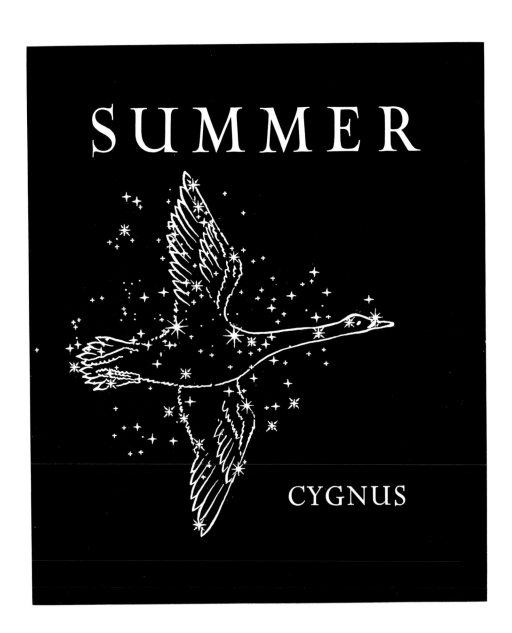

CYGNUS

THE SWAN

EARLY ON A JUNE NIGHT THE SWAN FLIES OUT OF THE east to announce, with astronomical certainty, that spring has gone and that summer is at hand. Of course, we have known right along that spring would not last forever. The pink azaleas and the mountain laurel have long since dropped their blossoms, old Leo, the Lion, is hunting in the west, and fledgling screech owls have been causing concern to their parents for some time; but not until the Swan sails into view early in the evening do we have official assurance that summer is about to begin.

There are geometrically minded people who refer to this constellation as the Northern Cross, but to most of us who have already had enough difficulty with Euclid, these stars are the celestial Swan, herald of summer, of the pasture rose and of elderberry blossoms and of wild strawberries on a hillside, of groundhogs blinking in sunlit meadows, of bass that leap in the evening on Kettle Creek and on the Juniata, of fields in Bedford County where young cornstalks whisper on still nights in late July. All these and more are promised by the gentle Swan as, in early summer just after nightfall, she sails serenely out of the east.

At that time, she is not hard to locate, though first we must find the bright stars Vega and Altair. Facing the south we see these two bright stars slightly to our east. The higher one is Vega, a little to the west of the Milky Way. The lower and more easterly is Altair, on the eastern edge of the Milky Way.

About halfway between them, and a little above a line drawn through them, is Albireo, the head of the Swan. Between head and tail, there are, depending on our eyesight, two or three other stars that form the neck and body of the Bird of Summer. And at right angles to the body are the extended wings, a

73

on a bluff above Pymatuning

star marking each wing-tip, and each of the wing-tips is just outside the Milky Way, one to the east and one to the west.

Why, we might wonder, does a bird as wise as the celestial Swan begin her southward migration early in the summer. The truth of the matter is that she does not do so, for if we watch her through the night we see that as the hours pass, she gives up her south-ern course and sails westward, as though the loveliness of a new summer had made her change her mind. Perhaps, of course, she is frightened by the Eagle of Altair, also flying southward, or by a backward glance at unfortunate Cassiopeia falling from her chair. Whatever the reason, she flies always down the Milky Way, an eternal though vacillating migrant along the brightly lighted flyway of the stars.

Pymatuning Reservoir

ON A BLUFF ABOVE PYMATUNING RESERVOIR WE PITCHED our umbrella tent one afternoon so that we could look out beyond the oaks, across a small lagoon, and over to the waterfowl sanctuary. The sun was warm and the sky a deep blue. Out on the lagoon a few small fish were rising, and on the grassy shore opposite us, ducks and geese were explaining things to one another.

A hundred yards or so behind us was the Pymatuning Laboratory of Field Biology, whose director, Dr. Arch Tryon, had suggested the bluff as a camp site. We could eat our meals with his students, he said, at the mess hall if we wished. Never did two campers have finer hosts than Dr. Tryon and his assistant, Dr. Richard Hartman.

We had spent the morning making a quick tour of the reservoir, the largest artificial body of water in Northeastern United States, a lake with over seventy miles of shoreline. Years ago, the area now occupied by the reservoir was a vast and dismal swamp, the home of the Delawares and their powerful chieftain Pymatuning, "man with the crooked mouth." It was a mysterious place from which rose the mephitic odor of swamp gas and into which only warriors would venture, the most daring. Out of the depths of the water, islands appeared, floated about for a few days, and then disappeared. Ferns rose higher than the huckleberry bushes, and orchids and pitcher plants grew under tamaracks, black ash, and swamp maple. On dry patches, tundra moss, relict of Arctic flora, covered the ground. Buffalo, elk, deer, bear, beaver, and otter roamed the region, and throughout the swamp, ducks and geese nested in incredible numbers. Chief Pymatuning and his Delawares had an abundance not known to many tribes.

Years passed, the white man came, and after a few bloody quarrels the Indian moved on. Shortly after the Civil War there was talk of draining the swamp, but nothing was done. Again, shortly before World War I, talk began to hum, and the Pennsylvania Legislature passed a bill directing that the swamp be turned into a tremendous reservoir. In 1934 the project was completed.

Once more, man had found it either wise or expedient to disregard the first rule of nature, which is, "Let me alone." To disregard is to run the risk that ultimately man and especially his children after him will suffer. Of course, there are times when we must run the risk, when we must run counter to the nature of nature: we cannot turn our cornfields over to the weeds or our kitchens to the ants or our bodies to harmful bacteria. The risk, though, remains, and we are just beginning to learn the far-reaching perils of weed-killers, insecticides, wonder-drugs, and radiation. Slowly we are also beginning to learn the perils of swamp draining and of dam building, particularly when they are recommended by selfish and unenlightened industrialists and by Army Engineers under the black flag of flood control.

The construction of Pymatuning Reservoir was a calculated risk, and a big one. The draining of the swamp, for instance, might well diminish the underground water supply for miles around. Sewage from Linesville, moreover, might contaminate the lake. If the reservoir filled with silt, as most artificial lakes and dams do, the whole project might return to a swamp within fifty years, and the course and nature of the Shenango River might be altered. With the draining of the swamp, the nesting sites of waterfowl would be destroyed, and the effects of the destruction would be felt as far south as the Gulf of Mexico and as far north as the Arctic Circle.

for boating enthusiasts

75

docks and liveries

Against these dangers there were possible advantages. The reservoir might stabilize the fluctuating water supply of the Shenango and Beaver rivers; it might be of some help in holding floods in check; barring contamination and swamp gas, it might furnish a large recreational area in which people could enjoy the outdoors and learn something about the everlasting ways of nature.

For several years after the completion of the project, scientists in many fields withheld judgment on the success or failure of the reservoir. But gradually it became apparent that the gains were greater than the losses and that nature, in this particular instance, was willing to cooperate with man.

Although many nesting sites for wildfowl were destroyed, a large sanctuary was reserved for the protection of those birds that remained, and the damage was in that way held to a minimum. The underground water supply of the district has not, so far, been materially reduced. In a peculiar contradiction, sewage from Linesville increased the food supply for small fish, which in turn furnished food for larger fish, and the possible contamination of the lake did not occur. So far, silting has not taken place in appreciable amounts. Today the Shenango

and Beaver rivers have an adequate water supply for domestic and industrial use and for sanitation, the threat of floods to the valley has been somewhat lessened, and Penn's Woods West has an outdoor recreational area and a wildlife sanctuary that surpass the dreams of most of the planners of the project.

Every year more than a million people enjoy the outdoors at Pymatuning. There are beaches for bathers, tents and trailer areas for campers, picnic groves for casual visitors. For boating enthusiasts there are docks and liveries. Outside the limits of the sanctuary, craft of all descriptions skim the dark water—sailboats and cabin cruisers, motorboats and skiffs and canoes and even rubber rafts.

The fishing, too, is good. In spite of numerous carp, Pymatuning has the best largemouth bass fishing in Northeastern United States. Dr. Tryon attributes the rapid growth of the bass and other fish to the abundance of microscopic aquatic life of the lake, higher amounts of which have been recorded at Pymatuning than at any other lake. In addition to bass, there are large numbers of panfish and walleyed pike.

As good as the fishing are the duck hunting and the bird watching. Since the lake is located on the

Atlantic Flyway, one of the four main highways in America, it has one of the greatest concentrations of waterfowl in the country. During migrations, particularly in April and October, the birds sweep in by the thousands, travelers from distant lands, to recuperate from their long flights and to feed on the lush vegetation and aquatic life before resuming their mysterious journeys.

As we ate our lunch on the bluff above the lagoon, we marveled at the success of this intelligently planned gamble with nature. Unlike most such exploitations, the Pymatuning project has had fewer losses than feared, greater gains than hoped for. Biologists, conservationists, engineers, geologists, and ecologists had worked together to court nature rather than to outrage her, and the result had been a peaceful union founded not on ignorance and contempt but on understanding and love.

travelers from distant lands

fishing is good

Roger sat down with us

It would be well for Penn's Woods West if all Army Engineers engaged in flood control were to spend one month out of every year in resident study at Pymatuning Reservoir. Other members of their class in ecology might be anglers who want to catch fish but who are unwilling to improve streams, old-fashioned operators of coal mines, farmers who plow their fields to the edge of the brook, people who pour sewage into streams from which the next community gets its drinking water, factory owners who have no regard for the rights of the factory owner farther down the river, hunters who are so chivalrous about does that thousands of deer die of starvation every winter, and, of course, owners of paper mills.

Such a class, taught patiently and kindly by Joseph Wood Krutch or by Samuel Ordway, might turn Penn's Woods West into the healthiest, happiest, and most prosperous community—for farmers, industrialists, and human beings in general—that ever existed in America.

While we were eating, we heard someone coming through the woods behind us—quick, energetic steps, heels hitting hard. Thirty yards away, we knew it was a young man with enough vitality for two. Ten yards away, we knew it was Roger Reed, Fish Commission Biologist for the northwestern part of the State. He had been a student of mine three years before.

We shook hands and he sat down with us. He had heard, he said, that we were visiting Pymatuning. He had come down to say hello. He had just a minute now, but would we like to go out on the lake this evening?

I looked at Tom.

Roger explained that he and Carlyle Sheldon, District Fish Warden, were transplanting twelve hundred bass from Pymatuning to Conneaut Lake and, as an experiment, were taking them by hook and line, seining being almost impossible among the spatterdocks and roots. He wished we could fish, too, but since that would be illegal, we could do the next best thing and just go along for the fun.

Again, I looked at Tom.

They would fish in water that had not been fished in twenty years, Roger said. He had found a special ecological niche, ideal for bass, and there should be a good evening of sport.

Tom laid down his plate on the leaves beside him. "I'll take my camera," he said.

Abruptly, his mission ended, Roger got to his feet. "We'll meet you at five-thirty then," he said, "down by the laboratory dock." He started back along the

78

path through the woods, and Tom watched him go.

"He'll meet us at five-thirty," Tom said, "if he doesn't have a heart attack first."

At five o'clock Tom and I were down at the landing and watching the dark clouds sweep in from the west. At five-twenty we were on our way to the fishing grounds, Roger, Ned Evans, and I in one flat-bottomed steel boat, Carlyle and Tom in the other. Each boat carried a large vat of fresh water into which the fish would be placed. A short distance out, we disturbed a flock of mallards and once, close to shore, we came upon a flock of Canada geese who tried to ignore us but could not keep from honking.

The other boat was speedier than ours and quickly pulled away, growing smaller and smaller as it sped down the lake. It was soon out of sight. We went about two miles to the south, I think, and then turned eastward. There, acres of spatterdock and lilies covered the lake, but Roger found a narrow channel through them. Sometimes we rode up on sunken logs and had to rock or push our way off, and sometimes we had to pole through masses of spatterdock, but Roger was a good pilot. After about half an hour of struggling and maneuvering we came to an open space of five acres or so, open except for floating islands of algae and for the black stumps of trees.

dark clouds from the west

79

we disturbed a flock of mallards

A wood duck only a few feet away gave us a quick look and then slipped under the cover of the spatterdock. Roger cut the motor.

"This," he said, "is my special, ecological niche. This is where bass live in great numbers. This is where . . ."

At the edge of the spatterdock there was a swirl of water.

"This," he amended, "is where we get our first bass."

As he spoke, he sent his plug curving in a low arc to the spot of the swirl. Ned and I watched. It struck the water within a yard of the spatterdock and floated there quietly. For a quarter of a minute, a half minute, almost a full minute, he let the plug float there, motionless at the edge of the spatterdock. Then he gave it a twitch. As he did so, there was a burst of spray with a flash of green in the center.

True to his kind, the bass did not take to the air again but bored deep, cutting to left and to right, catching the line temporarily on roots and sunken logs, driving towards the bottom of the lake. Roger kept heavy pressure on the rod, for the plug was sturdy and the line strong. With all its hidden hazards this was no place to play a bass warily; this was a place for brute strength and stiff rod. Slowly the fish gave up ground, coming closer and closer to the boat. Soon there was a swirl at the side of the boat, and Roger lifted the rod. The fish flipped into the boat, two or three pounds of solid largemouth.

Very carefully, Roger held the fish by the lower jaw and extracted the hook. "If you hold them by the lower jaw," he explained, "they don't thrash around and hurt themselves." Gently he placed the bass in the tank and threw a heavy tarpaulin over the top. "They stay quieter if it's dark," he said.

He reeled his plug up to the tip of his rod. "Look," he said, "over there." Two more swirls sent ripples from the edge of the weeds. Again he cast to the circles, and again there was a mighty splash that sent spray to the tops of the spatterdocks. By the time Ned was ready to cast, Roger's second bass was close to the boat.

Ned flung a long wooden minnow towards the weeds. It went halfway, backlashed, stopped in mid-air, and dropped to the water with a splash. Just as he started to reel in, the rod almost left his hands. There was no splash this time, just a tremendous pull downward. Twice the line caught on roots, and I thought he had lost the fish, but both times the line came free. In another minute or two, he had a Pymatuning largemouth. "Hold it by the lower jaw," Roger cautioned.

After Ned had taken the hook from the fish's mouth, he dropped the plug back into the water and lifted the tarpaulin on the tank. Suddenly the reel of his rod began to sing.

"Grab it," Roger yelled.

Ned dropped the fish into the tank and took hold of the rod. The reel was still spinning.

a line of Canada geese

"Another one must have followed the first one in," Roger said calmly. "They do that sometimes. Hey," he added, "I got a dandy on the line."

I watched Ned slow the reel down and go to work on his second Pymatuning bass. It was a big one this time, and he came back slowly in spite of the heavy tackle.

"About four pounds," Roger said, when at last Ned brought it in. "Maybe a little better."

For more than an hour, bass after bass came to boat and to tank. After a time, it took two casts to bring in a bass, then three.

"Seven-thirty," Roger said. "Time to quit. They'll stop hitting altogether in a few minutes." With characteristic decisiveness, he reeled his plug in, laid his rod away, and examined the bass under the tarpaulin. "They're all in good shape," he said. "Let's get them back to the hatchery. You know, we haven't lost one yet on the hook and line method." He started the motor. "How many did you get?" he asked.

"Eighteen, maybe twenty."

"I caught either twenty-two or twenty-three," he said. "That's not bad for a couple of hours of work. Forty bass, all in good shape."

It was growing dark as we left Roger's ecological niche. Heavy clouds were creeping in from the west, the sun streaking the edges with crimson. Wind was beginning to toss the big leaves of the spatterdock. We came to the narrow channel and sped through it much more rapidly than we had done on the way in. As we left it and pushed out into the lake, waves slapped against the prow and sent cold spray over us.

"Storm tonight," Roger said, "a dandy, too." In the semidarkness he steered a certain course, throttle wide open. He seemed to know every stump and every sunken log in the lake. "It's a long way off," he said, "but I'd just as leave take no chances. This isn't a nice lake in a storm." Occasionally he pulled back the tarpaulin to inspect the fish. Once we brushed against a floating log. "Wasn't there last night," he said. "In this lake you can't tell where the logs are. Here today, gone tomorrow."

only a few feet away

81

Presently we saw the lights of the dock ahead of us and over to the left the bright blurs of the laboratory windows. Biologists, I began to see, worked late, whether connected with the University or with the Fish Commission and whether storms were in the making or not. Carlyle and Tom had already arrived at the dock and were transferring their fish from the tank to a rearing pond. We beached the boat and at once set to work moving the bass. The evening's tally for the three was sixty-six bass ranging from two to five pounds. A few may have run to six pounds.

From the west we heard a roll of thunder, but it was far off. We said good-by to one another, and Tom and I walked up the dark path that led to the tent. As we passed the laboratory, we looked in the window. Dick and Arch and two students were still working.

Back at the tent Tom brewed a pot of chocolate. At nine o'clock we went to bed. Across the lagoon, at the sanctuary, the ducks and geese were nervous and disturbed the silence with strange honkings, but except for them and for the distant roll of thunder, the woods were quiet, ominously so.

When I awoke in the morning the sun was shining through the open tent door. There was a constant dripping of water on the roof of the tent, and outside such a chorus of birds as I think I had never heard before—trills and warbles, full-throated flutings,

whistles and chirps and gay arpeggios, an ecstacy of sound released from hundreds of throats. For a few moments I lay there, not quite of the world, part of something not myself, of sunlight and bird song, of rain dripping on the roof of a tent.

Then I heard someone moving outside. I turned my head. The pillowslip was wet. Near the door, sunlight flashed from a puddle of water. I crawled out of bed and called to Tom. "What happened?" I said. "Everything's wet."

"Storm," he called back. "About time you were getting up. Hurricane. Tornado. I spent half the night holding the tent down. And you slept through everything."

I threw a raincoat around me and stepped out into the dripping sunshine. Great branches lay on the ground. Our pots and pans littered the landscape. A plastic slicker hung from a huckleberry bush twenty yards away. Though rain still dripped from every leaf, the sky was a spotless blue, and the birds told of their relief in bursts of song that were spectacular.

"The birds," Tom said. "You've never heard anything like them."

He was right. They sang from every bush and branch. They sang from the oaks above us and from the shore of the lagoon below. Tom's telescopic lens caught a line of Canada geese on the opposite shore. The night of terror was over. If nests had been destroyed, they would be rebuilt. If fledglings had been

the narrow channel from the west

acres of spatterdock and lilies

lost, there would be new ones. Meanwhile, the world was bright and green, a miracle to be greeted with the miracle of song.

While we listened we put the camp in order and then went up to the mess hall for breakfast. On the way, Tom said it had been the worst storm he had ever gone through. At breakfast we learned that his estimate was shared by others. Trees were down all over the northern part of the State. The worst damage had taken place at Cook Forest, where hundreds of hemlocks in the Cathedral area, we were told, had fallen before the twister. There was little levity at the table that morning. We were thinking of the ancient trees crashing through the stillness.

❊   ❊   ❊

After breakfast, as we walked down the path to the tent, we said nothing, for it did not seem a time for talking. Strangely, the birds were still singing.

In the afternoon, as I walked along the edge of the lake, I brushed against a cherry bough that leaned out over the water. Immediately, there was a flutter of burnt gold among the leaves and sunshine, and the great wayfarer began his hesitant flight upward. The swallowtail butterfly may be larger and more spectacular, and the mourning cloak, that hints of deathly things and dark, may be more profound, but neither has been able to capture the imagination of man quite so well as the monarch.

I watched him ascend in gliding flight until he was far above me, a bit of dark fluff against the brightness. Then a current of air sent him gently off towards the horizon. How many horizons he had seen—here, this afternoon, in Penn's Woods West, a few days ago perhaps in Maryland, a few weeks ago in South Carolina, a few months ago in Central America. This black and orange creature with a directional apparatus no one understands had battled Atlantic storms and had basked in Georgia sunlight; it had known airy love against a blue sky; it had descended to earth to lay its mortal eggs on the green of the milkweed. And then, the golden mission ended, others of its kind would gather and begin the incredible journey back to the semitropics, to warmer breezes and to brighter wines.

What sustains, we wonder, the strength in the frail wings. For this creature of sun and sky, as if to show its contempt for mundane things, begins and ends its drifting days with neither teeth nor mouth. Only nectar—that mysterious love-essence of the flowers—is appropriate for the royal vagrant, and of it, in some manner not known to heavy-footed man, he compounds a strength and a courage to match the perfection of his wings.

And yet the monarch was not always royal. He began as a green egg on the bitter milkweed. As a lowly caterpillar, he ate the green, gorged on it as if in preparation for the time of nectar drinking. Then, after days of ignominious belly crawling, came the dark wonder of the chrysalis, which no man, for all his intelligence, has ever quite been able to explain. In total darkness, entombed by a case of pale green dotted with gold, strange forces worked, and

83

when they were done, the chrysalis opened, and out of its darkness emerged not a voracious, earth-bound caterpillar but a glistening creature of the sun. For a few minutes, he dried his wings; then, taking to the air as though born to it, he became the regal wanderer of sky and land and sea.

This afternoon I had seen him embark on another journey, earlier than he had intended, perhaps, because I shook the branch of the wild cherry on which he rested with folded wings.

I moved my clumsy feet forward along the path, about thirty inches a step. It was an uphill quarter of a mile to the tent and to a dinner not of nectar. Because I was still thinking of the monarch, I felt wonderfully unimportant, a clod beneath his flight, strangely humble and in my proper place, on the known earth and on a well-marked path.

❀   ❀   ❀

Early in the evening, with Dick Hartman at the helm, we started out into the sanctuary to look for snowy egrets. Fifty years before, in the days of the professional plume hunters, such a search would have been a waste of time. Even as late as 1940, W. E. Clyde Todd reported, ". . . it is a rare and infrequent visitor in our latitude." And indeed, before 1940, the snowy egret had been almost exterminated. It had been saved from the fate of the passenger pigeon by a change in the styles of women's hats, by laws that found a live egret more useful than a plume, and by such sanctuaries as the one at Pymatuning. This evening, Dick had promised, we should see not one but many of these beautiful creatures, saved for us and for our children partly by chance but largely by the awakened conscience of man.

The sun was getting low as we left the dock, and the lake was choppy. On our left, stumps, tree trunks, and clumps of spatterdock rose from the gray water and on our right a blue heron swept over the boat and disappeared into the darkness of the bluff.

After a few minutes Dick cut the motor and we drifted towards the shadowy shore. "There," he said suddenly. "By the rushes. There's one."

There was more than one. Dimly we saw them, snowy forms motionless at the edge of the water. They had been disturbed by the sound of the motor. They stood there as still as water lilies in the dusk, as vague as patches of swamp mist in the evening. After a time, one of them rose in ghostly flight, drifted northward low over the water, then curved upward into a tree that stood dark against the sky.

in ghostly flight

In a moment another rose softly and followed the course of the first, then another and another until seven had left and there were no white shapes among the rushes.

"It's the roost tree," Dick said. "There might be fifty in it. I'll try to get you a little closer." He started up the motor, and we moved very slowly.

Tom was sitting in the prow of the boat and peering at the roost tree, dark against the still bright sky. "It's too late," he said. "It's too late. There isn't enough light left."

Motor purring softly, we drew close to the tree and saw, though only dimly, white blurs against the dark. Again Dick cut the motor, and we drifted through the still water closer and closer to the tree. Then, very suddenly, the birds took to the air again. How many I do not know, but ghostly forms were winging across the evening sky. Three, four, and sometimes five at a time were visible for a moment against the light and then were swallowed up by the darkness of the shoreline. After a time, the tree was only a tree and not the evening home of phantom residents.

Tom was putting his camera back into its case.

"Any luck?" I said.

"No light," he said.

Dick started the motor and we went back to the dock.

"No light," Tom had said, but there was something about his voice that made me wonder.

85

Twin Lakes

Little Lakes and Large

WHEN NATURE MOULDED THE MOUNTAINS AND VALLEYS of Penn's Woods West, she gave us many streams and rivers, more than she gave to most of the people on earth. Then, fearing perhaps that she might spoil us with too much goodness, she refrained from dotting our landscapes with an abundance of lakes. Perhaps that is the reason we cherish so highly those that we do have. They are little lakes, most of them, fed by creeks and underwater springs. The largest natural lake in Penn's Woods West is Conneaut, and it is only three miles long and at no place more than a mile and a half in width. Much smaller are Twin Lakes in Elk County; Sandy Lake in Mercer County; Sugar Lake, Clear Lake, and Lake Canadohta in Crawford County; and Lake LeBoeuf, Lake Pleasant, and Edinboro Lake in Erie County—most of them natural and all of them looking as though they have been on the earth since the days of the retreating glaciers.

In addition, there are large impoundments, dozens of them, made by man—Pymatuning Reservoir with eighty miles of shoreline, Lake Gordon in Bedford County, the Quemahoning Reservoir in Somerset County, Crooked Creek and Beaver Run Reservoirs, and the great dams that are strung along the tributaries of the major rivers, dams that are used partly for flood control and partly for recreation. And then there are hundreds of little impoundments—private lakes, lakes built by sportsmen's groups, the fee-fishing ponds, and the small dams in State Parks, many of them as lovely as if nature had done the work herself.

Tom, Ray, and I started northward at dawn one August morning to see again a few of the little lakes and also our largest, Lake Erie, where the surf rolls in like the surf of the Atlantic. But since water was not all we wished to see, we took, as usual, the roads that are not heavily traveled. That was how we happened to see Evans City from the hill on Route 528, and the tricycle party at Prospect, Conoquenessing Creek from the little bridge, and, at Stone House, when we turned left on Route 78 towards Slippery Rock, the wonder of the Jennings Blazing Star Prairie.

Only a few hundred yards north on Route 78 from its junction with Routes 528 and 8 lies a small tract of land that is unique in Penn's Woods West. It is not impressive except for a few weeks of the year, the weeks when the Blazing Star blooms. Few of the people who travel the road are aware that it is bordered by two or three acres of midwestern prairie. Fewer still know that this small tract of land is in all likelihood a portion of the old shoreline of a glacial lake, Lake Arthur, which once covered most of northern Butler County. Nevertheless, there is reason to believe that an arm of the western prairie once reached all the way into Penn's Woods West, perhaps following the old shoreline of Lake Arthur. This prairie land puzzled some of the more curious pioneers, who noticed in the midst of the great forests small areas without trees and could not explain them. Actually the grassy areas had once been much larger, but slowly through the centuries the trees, by right of conquest, had taken over much of the

the Blazing Star in bloom

prairie land. Now there are only a few acres of the original prairie left in Penn's Woods West.

On Route 78 we stopped to look at them. Often before we had stopped and had not been impressed,

Evans City from the hill

on the dam at Slippery Rock

abandoned one-room schoolhouse

but now for the first time we saw the Blazing Star in bloom—and the sight was one to remember. It has been described best by the modest and lovable man for whom the area is named, Dr. O. E. Jennings:

"From early to mid-August the most glorious floral display of our region is to be seen at the Jennings Blazing Star Prairie, Stone House, northwestern Butler County, Pennsylvania, now a nature preserve,

the tricycle party at Prospect

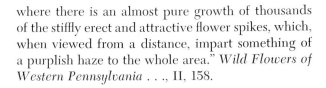
a bull wheel

the scarecrow in the cornfield

where there is an almost pure growth of thousands of the stiffly erect and attractive flower spikes, which, when viewed from a distance, impart something of a purplish haze to the whole area." *Wild Flowers of Western Pennsylvania . . .*, II, 158.

Forgetting that we were on our way to the lakes, we looked for a long time at the last of the prairie. A giant swallowtail fluttered from spike to spike, trying first one and then another a hundred feet away. Over the oldest blossoms crawled surfeited bees, so heavy with nectar that they moved clumsily and seemed in danger of falling from the blooms. Close to us a monarch butterfly clung steadily to a choice spike. Sometimes a breeze started at the far edge of the field and came towards us, and the vertical lines of purple leaned with the wind.

＊　　　＊　　　＊

"I'm glad," Ray said, as we left the field, "that we took this road and not the highway." And so we continued on Route 78, hoping for more good things. There were the mother and daughter on the edge of the dam at Slippery Rock Creek, an abandoned one-room schoolhouse with broken windows, a bull wheel that looked strong enough for all its years to pump oil again, and a little girl with a wagon who found her brother to be a proud cargo. North of the town of Slippery Rock a dirt road led us past Walker's farm and the scarecrow in the cornfield

and down to Wolf Creek, where we turned around and started back for Route 78. Somehow, in spite of stopping every mile or so, we managed to get through the beautiful town of Grove City and on to Stoneboro and Sandy Lake.

small sailboats on Canadohta

89

sparkling in the sunlight

Sparkling in the sunlight, it lay before us. Rushes and water lilies grew along its shores. A short distance away children played on the white beach, and across from the beach, in a wooded grove, were cot-

boating or fishing or swimming

tages that blended into the landscape. Sandy Lake is privately owned and operated. Summer after summer its visitors from Mercer and Franklin, New Castle and Pittsburgh, return to its quietness, there to fish or to go boating or to lie on the beach and watch the clouds sail by. A peaceful place, Sandy Lake, and beautiful, where the nights are not disturbed by that enemy of summer calm, the jukebox.

From Sandy Lake, back roads took us to Conneaut, frequented by people of more gregarious natures than those who like the sun and shade of Sandy Lake. At the amusement park children, mounted on angry lions and smiling antelopes, rode out their circles of adventure, or on the roller coaster, screamed their delight at sudden curves and terrifying drops. At the sandy beach parents kept watchful eyes on straying children, and beyond the beach motorboats purred up and down the lake, sometimes drawing behind them water-skiers, tense and

90

at the sandy beach

crouching. Away from the amusement park, fisher-men frequented the coves and the inlet, for Con-neaut is the home of panfish, bass, and mighty muskellunge.

From Conneaut, a narrow road took us to Har-monsburg and Meadville, and out of Meadville Route 77 led towards Lake Canadohta. They were good roads, edged with Queen Anne's lace, blue

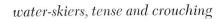

water-skiers, tense and crouching

enjoying the sunlight

a blackberry picker along the road

chickory, and wheat fields, yellow in the sun. Two young anglers of Blooming Valley discussed their luck with us, and a blackberry picker along the roadside told us that the drought had made the berries small. Then through trees we got our first glimpse of Canadohta Lake, as blue as the sky itself.

We parked at the public boat docks and watched the children fishing for bluegills. Out on the lake older fishermen sat patiently in anchored rowboats, and along the far shore, in the shadow of trees, an angler rowed slowly, trolling no doubt for one of the giant muskies occasionally caught in the lake. Small cottages fringed part of the shoreline. Not far from them a becalmed sailboat floated with limp canvas. Canadohta is less secluded than Sandy Lake, less commercial than Conneaut. There are public riding stables, a dance pavilion, a roller skating rink, shuffleboard courts, and a good beach.

Many years ago Canadohta had a marshy shoreline that was a favored home for waterfowl. Although the use of the lake as a summer resort has changed the character of the shoreline and has forced many of the birds to move elsewhere, it is not unusual to see mallards and blue-winged teal on the lake, and there are those who say that on a spring night, if you listen carefully, you can still hear the bitterns thump from the marshy shores that are left.

From Canadohta we found a fine back road that led to Cambridge Springs, the town of rest and mineral water, and then Route 99 took us to Edinboro Lake with its half-dozen beaches, its public docks, its canoe club, golf course, and riding stables. Edinboro Lake is about a mile long and about a half mile wide and is bordered on the north by marshy ground where swamp loving birds are reasonably abundant in spite of the activity on the lake. Small sailboats, canoes, and motorboats were plying the water when we arrived, and bathers were still enjoying the late afternoon sunlight. Though much of the shoreline was occupied with cottages, there was still plenty of room for rushes, cattails, and spatterdock, for a sky line of alder trees, and for a boy, strangely diminutive, trying to push his beached rowboat back into the water. We wandered about the lake for an hour or so and then, in the early evening, took Route 99 into Erie.

anglers of Blooming Valley

That evening, after finding a hotel and eating dinner, we walked down to the Erie wharf. The fishing boats had already left for their night runs, but out in the bay, in the distance, the lights of cabin cruisers, yachts, and speedboats flickered, green and white and red, and beyond the bay, far to the northwest,

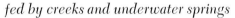

fed by creeks and underwater springs

93

a lakeside cottage

we saw, or thought we saw, a long avenue of lights where the fishing boats had anchored. They had left at about seven o'clock and would not be back before midnight. In the morning we would take one of these party boats and try our luck at a kind of fishing with which we were unfamiliar.

Meanwhile we wandered about the pier, where patient or indifferent anglers fished with rods and handlines, where spears of colored light shot across the water from the city, and where nets drooped damply from their winding racks. From the north a breeze had sprung up, and waves lapped against the sides of the boats moored to the pier.

Across the peaceful bay, lights glimmered on Presque Isle. But the bay and the land around it had not always been as peaceful as they seemed this night. There in 1753 the French had built their substantial fort of chestnut logs and had felt secure against enemies and time. Six years later the victorious English arrived and found "Prisque Isle in Ruins a Number of Gun Barrels Scalping knives and Seven Canoes with holes cutt in them." And in only a few years the haughty English themselves surrendered their mainland fort to Ottawas and Chippewas under the command of the great Chief Pontiac. Here in the peaceful harbor was launched the U.S.S. "Niagara," from the deck of which Commodore Perry wrote his terse message of victory over the English fleet: "We have met the enemy and they are ours, two ships, two brigs, one schooner, and one

sloop." Here Mad Anthony Wayne died and here at his request he was buried. Here is the grave of Captain Charles V. Gridley, who received and executed Admiral Dewey's command, "You may fire when you are ready, Gridley." And here was born Henry Thacker Burleigh, the not wholly peaceful composer of *Swing Low, Sweet Chariot* and *Nobody Knows de Trouble I've Seen.*

We looked again at the lights on Presque Isle, itself the result of six hundred years of strife and conflict, and then walked up the street to the city square. For half an hour, sitting on a green bench, we listened to an old-fashioned band concert. Between numbers, city crickets shrilled their own chorus and tree frogs chanted.

As we walked back to the hotel, Ray said, "What makes you fellows so quiet?"

"You're too young to know," Tom said. "I used to hear him at old Exposition Hall."

"Who?" Ray asked.

"Victor Herbert," I said, "in the evening. And in the afternoon there were popcorn balls in red tissue paper and the Battle of the Monitor and Merrimac."

"And the smell of gunpowder," Tom added.

"Erie," Ray said, agreeably, "is a nice city."

At seven o'clock the next morning we were down at the pier, and by seven-thirty we had paid the captain his fee, had assembled our rods, and with a dozen other fishermen on the boat, had passed through the bay and anchored a short distance beyond the protecting arm of Presque Isle. By that time each of us had been given a can of live minnows and a can of garden worms.

"Perch beds," the Captain said. "About fourteen feet of water."

We baited our hooks, let our lines down over the side of the boat, and waited. Already the sun was beating down warmly through a blue haze. A few hundred yards away another party boat had anchored, and clustered around that boat and ours were dozens of smaller boats.

A voice behind us said, "Coming up," and we turned just in time to see a beautiful perch being lifted into the boat. Then the handsome boy who was sitting next to us caught one, and then two rods on the other side of the boat bent under the weight of their catches. Everywhere but in front of us the perch were biting.

"Why," I asked the Captain, "don't they take *our* minnows?"

He took my rod for a moment, moved it up and down. "You're in the weeds," he said. "Bring it up about four feet."

After that we caught fish as fast as the others. Erie perch take the bait gently. First comes a light tug on the line, hardly perceptible, then a short run, when the hook should be set. Waiting longer results in the perch being hooked too deeply for release.

While we fished, we watched. The small fishing boats with outboard motors bobbed about on the waves. The large party boat rode motionless. Twice during the morning large tankers emerged indistinctly from the haze of the outer lake and passed close to us as they entered the bay. And all around, terns swept over the water and swooped suddenly downward for morsels of food. Sometimes they hung high above, and the next moment on powerful pinions they skimmed the surface of the lake so low that spray from the waves touched their silvery breasts.

perch were biting

Meanwhile through the haze the sun beat hotly. It was not the kind of day that makes photographers happy, but the boy beside us, still catching perch, looked as though he had never known a day so wonderful.

I asked the Captain how the fishing compared with the fishing of other years.

"Not so good," he said quickly. "Not nearly so good."

When I asked him why, he said. "We need fishing laws to protect the fish when they're on the spawning beds." Then he pointed towards the shore. "And

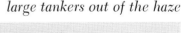

large tankers out of the haze

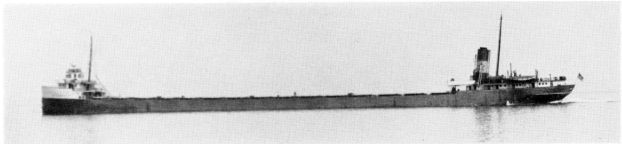

over there," he added, is a paper mill. There used to be good water over there."

He went to the cooling box for a bottle of pop. When he came back, he said, "Commercial fishing up here's an important industry, but it won't last long unless we use our heads. It's going fast."

"The lamprey eels . . . ?" I asked.

"That hurt," he said, "but the worst is the spawning beds." He shook his head. "Maybe the industry—and Harrisburg—will wake up some day. Erie needs this business."

"Maybe," Tom said.

Promptly at noon our good Captain weighed anchor, and for the first time that morning the face of the young angler near us was not beatific. "Do we have to quit now?" he asked Ray.

"I guess we do," Ray said. "Sorry?"

The captain came out of the cabin then and motioned to the boy. "We're all agreed you're the champion fisherman of this fishing party," the Captain said. "Would you like to pilot the boat back?"

The boy looked at his father, at Ray, at the Captain. "Gee," he sighed.

a new and able captain

bright boats

wharf fishermen

And so we headed back for Erie, a new and able captain at the helm. Terns following in the wake of the boat, spray breaking over the prow, we passed the lighthouse on the peninsula, the fishermen sitting on the piers, and the moored tanker that earlier in the morning had come out of the fog like the "Flying Dutchman." A few minutes later we had docked and were out on the pier again. There, at one of the restaurants, we had a delicious luncheon of blue pike, fresh from the lake, and then we took our final walk around the pier, looking at the bright boats, the gray peninsula across the bay, and the wharf fishermen, particularly the two anglers who were not, we hoped, brother and sister or even cousins.

Back in the car as we headed south, we began talking about the lakes in Penn's Woods West. Tom's favorites were little lakes like Sandy Lake at Stoneboro, Clear Lake at Spartansburg, and the reservoir at DuBois. "You can be friendly with them," he said, "but you can't get friendly with Lake Erie. It's too big. I like the little lakes with marshy shores."

Ray, who has a tattoo on his right arm, liked the big lakes. "You have room to move around on Lake Erie," he said, "or even Pymatuning. I like big boats and breakers. I like to hear them at night."

As for myself, I was thinking of Lake Gordon, ribbed with rock, in southern Bedford County, of a beaver dam I had not seen for years on Little Shade in Cambria County, and, still farther back, of a lake below a trickling spring, a lake not half so big as our

living room rug. I had made the lake myself, and there were crayfish in it, and when I was six years old I used to lie beside the lake and watch the crayfish, as they hid under rocks, wave their red feelers. Once I put fish from Mr. Braun's minnow bucket into the lake, but they died or went away.

In still waters there is a mystery that no one can explain. It is clearness and hidden things; it is shadows and the unexpected; if it is not the substance of things hoped for, it is their reflection; and surely it is the evidence of things unseen. Perhaps, as a scientist has suggested, it is a coming home to things primordial, a watery echo from the eons before life discovered lungs, a demand for regressional return to our earliest home of salt and water, before land became habitable.

Whatever its nature and origin, the mystery is part of the small boy's excitement as he wades tentatively into water that creeps up to his knees and of the older man's contemplation as he sits quietly on one shore and looks across towards the other. It lurks in every lake, whatever the size, that has in its depths or on its margins creatures that live and move and love and die. The perch that live in the shadows of weeds under fourteen feet of Erie water are part of the mystery and the love-thumping of the shy bitterns in the rushes at Canadohta are another part and we who look and listen and believe are yet another part. If we have not known the still waters, we have missed, I think, some indefinable but important fragment of life.

more wharf fishermen

more like a large trout stream

The Allegheny

WHEN WE ARRIVED AT THE RIVER ON MONDAY AFTER-
noon, Jim and Wayne were preparing lunch. They
had arrived the night before, had weathered a wild
storm, and were now drying out. After a quick greet-
ing, Tom and I went down to the river, impatient to
see the point of our departure for the long canoe trip
downstream.

A little murky from the storm of the night before,
the river shimmered in the sunlight. Small wonder,
I thought, that the French explorers called it "the
Beautiful River." Yet this afternoon it seemed hardly
a river at all. It was more like a large trout stream,
with shadowy aspens, willows, and maples along the
banks. As a matter of fact, huge trout do live and
thrive in this part of the river—rainbows, browns,
and an occasional brookie mingle with bass and
muskellunge.

It was hard to believe that this little stream, as yet
untouched by industry and by large communities,
furnishes life to the whole Allegheny valley including Pittsburgh, hard to believe that without this
blessed water, life in much of the valley would be
impossible and life in Pittsburgh would be less abundant than it is. Nature has been good to the people
of Penn's Woods West, and one of her more important gifts is the Beautiful River. In these years of
growing dryness the gift of a pure river is almost
like the gift of life.

We were a few miles above Corydon, Pennsylvania, and a few yards below the New York State
line. Here, as elsewhere, the Allegheny is a whimsical river of many moods. It begins in the eastern part
of Penn's Woods West, near the pleasant town of
Coudersport. From there, it strays to the northwest,
hardly more than a brook, and wanders inadvert-
ently into New York State. Near Olean, New York, it
seems to realize its childish error in direction, and,
eager to return to the woods that gave it birth, it

98

turns southward. With a gay rushing, it comes back home to Penn's Woods West almost where Tom and I were standing, still a little stream, one that we could have waded across almost anywhere, but somehow more mature for its venture into a foreign land.

A breeze blurred the reflections. As I watched the leaves of the willows turn whitely upward, I thought of another river and the trees along its edge. In her magic mirror, the Lady of Shallott saw

> Willows whiten, aspens quiver
> By the margin of the river.

Strange that she did not turn her head even before Sir Launcelot rode across her glass!

The breeze stopped, and the reflections came back, fringed at the edges and bright with little waves. Across from us there was a disturbance near the shore, like a liquid scattering of confetti, as minnows skittered across the water. I waited for the lunge of trout or smallmouth, but there was none. There were only the shadows of the willows, the sighing of wind in the treetops, the murmur of water, and, from far off, the dim trill of a wood thrush. Then I heard a metallic click, out of tune in this place of gentle sounds. I turned.

Tom lowered his camera and looked at me. "It's a beautiful river," he said quietly. I liked that. I knew, then, that we were going to have a good trip.

That evening, aided by maps and the light of our gasoline lantern, we made plans for the next day. The boys, of course, wanted to cover as much water as they could. "Thirty miles," Jim suggested. "Maybe forty," Wayne said.

We explained that distance was not our objective. We would take our time so that we could enjoy the River and get to know it. To see a river is one thing; to learn to know it is another. Each of us should feel free to stop, we agreed (the boys dubiously), to look at the rhododendrons, still in bloom, at a frog along the bank, at the sun-flecked spray of rapid water. We would follow the ducks if we felt like doing so, would stop to listen to a veery, would wait if we saw a deer drinking at the River's edge.

The gleam of fast adventure dimmed in the boys' eyes. Boys reared in the automobile age cannot easily change their way of life. From childhood on, they have been taught to speed across the earth rather than to learn about it. But Jim and Wayne were polite boys and courteous with their elders. They came along partly for the fun and partly for the job of pulling Tom and me from the bottom of the River if we fell in.

"Boys," Tom said, "how would you like to camp tomorrow night among the Indians?"

"Indians?" they said.

"Indians," Tom said, and he pointed to the map. Only seven or eight miles down the River was the

Jim and Wayne were preparing lunch

99

near the pleasant town of Coudersport

Cornplanter Indian Reservation, the last remaining home of the American Indian in Penn's Woods West —or East.

The gleam came back into the eyes of the boys and settled the matter of our destination. We would see if the descendants of Chief Cornplanter would allow us to share a night along the Allegheny.

When I awoke, it was still dark in the tent. For a moment I lay in a half dream, and then I heard the door zipper open and close. Tom was up. There was no point to lying in bed. I was rested, more rested, it seemed, than I had been for years. I wanted to get up and so I did.

Outside, everything was blurred. A luminous mist hovered between me and the tent in which Jim and Wayne were sleeping, a few yards away. I turned towards the River and saw an indistinct Tom. When I got to him, he said, almost apologetically, "Sometimes you get a good picture when the sun breaks through the fog."

But the sun never did break through the fog that morning. Instead, the mist merely evaporated, an imperceptible disintegration. We went back to camp after awhile and cooked our breakfast—slab bacon cut thick and eggs that were golden enough to please Midas.

"What about the boys?" I said.

"Let them sleep," Tom said. "They probably talked half the night anyway."

And so we let them sleep. Why not? We had no timetable. Tom wandered off somewhere, as a good photographer should, and I put my rod together and greased the line, as a fisherman should. Within an hour or so, I had caught and released three small bass and a rainbow trout that might have measured fifteen inches. They would be there next day for another angler, but a little wiser for the experience of this morning, a little harder to catch.

At ten o'clock the boys got up. At eleven the tents were down and we were ready to start.

100

The boys pushed off in their canoe, Tom and I in ours. They were big canoes and heavy, thoroughly reliable for the kind of water we expected. In sheer exuberance, the boys paddled in circles around their elders for a time, but half of each circle had to be upstream paddling. The Allegheny is swift. The boys soon settled down. Before long they were ahead of us and out of sight.

Above us, clouds floated across a bright blue sky. Before us, the River sparkled in the sunlight. And all around us were the Allegheny Mountains, the oldest mountains in the United States, brightly green against the blue, with cloud shadows moving across them, and everything, because reflected on the water, doubly visible and doubly beautiful. Often we stopped paddling altogether and let the canoe drift as it would. That way, we could look, from time to time, in all directions, and everything we saw seemed good.

Once, on a little plateau across the River, a doe and fawn, dappled with shade and sunlight, stared at us. Paddling slowly, we tried to get close to them, but when we were about twenty yards away, they took fright and bounded into the woods. We wondered if the boys had seen them.

Farther down, we watched a mallard and three ducklings swimming close to the rushes of an island. As we approached, the ducklings fled to the rushes.

dappled with shade and sunlight

For half an hour we tried unsuccessfully to find them. But we had not gone downstream more than a hundred yards before we looked back, and there they were, the three ducklings and their mother resuming their normal way of life, searching for tidbits beside the water rushes. Though they did not know it, they had less to fear from us than from their ancient enemies, the snapping turtles that lie in wait for them under the knee-deep water.

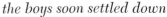

the boys soon settled down

Chester Redeye

We idled away much of our time, but by two o'clock we were opposite the land of the Cornplanters. Where the boys were we did not know, but something had gone wrong. Near a great sycamore that leaned out over the water we beached our canoe and made it fast. The boys could not fail to see it if they should pass. Then we scrambled up the bank to an old dirt road that, our maps told us, followed the course of the River. About a quarter-mile down the road we came to a frame house near which an old man was whetting a scythe. We told him who we were and what we wanted. Did he know where we could go to get permission to camp? He smiled then, and the sunlight was bright on his face. He told us his name was Chester Redeye, and that he was, himself, a direct descendant of Chief Cornplanter. He was eighty years old, he said, and had always lived in the reservation. Of course we could camp on Cornplanter land.

With an arm that was not withered, he pointed up the River. There was a place to pitch a tent, he said, and he described the place. There was a spring, too, and the water was good. He, himself, often drank the water. It was better than the spring he had at his own house.

We thanked him and went back to the canoe. A hundred yards upstream we found the camping site and a spring brook. There were fingerling trout in the brook, and the water was as cold as a trout stream in April. By four o'clock our tent was up, and we were sitting in front of it looking across the Beautiful River.

But by now we were beginning to worry about our boys. We could have passed them when there was an island between us. That did not seem likely, however, for when we had last seen them they were far ahead of us. On the other hand, it did not seem likely that they could have overshot their mark, for we had explained the map to them carefully.

After dinner, we climbed back to the road. Tom would go up the road about two miles and I would go down the same distance. If we did not see the boys, we would return to camp.

It was nearly six o'clock before we got back to the tent, but almost as we got there, we saw the two boys paddling wearily *up* the River. When they caught sight of our tent they changed course and slowly made their way in our direction. We helped them land and make their canoe fast, and then they told us the story. It was simple enough. Paddling rapidly down the River, they had gone past the reservation without noticing it.

After a long time they had realized their mistake, had turned around, and had paddled back. Paddling up the Allegheny, they assured us, was harder than paddling down. That night they went to bed early and did not talk, but not before we had agreed that hereafter the two canoes would always keep within sight of each other.

Long after the boys were asleep, Tom and I sat by the fire in front of the tent and looked out over the River. A thin moon shot slivers of light across the water. High in the treetops the wind moaned. Screech owls sent quavering calls from shore to shore. Tonight there was no doubt that they were the calls of owls, but two hundred years ago . . . Two hundred years ago, *Gaiant waka*, the Cornplanter, and his Seneca warriors paddled their canoes in silence along this same River. In the dark forest that covered the mountain behind us, they hunted deer and bear and elk. In the spring, they snared the trout and speared the great sturgeon in the River that belonged to them. For then, this ground was *Jennesadaga*, home of *Gaiant waka*, the betrayed and honorable *Gaiant waka*, whose ghost this night stood for a long time between us and our sleep.

cloud shadows on wooded hills

Early the next morning, Tom and I left camp to look at the vestiges of an old and noble civilization. We wanted to see, first, the burial ground. We walked the road silently, and our thoughts were of *Gaiant waka,* the Cornplanter, the warrior, the honorable man, the diplomat, the satirist of the white man's logic and behaviour.

Even in early childhood, the Cornplanter had reason to wonder about the ways of white men. His skin was lighter than that of his friends. Sometimes his friends spoke of the difference. When, one evening, in the teepee, he asked his mother why this difference should be, she put her brown arm around him and told him about John O'Bail. John O'Bail was a white man with whom, years before, she had been in love. *Gaiant waka* had been born of this love. But in a manner strange to the Senecas, John O'Bail had wearied and had wandered off.

After he had become a warrior, *Gaiant waka* located his father and went to visit him. The Cornplanter's short account of that meeting has overtones of satire and contempt. "He gave me victuals while I was at his house, but when I started to return home, he gave me no provision to eat on the way. He gave me neither kettle nor gun . . ." The strange morality of the white man had been made clear. With his own son, *Gaiant waka* would not have acted so.

103

Cornplanter's marker

the names of the dead men

About a mile up the road, we saw his marker. It stood gray and inconspicuous among the weeds. Though we felt like intruders, we walked towards it through the dewy weeds and grass. We read the half-obliterated inscription. Is it the white man's apology for the betrayal of a nation? If so it is strangely paternal. Is it an effort to make amends? If so, it came thirty years too late, thirty years after the wise Indian's death.

Chief of the Seneca tribe, and a principal chief of the Six Nations from the period of the Revolutionary War to the time of his death. Distinguished for talent, courage, eloquence, sobriety, and love for tribe and race, to whose welfare he devoted his time, his energy, and his means during a long and eventful life.

It was he who told his friend President Washington, "What the Seneca Nation promise, they faithfully perform." It was he and his nation who were granted by formal treaty in 1794 a pitiful remnant of their empire "so long as the Allegheny flows and the sun and moon shine."

We wandered through the ancient burial place and looked at the gray stones, at the names of the dead men, ghosts that still haunt, it seems, the little that remains of their native land. If we did not hang our heads as we left the plot of the dead, we felt like doing so. And yet, I think, we took a ragged wisp of

104

comfort back to the road with us: on the morning of our walk at least seven hundred acres of Penn's Woods West still belonged to the Senecas.

We walked on along the road. Once it had been the trail through *Jennesadaga,* the Seneca village that was a mile long. Now it was Legislative Route 61037. We passed a little stream. Along the old road, blue chicory bloomed. We forgot about Route 61037. A yellow chat talked nonsense to us from a branch on a wild cherry tree. He had been talking that same discriminating nonsense since Cornplanter was a baby. He had sung it, no doubt, long before the Cornplanter had been born. He had sung it to the Mound Builders and to those who had lived here in the unremembered and unpictured past before even the Mound Builders had first seen the Beautiful River. Older than the Senecas, older than the Mound Builders, the yellow chat sang from a wild cherry bough.

For a moment we stopped and looked at the River, bright and singing, and youthful yet older than *Gaiant waka,* older than the Mound Builders and those who lived before them, older than the yellow chat: the River that once knew the cold of the glaciers and the torment of mountains being leveled to icy plains and the dead mammoths frozen in millions of tons of glistening ice that once covered the road we were now walking on, the familiar trail that the Cornplanter trod only short centuries ago.

older than the Senecas—the yellow chat

From the trail of the Cornplanter and of prehistoric ice, we saw a house made of wood that had been sawed in a mill but never painted. On the porch of the house were two women, one of them, we could tell, very old. In front of the house was a man. We walked up the road to the house.

I told the man in front of the porch who we were, and he told us who he was and introduced us to the women on the porch. One was his mother. She was eighty years old, he said. The other was his wife, crippled with arthritis. The doctors, he said, had tried hard but she still had arthritis. He guessed she would always have it. She could not go to the spring anymore. Sometimes, though, if he helped

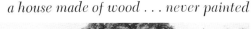

a house made of wood . . . never painted

Frank Logan

her, she could go down the porch steps and pick flowers. And together, she and his mother could do the washing.

After awhile, I asked him about the new dam at Kinzua. He did not know what would become of them, he said, but he had heard that They would do something for them. There were only eight families left of the nation.

I heard Tom's camera click once and then again.

It is hard to forget the face of Frank Logan, descendant of *Gaiant waka*. Perhaps it is a sad face, but it has the serenity of sunsets, and the fortitude of the rocks along the River, rocks that the glaciers displaced but could not destroy.

When we got back to camp, the boys were up and were eating a breakfast of bread and jelly. "When do we start?" said one. "And how far can we go?" asked the other.

Within an hour, we had broken camp and were on our way down the River. Through the slow eddies and down the fast riffles we paddled, watching for the oily swells that meant hidden rocks. Soon we fell into an easy rhythm, and the trees and grass and rocks along the shore seemed to be going past us very

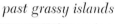

past grassy islands

rapidly. The flowering raspberries were in purple bloom, and the last of the rhododendrons blossomed in pink masses on the banks. Sometimes the drops from Tom's paddle caught the sunlight and sparkled like iridescent beads.

Down we went, past Olmstead and the Boy Scout Camp, where two youngsters were racing their canoes without paddles, past grassy islands and sand bars, past Sugar Run, and then through the little town of Kinzua. For a moment, I wanted to stop there and to turn up into Kinzua Creek, a beautiful stream, where the trout grow large and brilliant. But before I knew it, we had swept past in the swift current, and the creek was far behind us.

Below Kinzua, at the Big Bend, the mountains grew steeper and came closer together, until we felt, at times, as though we were going through a canyon with the sun hidden behind the mountain side and the whole valley steeped in shadow. When we came to Dixon Island, we stopped for lunch or dinner, whichever we cared to call it. And while we ate, we watched the bass chasing minnows through the riffles and, far above us, a hawk that had found a current of air to his liking.

After lunch I took a walk for a few hundred yards up the River. I kept thinking about the canyon we had passed through. It is the site of the proposed dam that, rising 180 feet above the River, will form the Allegheny River Reservoir and inundate not only the canyon but square mile after square mile of land above Kinzua, above Corydon, above the State line, and on into New York State. On this much-disputed project the sum of $100,000,000 will be spent.

There is much that can be said in favor of the reservoir. In one week in 1954, for instance, other flood control projects that cost $107,000,000 saved the Allegheny Valley more than $140,000,000 in flood damage. And there is no doubt about the skill or the integrity of the Army Engineers. If they build a dam, it will be sound. They will do exactly what Congress authorizes them to do. They will do no more—which is proper. When constructed, the reservoir will accomplish three things: (1) it will store water when there is an excess of it, thereby diminishing the damage of floods, (2) it will release water when there is not enough in the River for navigation or for industrial use, and (3) in periods of low water it will dilute the downstream contamination already in the River. Of course it will end the dream of the River Improvement Association for a system of locks and dams that would make the Allegheny navigable

to Olean, but in other ways the reservoir will be of great financial value to the people of Penn's Woods West.

Nevertheless, one wishes that more thought and research could be given this project than the Army Engineers have given it or, by virtue of their limited training, are able to give it or, by Congressional authority, are permitted to give it. An incomplete job is often an economic waste, and this project is likely to be incomplete unless a way is found for other agencies to participate in it at the planning stage— specifically, such agencies as the Pennsylvania Department of Forests and Waters, the Pennsylvania Department of Agriculture, the Sanitary Water Board (especially if reconstituted), the Fish and Game Commissions, and perhaps civilian experts in sanitation, ecology, and engineering.

Much of the difficulty in undertakings of this kind arises from a division of authority. When the Army purchases land for a flood control project, it pur-

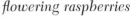

flowering raspberries

mountains grew steeper

chases only the land that will be covered by the water and a small area surrounding the perimeter of the lake. The drainage basin itself is not the concern of the Army. Yet in this particular project the drainage basin contains 2,190 square miles! And on the management of that tract of land and the streams that flow through it depends, in a large measure, the life and the usefulness of the reservoir.

When the reservoir fills with water, the management of the vital drainage basin is either nobody's business or the State's, and the agencies of the State may or may not be prepared to cooperate with carefully drawn plans and with necessary finances in their budgets. After the Army has placed a reservoir in the middle of an unprotected drainage basin, it may be a little late to ask questions. It would be better to ask them now.

Will, for example, New York State and the Pennsylvania Sanitary Water Board permit the cities of Kane, Bradford, and Jamestown and the towns of Smethport, Coudersport, Port Allegany, Eldred, Portville, Allegany, and Salamanca to drain their sewage into the reservoir? Will the Sanitary Water Board see to it that the coal mines in the drainage area are more adequately sealed than they have been in other projects? Will the Department of Forests and Waters reforest the drainage basin for miles back from the water line in order to keep the level of the dam more nearly constant and to minimize the siltation that sometimes renders a dam useless in twenty-five to fifty years? Will the Department of Agriculture insist upon the construction of small upstream dams—the value of which is more obvious to conservationists than to engineers—to help control silt? Will an honorable effort be made to relocate the Seneca Indians on ground that is better than they have now in partial compensation for our violation of our treaty with them—a moral question, to be sure, but an important one? In planning new roads through the area, will the Highway

Department drain and plant its right of ways so that ill-planned roads do not wash out the work of the Department of Agriculture and the Department of Forests and Waters? Will they cooperate with the Fish and Game Commissions in planning small ponds at bridges?

All that the Army Engineers are asked to do is to build a dam. They will build well. But they do not have either the knowledge or the authority to finish the job in terms of water conservation. And a finished job is necessary, for water has already become our most precious and most imperiled natural resource. Today we use four times as much water as we did in 1900—but there is less water in Penn's Woods West than there was then. By 1975 we will need eleven times as much water as in 1900. And as things stand now, it will not be there to use.

When nature designed Penn's Woods West, she endowed it with an almost profligate supply of wonderful water, more by far than she gave to most parts of America. Because we had so much water wealth, we used it generously and often unwisely. We could not have known then that someday there would not be enough.

Now we know. Our industry, our culture, and the lives of our children depend upon saving what is left. The building of dams will help, but they will not be enough unless we add the knowledge and the coordinated efforts of all the agencies in the State that can maintain and improve a first-class watershed, here and throughout our region.

And there is something more. We must add, also, the industrial and political courage (1) to take away the special privileges of pollution now granted to a few industries and (2) to assist these industries, in all fairness, for the period of their readjustment to the common welfare. If we can do these things, our resources of pure water will, in ten years, be the envy of the nation.

This is a large bill, but our future as a community depends upon it. The year 1975 is not far away.

When I got back to the canoes, the boys had already washed the dishes and were eager to depart. We pushed off and were on our way again down the Beautiful River. There are many islands in this portion of the River, islands that force the canoeist to make up his mind which channel is the better. The water was high, though, and we seldom had to step out of the canoe to lighten the load. Often we slowed our pace to look at the shore birds on the stones or near the rushes. There were spotted sandpipers and

the killdeer tilted impudent tails

Virginia rails and killdeer that tilted impudent tails. Twice that afternoon we saw bitterns and once a woodduck hen hiding her ducklings among the spatterdocks.

We skirted Harmon Island, swept past Hemlock Run and the half-dozen houses near it, counted the next three islands and kept to the right of them, and then, in the middle of the afternoon, began looking

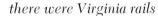

there were Virginia rails

a dinner of slab bacon

We did not care, of course. They climbed the hill to the road, and we heard them talking excitedly as they started off for Warren.

It was almost dark now. The fireflies were out. The whippoorwills were still singing, and an old bullfrog monotonously announced his presence to the River and to all who lived around it. Another bullfrog said that he, too, lived there. They talked the matter over gruffly but politely, each waiting until the other had spoken. Moonlight drifted through the fog and brightened the riffles above us and glimmered on two rocks that stood gray between us and the brightness. In the air was the smell of hemlock. When either of us struck a match, we could see the blur of rhododendron blossoms. Once, behind us, we heard the bark of a fox.

And all around us were the night sounds, the almost imperceptible but swelling chorus of the creatures that live in the woods and move and sing when darkness comes: the crickets and katydids and tree frogs, the scratching of a mouse among leaves, the muffled beating of the wings of an owl, the shriek of a rabbit, caught, perhaps, by a weasel, the soft

washing the dishes

for a campsite a few miles above Warren. We found a beautiful spot on the left side of the River, beached our canoes, and made camp among the hemlocks and the rhododendrons. We had dinner then, Tom and I cooking it, Jim and Wayne washing the dishes.

After a dinner of slab bacon we sat among the rhododendrons and looked out over the River. Mist was beginning to rise from the water in uncertain layers, and from the lowlands opposite us the whippoorwills were singing. Far off a train whistle moaned among the hills. The shadows in the valley deepened, and above us, high clouds caught the last light of day and turned dark and purple against the blue.

After awhile, the boys grew restless. They went back to the tent. When they appeared again, they were conspicuously fresh in clean T-shirts. There must be a picture house in Warren, they had decided. Did we care if . . .?

stomping of the hooves of a deer, and through it all, the River itself, telling in a strange tongue of things ancient and intangible.

We sat there a long time in the darkness. If we said anything at all, I do not remember what it was. When the River is speaking, the humble man listens and is silent.

Later on, we went back to the tent. I did not go to sleep at once. After about an hour, I heard the boys coming along the road. Their voices sounded happy.

Maybe the River is for older folk.

Early the next morning, we were on our way again. The sky was bright but overcast, and there was a blue haze in the air. Whether it rained or not, we had decided, we should camp a short distance above Tideoute, provided, of course, that we could find a site on the rugged mountain sides.

We had gone but a short distance when we saw below us the little city of Warren and the steel bridge across the River. The current was swift and carried us rapidly towards the bridge. As we crossed under the central span, Tom and I cut sharply to the right, for we wanted a good glimpse of Conewango Creek. The boys were ahead of us, almost at the bend in the River.

We had not long to wait. It came upon us suddenly, sweeping in from the northeast, a fast stream and wide, so wide that it seemed a little river itself.

For a moment I found myself looking for a great red oak, though I knew it must have died many years before.

Here, where we held the canoe for a few minutes at the mouth of the Conewango, Celoron almost two hundred years ago had caught his first glimpse of the Beautiful River. He and his company had come down the Conewango by birch-bark canoes from Lake Chautauqua. He recorded in his journal that he arrived "at the entrance of the Beautiful River, the 29th of July (and) buried at the foot of a red oak, on the southern bank of the river Oyo and Kana-ougon, and at 42 5' 23" a leaden plate." A short distance up the Allegheny, along the shores we had just passed, he soon discovered, was the Indian village of Conewango, consisting of "twelve or thirteen cabins." He visited them. "The women," he wrote, "brought me presents of Indian corn and squashes, for which I gave them little presents." More significant than the "little presents" he gave them, though, was the lead plate he planted at the foot of the red oak, a plate that announced to any who cared to dig it up that the river and the land belonged to France. Had the Indian dug up the plate and had he been able to read the French inscription, he might have marveled at the white man's arrogance.

We went on down the River, catching up with the boys at the next bend. They had waited for us. Occasionally, we passed an angler fishing along the

111

we passed an angler

shore. Once we saw a boy landing a large fish, but what kind it was we could not tell.

We passed Meade Island, Leek Island, Grass Flat Island. There were fewer houses now, fewer boats, and fewer fishermen. Then, to our right, we saw Brokenstraw Creek entering the River. Celoron called it "Cutstraw." Once, there was a Seneca village along the Brokenstraw, that pleasant trout stream that empties into what was described, back in 1754, as "one of the most beautiful rivers in ye world." Indeed, it was . . . and still is.

We were tempted to go up the stream to try our luck for trout, but a light mist was beginning to fall, and we thought we should continue.

All afternoon, the rain kept up, not a heavy rain but steady and gentle. The clouds hung low, blotting out the tops of the mountains and settling in the valleys. Fog drifted in wisps along the surface of the River. We passed Crull's Island, where a blue heron stood calmly in the rain and where a muskrat started to swim across the River ahead of us. He dived under when he saw our canoe, came up about fifty feet away, and went on about his damp business of crossing the River. Sometimes Tom would lay down his paddle, unwrap his camera, and try to get a shot of cloud and hill and river. Then he would dry the camera off and put it away again in the water-proof bag.

After Crull's Island came Thompson's Island, where, in 1779, General Brodhead attacked and defeated "between thirty & Forty warriors coming down the Allegheny River in seven Canoes."

Island after island split the River below Thompson's. Once we took the wrong channel and found

the water churned and swirled

ahead of us loomed two boulders

ourselves in a stream of fast moving water not more than twenty or thirty feet wide. The water churned and swirled and, when it hit a boulder, threw up a wild spray. Twice waves spilled into the canoe and once a crosscurrent almost spun us sideways. Then ahead of us loomed two boulders with maybe enough space for the canoe to squeeze between them. There was a quick scrape of stone on the bottom of the canoe, and then we swept swiftly out of the fast water and into the main channel of the River.

In a few minutes, we saw the boys paddling leisurely down the channel on the other side of the island and out into open water. Theirs had been the right way, and ours had been the wild one.

Even in the rain, the mountain on the left side of the River looked beautiful and exciting. It came down abruptly, and rhododendron clumps shone in the wetness. If only we could find a level place large enough for two tents! A mile or two down the stream, as we skirted the left shore, we saw a path that began between two boulders and crept steeply up the hillside. We nosed in, made our canoes fast, and climbed the path.

At the top, the ground leveled off into a fine grove where there were gravel paths and fireplaces and picnic tables and benches. We walked along a gravel path until we came to a sign that read "Roadside Rest." Near it, a man in a rain slicker looked at us curiously. He was the caretaker of the place, he said, and of other grounds nearby that belonged to the State. No, he did not think he could let us camp

here, although, considering the kind of day it was and how hard it was to find a good camping site . . . I showed him a letter from the Department of Forests and Waters, a letter that asked the Department's personnel to help us in whatever way they could.

"Over there," he said, pointing, "is a good place for your tents. And right there," he pointed again, this time to a stone drinking fountain, "is the best drinking water in the State. Hope you have a good night," he said, "but it's sure gonna be a wet one."

Getting our gear up the slippery path was not easy, but there were two old backs and two young ones, all of them willing. It was not long before we were set up. We cooked our dinner late that afternoon in the rain, and we ate it in the large tent. And we had long drinks of "the best drinking water in the State."

Rain or no rain, it had been a good day, about thirty wet miles on the River, and there had been the herons and ducks, and the muskrat, and Conewango and Brokenstraw, and a stretch of wild white water, and the clouds touching the mountain ridges and creeping down into the river valley. We were wet and tired and content.

At about six o'clock, the rain stopped. The boys decided to walk to Tideoute. I asked them to telephone their parents while they were in town and Mr. Beachler of *The Pittsburgh Press*. He had said, before

we came to a sign

113

best drinking water in the State

we left, that he would like to come up and spend a day or two fishing. They could tell him where we were, and if he felt like coming . . .

Tom and I did not do much river gazing that evening. We did walk along the bluff for a time and looked down through the hemlocks and the rhododendron at the fog that curtained rock and riffle. There was fog on the bluff, too. As we walked, a great sea of it drifted in, blurring sight and sound.

After a time, we went back to our tent. It would be foggy and rainy the next day, Tom said, and so, from a photographer's point of view, there was little use in planning to go on down the River.

As I went to sleep, the rain had started in again. It dripped on the roof of the tent. Quiet rain on a tent at night is a soothing sound. It is persuasive and hypnotic. For awhile, you try to listen to it, do listen to it, to the separate and distinct drops striking the tent, to the flurries of them, and then the awareness slips away from you. The drops become an indistinct and conglomerate tapping, monotonous

and lulling, farther and farther away, until the sound of them is no longer an indistinct tapping but a drowsy humming, and you move your head on the pillow and the humming turns to darkness.

I did not hear the boys come back, but I did not worry. They are good boys and strong and capable.

The morning fog was heavy, a gray, ubiquitous cloud that blurred the edges of sight and sound. The tent was a gray mass without shape or size. Tree trunks were fuzzy lines of darkness. The sky itself, without horizons, was only more of the milky vapor, but lighter and more luminous. Below me, the crisp sound of the riffles had dulled to a murmur. No birds sang. From all around came an indeterminate dripping, and as we prepared for breakfast, the pots and pans clinked like pewter vessels.

It was a mysterious world, indistinct and incredible. We trod the earth without sound, ourselves as unsubstantial, it seemed, as the dream world that surrounded us. So the days must have dawned a hundred million years ago, when, from time to time,

114

the earth heaved heavily and these same Appalachian Mountains were born into the fog. So the dawns must have been in the days of the dinosaurs as they crept through forests of dripping ferns and cycads. For this ghostly, intangible vapor that had come over us in the night is older than man, older than dinosaur, than spider and protozoa, older than the earth itself. If mist was my primal home, I think I shall be content, after the final moment, to return to it.

Before noon, we heard a wind moving among the treetops. It came from the north. We heard it from a long way off, and it swept the wetness from the leaves in sudden showers. It moved the fog in uncertain swirls and eddies, like the currents of the River, like a school of minnows scattering in fright. For a time, the grove would be free of mist. Then the fog would flow in again and again flow away.

Shortly the grove was clear, and we looked upward. The sky was dull, and we knew that the clearing of the fog was less a promise than a threat. We got the boys up and gave them the best lunch we had had on the trip. It would not be long before they would be leaving us. Tionesta was our next stop, and at that point we would be parting. We knew we would be lonely when we saw them leave.

Early in the afternoon, I started down the path for a bucketful of "the best drinking water in the State," and at the pump I saw David. I had never seen David before, but I knew he was David the moment I saw him flashing the Beachler smile. Far behind him came Ed.

"Are you David?" I said, just to be sure.

"Yep," he said. "When can we start fishing?"

Ed had come up.

"Well," I said, "what about right now?"

it had been a good day

115

David sat on the stones

David's face was the brightest thing I had seen all day. "Let's hurry," he said. "I've never been fishing before."

In a few minutes, we had skidded down to the River. I looked up at the sky. It had trouble in it.

David sat on the stones at the edge of the water. "How do I put the worm on?" he whispered.

"I'll show you," his father told him. "Once. After that, it's up to you."

Ed baited the hook and both of us watched the boy. There was a clap of thunder, then, and we looked up. The even gray of the sky had changed to heavy clouds with black edges.

David flung the worm awkwardly into the River, and as he did so, the rain began to fall. This was no gentle rain. It swept up the valley in slanting curtains and spattered the River.

But we accepted the storm as part of the day. David sat in an attitude of oriental patience, his blue jeans turning dark, rain dripping from the peak of his cap. Then his whole body stiffened and he leaned forward. "I got a bite," he said. "I think I got a bite."

His father stooped down beside him. "You sure, David?"

The line cut cleanly out into the River. "You're darn tootin'. What do I do now?"

"Jerk your rod hard and then reel."

David did, and line began to whine from the reel. Forty feet out in the River, a bass leaped clear of the water. It was not a large bass, but at that moment, it was the most important fish in the world because it was his first.

David was reeling in. At the edge of the rock, the bass turned over—having come a long way and fast. David heaved on the rod, and fish and sinker flew through the air and landed on the bank behind us.

"I got it," David yelled. He scrambled off the rock and grasped his prize between his hands.

Then I heard Ed saying in a voice strangely gentle, "It's your first fish, David."

When the boy looked up, there was something in his face that I think I shall always remember. Maybe it was only the gleam of rain, maybe it was blessedness or faith, or maybe it was my memory of another boy and his first fish and a still remembered pool in a far away river. Whatever it was, it was good to see and to store away for an empty time.

"David," I heard Ed saying, "we've got to go now."

"Gee," David said, "can't we fish anymore? We just started."

"After the storm," Ed said. "Maybe after the storm."

We climbed up the slippery hill, David leading the way.

That night, with the rain still pelting down on the tent, we made our plans for the morning. If the rain stopped, we decided, we would start for Tionesta. That was to be our last day with Jim and Wayne, whose vacation had come to an end. Ed and

cutting into the white caps

116

the bridge near Tionesta

David would drive to Tionesta, would meet us there, and would take the boys home.

Before we turned out the lantern, I took a last look at David. His hair was still wet, and so was the blue jacket he had rolled up for a pillow. But he was sound asleep in his sleeping bag, and his face still smiled.

In spite of the fresh wind that blew in our faces and ruffled the water into slapping waves, we came to Tionesta in the afternoon. The boys had raced ahead of us most of the time, cutting into whitecaps, challenging the wind, then turning and coming back to us with all the speed that they and the wind could gather. After we passed under the bridge, we began to look for a campsite and came upon one, a wide sand bar, a few yards above Tionesta Creek. There we pitched our tent, just one this time. Looking at it, we felt a little lonely. A half hour later, we met Ed and David at the bridge, shook hands all around, and parted. We would miss all four.

The next morning we slept later than usual. When we awoke, the sun was shining through the doorway, and beyond the doorway the sand bar glistened white. Tom stepped out of the tent first but stopped immediately. He was looking towards the River. "Take it easy," he whispered, "but come on out."

I did, cautiously, and looked where he was looking. At the edge of the River, spaced about six feet apart, were seven turtles. Motionless, they lay in the morning sunlight, seven brown ovals on the white sand, seven spiny softshells recovering from the chill of a summer night in Tionesta.

Camera in hand, Tom started to move towards them, very slowly, but they did not approve of his presence. Simultaneously, twenty-eight flippers flipped into action, and seven softshells scrambled into the water. The ovals were gone, and the morning sunlight began to warm the chilled spots they had left.

After breakfast we walked to town and telephoned Boy Scout Headquarters at Tionesta Camp that we

117

had an excellent canoe to return to them with thanks. In about a half hour, the canoe was on its way in a truck to Tionesta Camp, and we were with it.

Set among the woods and close to Tionesta Dam, the Camp is large and beautiful. Here, hundreds of Boy Scouts become better acquainted with trees, sky, and water and learn something of their importance. We walked around for an hour or so, Tom taking pictures all the while. By ten o'clock we were back at our own campsite and were ready to resume our trip down the River.

Before we pushed off, though, we took a last look to make sure that we had forgotten nothing. Tom was the first to notice the little hole in the ground directly under the spot where we had pitched our tent. "Look," he said, "what we were sleeping on."

Almost where the pole of the tent had rested was a hole about two inches in diameter. In the hole were little white eggs, turtle eggs. Gently, I jiggled three of them out of the hole and Tom took a picture. Then we put the eggs back and filled the hole with sand. I thought of our arrival the day before. Clearly, we had interrupted the mother turtle, who had not had time to fill up the hole with warm sand. No wonder she had been unwilling to share breakfast with us!

As we paddled down the River, I thought about the fate of the eggs. Would the young turtles hatch in four or five weeks, as they should, wisely survey the world from the height of their abandoned shells, and depart for the water in their instinctive way without benefit of parents? I have no doubt they did. If Mother Turtle was in any way disturbed, it was only because part of an ancient process, the covering of the eggs, had been interrupted. In her Paleozoic concept, were she able to have a concept, her duty would have been fulfilled with the digging of the

better acquainted with trees, sky, and water

Tionesta Camp

hole, the laying of the eggs, and the filling of the hole. We had interfered with only one-third of the total duty. She would probably sleep well in spite of our intrusion. And her children, forgotten by her and unknown to her, would enter her river a few minutes after birth and would live their lives much as she had lived hers, much as her ancestors had lived theirs long before man had put in his appearance upon the earth.

In a few minutes we had passed the cluster of sandy islands below Tionesta Creek. The hills rose sharply on both sides of us, green hills and bright. Shortly after noon we passed Stewart Run and the two islands opposite. Then came a mile where the hillside on our right rose almost straight up, then Hemlock Creek on our left. We paddled steadily. By two o'clock we had swept past Eagle Rock and Henry's Bend and were at the mouth of once-famous Pithole Creek. There we stopped to cook lunch, but we were thinking of other things.

"Tom," I said, "according to the map, it's only a few miles to where the City used to be."

Tom looked at the sky and then at his watch. "If we passed up our lunch," he said, "we could probably make it there and back before dark."

We hid the canoe among some bushes, found a path along the stream, and began the walk up the valley towards what was once Pithole City, a rival

of Pittsburgh and Philadelphia, a city with the third largest post office in the state of Pennsylvania.

The valley was heavily wooded, but even among the shadows, Pithole Creek caught patches of blue sky and glimmered brightly on its way to the River. Once I saw a trout come clear of the water with a

turtle eggs

119

green hills and bright

wild splash, and a half mile up the stream we came upon a doe who let us get within twenty yards of her before she turned, flipped her tail, and bounded off through the woods.

Along the overgrown path we walked towards the forgotten City. In 1864 the City did not exist. Its site was an almost uninhabited valley through which

frightened eyes

flowed the quiet trout stream, Pithole Creek. In January, 1865, a newly drilled oil well in the valley began producing at the rate of 650 barrels a day. Hundreds of people flocked to the valley and drilled more wells. By the end of May a city had been laid out, Pithole City. By the end of November the City housed more than 15,000 people. Then the wells began to fail, and within two years most of the people had moved out. Ten years after the founding of the fabulous City, only seven voters remained.

After we had walked an hour or two, the left side of the valley began to level off. We found an old road, then, and the walking was not so difficult. Chipmunks scurried across the road, and an opossum with frightened eyes clung to a rail fence. At last we came to a bridge that spanned the creek, then to a couple of houses and a pumping station, and a few minutes later to a black-top highway, numbered 60049. We were standing on the site of Pithole City. The road we had followed for a few hundred yards had once been the main street of a wealthy, exciting city.

We walked up the black-top road to the crest of the hill and looked down into the valley. It must have looked much the same in the summer of 1864. That was the summer before Sal Fargo went to her pump for a bucket of water and got, instead, a bucket of oil, before five hundred houses lined the quickly laid-out streets, before the bars and hotels rang with bawdy songs sung by girls in rich brocades. It was before the days when teams of horses and mules, hauling barrels of oil, were drowned in the mud, before the plank road reached all the way to Titusville, before hundreds of derricks towered skyward, before Sam Van Syckle's pipeline was built, before Analisa Lund sang in Pithole City's one hundred thousand dollar opera house. And it was before the last editorial in the Pithole *Record* said, ". . . to record the rise and fall of Pithole is like marking the flight of a bird as it passes."

We walked around on the hilltop and at last found the remnants of a stone foundation wall. From its

"the little white church" at Pithole

location, we guessed that it was the foundation of "the little white church on the hill," the only church in Pithole, the church that was attended by Protestants, Jews, and Catholics alike, and also by the hotel girls, whose silken purses bulged with the profits of Saturday night.

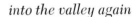

into the valley again

121

site once of a city

we watched the moon and listened to the river

As we left the stones and started across the barren field that sloped to Pithole Creek, I thought of Robert Browning's lines about another city.

> Where the quiet-colored end of evening smiles
>   Miles and miles . . .
> Was the site once of a city great and gay
>   (So they say) . . .
> Now the city does not even boast a tree,
>   As you see . . .

Down in the valley again, we stopped on the bridge and looked at the stream. It mumbled over the riffles above the bridge and spread into a placid pool below. For a few minutes, we stood there looking and listening. It had lived in this valley a long time.

When we got back to the River, it was almost dark. Tom started a fire, and I put up the tent. After dinner we sat for awhile and watched the moon and listened to the River. Both seemed very wise.

Later that night, we were sitting in the tent, talking about the day just past and planning in the laziest

a placid pool

of manners for the day to come. Moonlight streamed through the doorway, and the low-hanging branch of a maple cut across the bright sky. From far away, an owl called into the valley and into the brightness —a hesitant call, quavering and mellow. Crickets chirped with a high monotony of sound, and tree frogs saluted one another with voices of uncommon dignity.

I flicked on the electric lantern for a moment. The beam shone through the doorway and, catching the maple leaves in front of the tent, turned them to liquid silver. Suddenly, out of the silver and into the stream of light, came motion, fluttering, frantic motion. For a moment I thought it was a bird that had been dazed by the brilliance. Then I heard the scratching on the plastic screen and saw the frenzied beating of wings.

We moved closer to it. It was not a bird, but a moth, a large moth, crazed by the stream of steady light. Desperately, it fought to get to the source of

that light, to its ultimate brilliance, whether death lay in wait for it or not.

"It's an Underwing," Tom said. "Darling, maybe."

And so it was. The upper wing was a mottled brown, the under wing bright scarlet arced with black. The eyes glowed fiercely with pink and opalescent fire. And while we watched, the creature's legs clutched at the plastic screen, and the wild wings kept on beating, and the markings on the under wings were only a scarlet blur.

I turned off the lantern, and now we watched the moth against the sky and the moon. The fluttering continued for a long time, but after awhile it stopped, and the Underwing rested quietly with folded wings, a shadowy triangle against the sky.

How strange it is that the moth, brother of the butterfly, should prefer darkness to the brightness of the sun! While the sulphur butterfly dances along the roadside at noon and while the black and yellow tiger swallowtail hovers over sun-drenched cherry

123

the dark sobriety of hills

companion of the owl

blossoms, the Underwing clings to the shady side of the trunk of a tree, preferably a maple tree. All the bright day he folds his brown wings over the startling beauty of his scarlet under wings. Then, when shadows begin to creep along the ground, he rouses to explore the evening and the night, to become companion of the owl and bat and toad, to discover the unknown nectars of the dark. Is nectar sipped by night sweeter than nectar sipped in the sun? What happened, a million years ago, to make one brother seek the high lights of the sun, and another brother seek the shadows of the moon?

Again the Underwing began to move against the screen. This time, its motion was not frantic. It fluttered its wings gently, deliberately, feeling them out. Had the light of desire been forgotten? In the next moment, the dark triangle was not there, though I did not see it leave.

For a long time that night, I seemed to hear the crazed, pathetic beating of wings, to see the glow of love in eyes that were luminous and wild, to feel the uncontrolled aching for the light. My friends tell me that all this primal longing is simply phototropism, the attracting power of light. And no doubt they are right. Of course they are.

124

But the word leaves something unsaid. For a moment I felt vicariously the anguish of those who have renounced the light but who are forever drawn to it, even unto the singeing of wings, the burning of the abdomen, and the brightness of death.

❋ ❋ ❋

Early in the morning, we left Pithole Creek. We left early because we wanted to spend the night far below Oil City and Franklin, at least as far as Indian God Rock. Although the sky was cloudy, the River was as beautiful as ever. Ahead, the mountain rose sharply to a height of four or five hundred feet and cast across the gray water variegated greens and browns through which we paddled. Weather changes the mood of the River but not its character. It is always the Allegheny.

Today its dark sobriety was not matched by the hills that scampered along with it. If, while canoeing down the River, one ever gets tired of watching the water and the shoreline, he can always entertain himself by watching the whimsical behaviour of the Allegheny Mountains. For all their age, they are like fox cubs as they bounce off towards the sky, then lie down and hide in a grassy plain, then scamper away from the River, and at last scurry back to it to keep from getting lost.

For the first mile, the mountain on our left stayed close to us, though on our right it ran away a half mile towards the sky. Then, as we came to the two islands at Walnut Bend, the companionable mountain on our left dropped down suddenly and hid in a broad plain that was almost at river level. In a few minutes we had rounded the Bend, and the hill that had run away came back and grew to mountain size and looked down on us. We looked up at it, and so we paddled for another mile, the mountain on our right this time and the lowland on our left.

But suddenly the mountain we had lost when it flattened into a plain appeared again and began to rise and came racing towards us until it got to the edge of the River. There it stopped. For two miles after that, a mountain on each side to keep us company, we paddled through a gorge so narrow and so deep that sunlight could reach the water, I think, only between ten o'clock and two. It was a beautiful gorge, shadowy and brown and green.

We came out of the gorge at a little settlement called Rockmere, and there, for the first time, we caught the faint odor of oil. After the cool scents of the valley, the new odor came as a surprise. In the beginning, it is not unpleasant, though it is warm and rich and pervasive. But when it gets stronger, after you have paddled through it for a mile or so, it moves in your hair, saturates your clothing, clings to your tongue.

As we rounded a bend in the River, Oil City lay before us. We dug our paddles in more firmly. I think we would have closed our eyes at that moment, and, unseeing, would have floated past the town if we had not remembered the abandoned bridge piers that lay ahead of us and that nobody had ever taken the trouble to remove. Seeing and smelling as little as we could, we swept under the railroad bridge, around the dangerous piers, under the highway bridge, and beyond the city limits.

Afterwards, the experience of Oil City seemed strange. Here was the only unlovely stretch of water we had seen since we had left Corydon. Man had crept in and had shamed not only the River but himself. I thought of the pleasant waterfronts of Kinzua, Warren, Tidioute, and Tionesta, and the beautiful, new waterfront of Pittsburgh. Someday Oil City, too, may wash its face.

as beautiful as ever

past Cottage Rock

About two hours after we left Oil City, we were eating lunch near Franklin. Most of Franklin is built along the shores of French Creek rather than along the River, and so we saw only a small part of the little city. There is an explanation for its shy location. In 1787, a group of about a hundred people, most of them soldiers under the command of Captain Hart, arrived at the junction of French Creek and the Allegheny. They had come overland from Fort Pitt and had been instructed to build a fort near the junction of the two streams. In its lower reaches, they soon discovered, French Creek was a dangerous stream. The best place to ford it was along an Indian trail more than half a mile above the River. There the soldiers built Fort Franklin. A village grew up around the fort, and the village later became a little city. The city has remained there ever since, quietly contented, where once a narrow Indian trail crossed French Creek.

After lunch we walked into town for a few supplies. The grocery store was humming with talk about a paper mill that wanted to set up shop in Franklin.

"I'd hate to have to sell my camp down river," said a sunburned young fellow. "I have a boat, too. I guess they wouldn't be worth much."

"It might not be so bad," another man said. "They claim they have a new method of waste disposal."

A wholesale grocery salesman said, "I live in Erie. There's a paper plant there, too, and they have a new method. God, how it stinks! And even the Lake fish die."

A woman joined in the conversation. "My married daughter lives in Johnsonburg. That's up on the Clarion. I can't even stay at her house, everything smells so bad. When we visit, she has to come down here."

"Lady," said a policeman, "if that plant gets in, the whole Allegheny River will be like the Clarion all the way to Pittsburgh."

We took our packages and left. "Sounds bad," Tom said.

126

"I don't think it will happen," I said. "It *can't* happen."

Tom said nothing.

"I know what you're thinking of," I said, "but this isn't 1900. Businessmen know better, legislators know better, and the people know better. Pure water is getting scarce."

"I hope you're right," Tom said.

And I think I am. In the end, good sense prevails, and good sense will not permit a single mill to cancel out a one hundred million dollar investment in a dam at Kinzua and an even greater investment in a sewage disposal plant in Pittsburgh.

"Right now," Tom added, "your optimism isn't very contagious."

I am not an optimist, but man has come a long way since he left the jungle, and I do not believe that at this late date, he plans to commit suicide.

By the time we started off again, the sun was shining, and a brisk wind was blowing up the River. We swept past the tall, abandoned piers of a railroad bridge (A little tree was growing from the top of one of them.) and then past Cottage Rock.

After that, we began counting the islands, for at the foot of the third one, we should come upon Indian God Rock. The first came quickly, Three Mile Island. We kept to the right and soon saw Four Mile Island ahead of us.

"Let's take it easy now," Tom said.

We paddled over to the left and drifted past the island. Then, close to the left shore we saw the third island, Foster's. As we came even with it we moved as close to the left as we could and slowed the canoe down until the current of the River was going faster than we were. There were many rocks along the shore, large rocks, but there was only one that mattered.

We were almost at the end of the island now, and we had seen no stone that looked different from the rest. As we passed the lower tip of the island, Tom said, "Let's beach the canoe and look for it on foot." I turned the canoe in to shore and Tom hopped out with the rope.

But the precaution was unnecessary. Only a short distance down the River we saw it, a slab of stone sloping into the water. How many hundreds of freshets had washed against it since the original symbols of another way of life had been carved into it! And yet they were still there, dim and indistinct. We peered at them from different angles, hoping for a sunlight-and-shadow combination that would make them clear. We touched them with our fingers, trying to trace the contours and depressions. This, surely, was a sun, that a rude deer, and this wavy line a snake. But the chiseled lines were very dim, and it was hard to tell whether we were seeing them with our imaginations or with our fingers.

Spring after turbulent spring, the River had done its best to erode this early record of man's existence in Penn's Woods West. The River has done well. Soon the rock will be as smooth as it was before the wapiti roamed the mountain sides. Nothing will be left except an anonymous stone that slants into the water, a legend that may be cast aside as merely that, and a little pencil sketch made in 1853 by Captain Eastman, who wanted later generations to see what he had seen.

More than two hundred years ago this same rock was described by Celoron and Father Bonnecamps. In his camp in the wilderness, Celoron, referring as usual to the Allegheny as the Ohio, wrote:

the pencil sketch by Captain Eastman

127

In the year 1749, we, Celoron, Knight of the Royal and Military order of St. Louis, Captain commanding the detachment sent by the orders of M. the Marquis de la Galissoniere, Governor-General of New France, on the Beautiful River, otherwise called the Ohio, accompanied by the principal officers of our detachment, have buried on the southern bank of the Ohio, at four leagues distance below the River aux Boeufs, directly opposite a naked mountain, and near an immense stone upon which certain figures are rudely enough carved, a leaden plate, and have attached in the same place to a tree the arms of the king. In testimony whereof we have signed the present official statement. Made at our camp the 3d of August, 1749. All the officers signed.

That night in his journal, Father Bonnecamps added to Celoron's information and altered it slightly:

In the evening, after we disembarked, we buried a 2nd plate of lead under a great rock, upon which were to be seen several figures roughly graven. These were the figures of men and women, and the footprints of goats, turkeys, bears, etc., traced upon the rock.

No one has ever found the plate of lead. Was it buried "near" the rock, as Celoron stated, or "under" the rock, as Father Bonnecamps said? And what did Celoron mean by "four leagues"? The distance between the mouth of French Creek and the rock is about eight miles, not four leagues. Celoron, however, measured distance in a wonderfully inaccurate way, by paddle-strokes, the same number of feet to a stroke whether paddling through still eddies or through foaming rapids. Small wonder that his map of the Allegheny is confusing.

Back in the canoe, we drifted past the Rock and on down the River. The sun was shining and the sky was bright, but I felt lonely, thinking of the man who, long ago, had tried to speak in stone. There is a quality in man, whatever the color of his skin, that makes him try desperately to preserve in words or pictures his brief identity and with it his faith in something better than here and now. How naked and noble he is in his faith! Then spring comes to the

East Sandy Creek

under the railroad bridge

earth and to him and his river, and after many floods he dies. And with each April freshet the words and pictures grow dimmer until at last they are even with the stone and all that is left is a smooth blankness. What matters then? Nothing, perhaps, except the writing of the word itself. That could be enough. In the beginning was the word. And in the end.

A half mile down the River we turned into East Sandy Creek and paddled upstream for a hundred yards or so. It was still early in the afternoon. Red-finned suckers moved leisurely out of our way when we floated over them. As we drifted back down, there was a tremendous swirl of water under an overhanging tree to our left, then a splash close to shore. A bass or muskie was looking for his dinner.

We left East Sandy, went under the railroad bridge that crosses the River, and then looked forward to Big Sandy, only a few miles away, as a possible camping site. There in less than an hour, we paddled into a long, quiet pool crossed by another railroad bridge.

On the right a high stone cliff dripped with wetness, but on the left, about a quarter of a mile from the River, was level ground three or four feet higher than the stream. We tied the canoe to a tree on the bank, scrambled up to the level place, and made camp.

Tom left to gather firewood from a willow grove. In a few minutes he was back with an armload. "Wouldn't it be nice," he said, "if we could have a fish dinner tonight?"

Before he could leave for a second load, I had put the spinning rod together and had attached to the line a small wobbler spoon. Standing in front of the tent, I made the first cast across the creek to a shelf of rock hardly covered with water. For a moment I let the spoon lie on the shelf, then gently eased it off. As it began to sink, there was a wild surface rush and a hard strike. The line started upstream, turned, and moved back towards the rock shelf. Just short of the shelf a nice bass flipped into the air, shook its flashing body, and dropped back into the water. Two more leaps upstream, and it came back slowly, zigzagging to right and to left. In a moment, I reached down over the bank and netted it, about a pound and a half or two pounds of bass.

"Maybe we *will* have fish," Tom said as he left for his second load of firewood.

129

out of Sandy Creek into the Allegheny

bass for dinner

The next cast brought a small rock bass to the bank and to release. Two more casts brought nothing but expectation. On the fifth cast, another smallmouth, larger than the first, came to net after much leaping and head shaking. I walked on down the stream then and caught three more smallmouths, all of them released unharmed—as easily as if they had been caught on a fly. That is the advantage of a single hook on a bass spoon or plug instead of the lacerating treble hook.

Back at camp, we cooked the bass for dinner, and peas and potato sticks, and steaming date-and-nut bread. I cleaned up the dishes, and we sat by the fire for awhile. It had been a good day, we decided: thirty miles on the River and a dinner that could hardly be improved upon. And there was something else, though we did not talk about it: the thought of a dark figure that crouched, ages ago, on a slanting rock and tried to make permanent, forever and forever, a record of himself and of the world he knew.

When we awoke in the morning, rain was dripping gently on the tent, and a blue-gray mist veiled the cliff. Behind the tent a song sparrow trilled wetly, and down the stream somewhere a frog plunked into the water.

"Fine day for pictures," Tom grumbled.

As we ate breakfast, I said, "What do you think? Shall we go on down or wait for good weather?"

"Let's go," he said. "We might get some fog pictures."

But before we broke camp and loaded the canoe, the fog had lifted and had given way to a misty drizzle. We pushed off from the place of many bass and headed for the River. For myself, I should have been content to stay on Sandy Creek all day. I think there were pike in that pool and muskies, too, but photographers are more interested in pictures than in pike. In a few minutes we paddled out of Sandy Creek and into the River.

Into the River, and then I was no longer sorry we had left Sandy Creek. There is something hypnotic and magical about the Allegheny. As soon as you are on it and feel the current pulling, you are caught up in the spell. You forget other streams and other loveliness. Every morning, when you start out on it, it is as fresh and new as dogwood blossoms in May or a gum tree in October. Every morning it has a different look on its face, yet it is always the same face. One morning it is dancing with high lights; another morning it is as sober as its shadows. One morning it is chaste and frivolous with whitecaps; another it is as fertile and calm as the valley it inhabits. And yet in a magical way it contrives to be always the Allegheny, always the same face, whatever the expression on it, and always beautiful.

This morning as it caught us in its current, the River was somberly alluring. The current frankly led us on. From Sandy Creek to Emlenton, the Allegheny is flirtatious. It coaxes you from north to south and from east to west, a half circle one way and a half circle the other, east along a mountain side, then a quick turn and west along the other side, and every turn makes a new promise, shows part of a new vista, hazy and mysterious in the distance. You follow the enchantress because you must, but you are not unwilling, for you know that however the compass points, the vixen is worth the following.

somberly alluring

131

the misty loon

The distance between Sandy Creek and Emlenton, for a wise crow, is only eight or nine miles; for the canoeist it is twenty-five. All morning long and part of the afternoon we followed the wandering one through green, enchanted valleys, drifted along with her in the eddies, tried to catch up to her on the riffles. Throughout the day images flooded in upon us—the misty loon that left its wake on the water behind it; a colony of ferns on a rock we could have touched in passing; the grave reflections all around us; the bridge at Kennerdell, then Scrubgrass Creek; a few miles farther down, the water spilling over Falling Springs; mountains that seemed to block the valley; in the afternoon the bridge at Emlenton; a mile farther down, the ducks that felt we were intruders.

"I cou'd say much here in Praise of that sweet Tract of Land," wrote Gabriel Thomas in 1698. Indeed, he could have. To have this River makes the people of Penn's Woods West among the luckiest in the world. Centuries later the casual canoeist could still say much in praise of the valley and the River and "that sweet Tract of Land" through which they wander. But Tom's pictures are both praise and proof.

In the middle of the afternoon we passed Foxburg and then came to Clarion Island, where we pitched our tent. There were red-winged blackbirds on the island, and along the shore sandpipers tilted indecent tails.

Early in the evening, after dinner, Tom explored the little island for pictures he might take the next day. I sat on a bit of driftwood and looked at a map I had copied before we had started on our trip. It was a map that showed the drainage of the rivers in Penn's Woods West millions of years ago, before the great glaciers crept down upon us from the north.

In those prehistoric days when the mammoth roamed our hills and valleys, Lake Erie was not so big as it is now. Most of the land in our part of the country sloped gently northward, and the streams and rivers as far south as what is now Clarksburg flowed in a northerly direction and at last emptied into the lake. There were at least three major rivers that had cut deep channels to the lake.

One river started in Pennsylvania near Coudersport, flowed north and west to Olean, in New York State, and entered Lake Erie near Dunkirk. Another started near Warren, flowed south through Tidioute, Oil City, and Franklin, and then swung north and

132

west past Meadville and into the lake. A third started far above Clarion, flowed southward through Kittanning to Pittsburgh, and there turned north and west. A short distance out of Pittsburgh it picked up the Youghiogheny and the Monongahela, moved northward through Beaver, joined the Ohio near New Castle, swung over towards Youngstown, Ohio, and then turned north and emptied into Lake Erie near Ashtabula.

Today it is hard to believe that our streams and rivers that now flow south and west until they empty into the Mississippi and the Gulf of Mexico once flowed in the opposite direction, northward to Lake Erie and then to the St. Lawrence and the Atlantic. But so it was in the days of the diplodici and the fern forests.

A million years ago, if we had started our canoe trip where we did, at Corydon, or at Coudersport or Olean, we should have gone but a short distance before we came to Lake Erie. If we had started a little south of Warren, we should have gone through Tidioute, Oil City, and Franklin, as we did, but then we should have swung to the northwest and in a single day have entered the lake. And if we had started where we were this evening, we should have

a colony of ferns we could have touched

had a weary way to go indeed—to Kittanning, Pittsburgh, Beaver, New Castle, Youngstown, and at last Ashtabula.

For thousands and thousands of years the rivers had been flowing so, as their deep gorges testify. And then, one bitter day, a great glacier from the north began to creep down upon Penn's Woods West. Some of the mammoths escaped to the south;

grave reflections

133

others were caught and buried in the snow and ice. Still the glacier crept slowly southward like a gargantuan snail, moving mountains or crawling over them, eating out gorges, picking up millions of tons of earth and pebbles and boulders and carrying them with it. It kept moving southward until its outer fringe made a curving line of ice and rocks and frozen soil that extended, very roughly, from Olean to Warren to Tidioute, to Oil City and Franklin, to Slippery Rock and to a point north of East Liverpool.

No longer could the rivers of Penn's Woods West flow northward to the lake. Their way was cut off by a gigantic wall of ice. The lake itself was buried under miles of ice and its floor was sinking under a tremendous weight it could not sustain.

Falling Springs

Finding its access to Lake Erie cut off, the upper river, the river that started at Coudersport and went to Olean, turned southward there, along the wall of the glacier. It joined the river that started near Warren and rushed with it down along the edge of the glacier to Franklin. Again its access to the lake was cut off by the wall of ice and so it turned southward and met the Clarion and, together, all three flowed down to Pittsburgh. Still there was no way through to the lake. The Ohio, itself, had been dammed up and of its own accord had started moving to the south. And so, at Pittsburgh, the Monongahela and the Allegheny mingled their frustrated waters, rushed on to Beaver, and then with violence cut a new channel out of Penn's Woods West and into East Liverpool, Ohio. All this happened so many million years ago that no man was alive to witness it.

At last, on some unrecorded day, hot winds from the south swept up to meet the glacier. Summer after summer, the winds swirled and eddied around the surface edges of the glacier, turning ice and snow to water, slowly forcing the glacier to go back where it had come from. As the glacier melted and retreated, it left behind it, to mark the farthest edge of its advance, a deposit of pebbles, rocks, and boulders—the terminal and lateral morraines. Back to the north the glacier went, leaving Lake Erie not the little lake it had been before, but a huge body of water, its floor sunken to a great depth. The rivers never returned to their northward flowing. They had cut new channels and were satisfied.

This evening, as I sat on a bit of damp driftwood and watched the Allegheny swirl southward, I marveled at the strength of flowing water, water that triumphs over a mile-high glacier and feeds upon it, that grinds its way through solid rock and alters mountains as easily as it pulls the expert swimmer into its secret currents of death, flowing water that in its due time ("Time is long," said Hutton.) will fill with sediment and will destroy the finest dam that modern engineers can devise and will continue its eternal rush to the sea.

And I marveled that the River which had been carrying us southward from Corydon once flowed the other way.

As we pushed off the next morning, Tom said, "I'll be sorry to leave this little canoe."

I felt as he did. East Brady, which we expected to reach by noon, is almost a hundred and fifty miles from Corydon. Our canoe had been good to us. Through riffles and still waters it had made its way

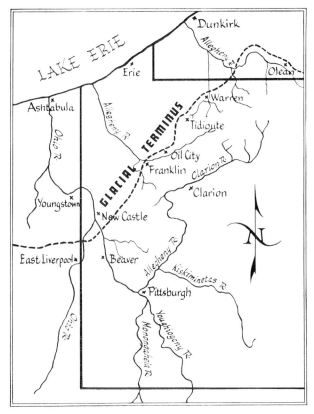

when waters of the Allegheny flowed northward

furnace in the United States. Bear Creek Iron Furnace it was called and it produced forty tons of iron a week. From this furnace came the first run of coke iron produced in America, when Penn's Woods West supplied the New World with most of its iron. Today Bear Creek and the Allegheny are much the same as they were then, but nothing remains of the furnace except a memory.

In the middle of the morning we passed the village of Monterey and before noon Sarah Furnace and the town of Catfish. We knew then that we were close to Brady's Bend, one of the most spectacular turns in the whole River. The distance across the neck of the bend is about a half mile, but that half mile is a high and rugged slope that blocks the course of the River. To get around the ridge, the River makes a great sweep of six or seven miles.

As you paddle down, you are hardly aware of the bend. You drift serenely with the current and look up from time to time at the ridge, but the bend is so gradual that you do not notice the shifting points of the compass—from south to northwest to southeast to west and to north. After an hour or two of paddling you are back to within a half mile of the point from which you started.

As we entered the bend we noticed, high on the ridge, an observation tower. From the tower, I thought, the bend would make a magnificent picture. "I wish we could be up there," I said to Tom,

high on the ridge

among the reflections, it had skimmed lightly over hidden rocks, it had skirted the shoreline so closely and so slowly that we could see the tracks of raccoon and of deer. Shortly we would say good-by to it and make the next seventy miles down the River in Captain Way's "Lady Grace."

In a few minutes we had passed through the dark water of the Clarion. The Clarion is a pitiable river sick and close to death. It is a sister river to the Allegheny and was once as beautiful. Someday, and the day is not far off, it will regain its health and loveliness. When that time comes, this will be a happy meeting place of two beautiful rivers.

Shortly, we were drifting past Parker City, which, like Pithole, could look back on a history of wealth and gushing oil, of Ben Hogan's and French Kate's and Floating Palaces. Then the wells failed, fires swept through the city, and those who sought for oil moved northward. As we floated on, Parker City slept peacefully in the morning sunshine.

At Bear Creek we hesitated a moment, remembering past glory here, too, but seeing none of it. Less than a mile up the creek was once the largest iron

to get around the ridge the Allegheny makes a great sweep of six or seven miles

one of the most spectacular turns on the beautiful river

"and down here at the same time so that we could see the whole show."

"I do have some pictures from up there," Tom said, "but I took them last fall."

"Let's use them," I said. "It's the only way to see the bend, all of it."

We had been paddling in a southeasterly direction before we reached the bend, but now we swung around to the north and west. A mile or two down the River, as we swung south again, we saw the bridge at East Brady. To us, that bridge was important, for it marked the end of our trip down the Allegheny in a canoe. We drifted under it, slowly, and then tied up to the little wharf.

Since we did not know when Captain Way and the "Lady Grace" would arrive, Tom and I ate our lunch in a restaurant in East Brady. There we made a telephone call that assured the return of the borrowed canoe to the American Youth Hostel, which had generously loaned it to us. We stretched our legs with a walk through town and then went back to the wharf to look at the River and to wait.

"It's funny how you always come back to the River," Tom said. "There's always something inter-

esting to see—like those reflections of the bridge." While he talked, he was busy taking a picture of the reflections. "This isn't the prettiest part of the River, but it's still the River. There's always something to see."

From upstream we could hear the chug of a motorboat. In a few minutes the boat came racing down the River. Then, short of the bridge, it made a sharp turn and sped back. Little waves surged past the bridge, broke the reflections into grotesque curves, and began to lap at the wharf. I heard the camera click again. "There's always something to see," Tom said.

Three piercing blasts shattered the quiet of the River. We turned and looked downstream. There in the sunlight, her stern wheel a glistening arc of drops, came the "Lady Grace." She looked young and fragile, a youthful sister to a "Nellie Hudson," a miniature too small to be out on the Allegheny River alone even in broad daylight.

Steadily she chugged her way towards us, a twenty-foot skiff with a five-foot paddle wheel powered by a two-cylinder gasoline engine. She had challenged the Ohio from Sewickley to Pittsburgh

137

the bridge at East Brady

and the Allegheny from Pittsburgh to East Brady to meet us. Now she was approaching the wharf—the skipper, like a stout Cortez, at the wheel and Ray at the whistle. Again three blasts cut through the valley.

The Captain was smiling. He is a man of smiles. Every voyage is a personal victory for him and for his ship. Once he brought a river steamboat from San Francisco through the Panama Canal into the Gulf of Mexico and up the Mississippi to the Ohio and the Allegheny. That victory was worth a smile. Now he had successfully piloted his little "Lady Grace" from Sewickley to East Brady. The new triumph was worth a new smile, bright and broad. When "Lady Grace" touched the wharf, there was no sound of her touching. She touched like a Faerie Queen.

As though he were a boy of twenty, Captain Fred leaped out of the boat and made it fast with a few deft turns of the line. Ray stepped out more gin-

gerly. Ray had been a blessing to Tom and me. He had acted as chauffeur, typist, research assistant, proofreader, apprentice photographer, and general laborer, always in good humor and always ready to shoulder the heaviest load.

We chattered for awhile about their trip—it had taken three days—and then Captain Fred said, "I have some friends here. I think I'll go up and give them a call."

As the Captain ran up the steps leading to the bridge, Ray said, "That man knows every fellow who ever got his feet wet in the Allegheny. I'll bet he won't be back until five."

He wasn't. While we waited, we transferred all our gear from the canoe to the "Lady Grace" and Ray tried his right arm at spin casting and at fly casting. He learned quickly. A determined fellow, Ray—determined to learn as much as he could as quickly as he could. After he had worn out his right arm, he

138

asked for a lesson in canoeing. I took him out on the River for an hour or so. When we came back, Ray steered the canoe alongside the wharf with the skill of an experienced paddler, and when he stepped out he had a look of triumph on his face, like the look on David's face when he caught his first fish.

Shortly before five o'clock Captain Fred came bouncing down the steps, flushed with renewed friendships. He had met a number of people he hadn't seen for years, rivermen most of them. We were to have dinner, if we were willing, at the hotel with him and with his good friends Mr. and Mrs. Kempel. As for the night, we *could* pitch the tent directly across the River or, if we preferred, Mr. and Mrs. Kempel had offered the use of their yacht, the "Fern M." . . . It was a beautiful yacht, Fred added hopefully, and the night might be cold and foggy.

And so, at six o'clock, unshaven and looking like nineteenth-century roustabouts, we had a delicious dinner in good company. At eight o'clock we were enjoying the luxury of the "Fern M.," its warmth and light and abundance of hot water. At ten o'clock we were lying in real beds and listening to the slap of water against the hull of the boat, to the sober croak of bullfrogs along the river shore, and to the moan of a train whistle many miles away.

The morning was cold and foggy. We ate a leisurely breakfast on the "Fern M.," blessing Mr. and Mrs. Kempel as we did so, and went down to the wharf at about ten o'clock. By that time the fog had lifted and the sun was shining warmly. The "Lady Grace," dainty and diminutive, looked like a royal craft of the Lilliputians.

Captain Fred started the engine, we cast off, the paddle wheel began to churn, and the "Lady Grace" curved away from the wharf and out into the River. I looked back. A little boy was waving to us from the bridge. Above the bridge a crow flapped lazily against the blue. Below the bridge, our canoe, lonely

out on the river for an hour or so

139

enough to be desolate, bobbed about at the end of the wharf.

From Corydon to East Brady we had traveled as the Indians had traveled. Now we were skipping a hundred years and were adopting the white man's boat, the boat that had brought commerce and prosperity to the towns along the Allegheny. We soon discovered that Captain Fred knew something about every boat that had ever churned the River. From time to time he spoke of the old boats as though he had known them personally—of the "Venango" that brought out the first shipment of barreled oil from the Oil City Regions; of the "Tidioute," a sixty-three-ton boat that drew only eight inches of water; of the "Albion," which in 1827 became the first steamboat to get up the Allegheny as far as Kittanning; of the "Belle," largest packet on the River, that set a record on May 24, 1866, by going from Pittsburgh to Oil City and back in forty hours; and of the "Allegheny," which on May 21, 1830, became the first steamboat to ascend the River as far as Olean, N. Y.

But though the Captain spoke of the days of commerce—of the great rafts of lumber from Warren, the iron shipments from the furnaces at East Brady, the oil barges from Pithole and Franklin—the River itself was much the same as the River we had learned from the canoe. Again the little mountains began to close in upon us, mountains too steep for human habitation. Again we moved through a River wilderness, two bitterns leading us on. They would fly from us as we approached and would settle on the River again a quarter of a mile below. There, they would wait in shallow water, and when we caught up with them, they would swoop on ahead. Near Redbank Creek we lost them, but a few minutes later as we looked back, they were feeding sedately in the shallow water behind us.

In a few minutes we were approaching Lock No. 9. Tom polished the lens of his camera. Ray made sure that the whistle was operating properly. Captain Fred, of course, manned the steering wheel and instructed me to seize a rung of the lock ladder as we

we would say good-by to it

140

the Fern M., a beautiful yacht

Capt. Fred Way's royal craft

came alongside it. My responsibility alarmed me. But we passed the upper gate and came gently to the ladder, and all I had to do was reach out with one hand and pull the "Lady Grace" close to the concrete wall.

I looked up. A face was peering down at us. The lock tender and Captain Fred began a distant but amiable discussion of river conditions. Meanwhile, behind us, the gates had slowly closed and great swirls and eddies began churning the water around us. My hand, which had been at shoulder level as I grasped the ladder, was now above my head. I took a grip on the next lower rung as the water level sank and as the "Lady Grace" began the long descent to the depth of the water below the lock. Twenty feet down into the chasm we descended, lichens and water mosses appearing on the walls as we went down and heavier and heavier coatings of slime covering the rungs of the ladder. After awhile, I noticed that I no longer had to reach for a lower rung. We had dropped to the level of the lower River, and the gates in front of us began to swing open. A blast of the whistle, then, and we were steaming out of the lock and on down the River.

Again the mountains crept close to the bright water, and rolling clouds drifted up the River. Once, a fawn allowed us to come very close; then she gave

141

the guardian of Lock No. 9

us a startled glance and bounded off into the safety of the tree shadows. Though I could not see her, I know that in some secluded spot she turned to look again through the leaves at the "Lady Grace," just as her ancestors a hundred years before had turned to watch the "Echo" come steaming down the River and as her earlier ancestors had turned to watch the silent war canoes of King Shingas and his Delawares sweeping on to rendezvous with Captain Jacobs at Kittanning. In two hundred years, the River and its mountains have changed but little. Could the ghost of the King of the Delawares return, he would know the valley as his home. May it stay as it is a long time!

At Nelly's Bend we put in for lunch, and a good lunch it was though King Shingas might have been mystified by it—tomato juice, ham and fried potatoes, hot chocolate for drink and fruit cocktail for dessert. After lunch we decided we were in no hurry to go anywhere. Ray began perfecting his newly acquired skill with the fly rod, and Captain Fred went down to his boat and tinkered with the engine.

Up the River, I remembered, was a large, flat rock. I had noticed it just before we beached the "Lady Grace." It seemed like a good place to be and so I went there. For awhile I sat on the rock and watched the River, green and brown from the mountains, white and blue from the sky. Cloud shadows raced against the riffles, and a rock halfway across the River tossed a cascade of spray into the sunlight.

At the foot of the rock, where the water lay still, silver-sided minnows flashed little arrows of bright-

ness; algae waved from a stone; a crayfish, half-hidden under another stone, stretched his pincers with no obvious intent. I lay back on the rock and closed my eyes, as lazy as a crayfish under a stone, as lazy as a bullfrog on a stump. The hot sun beat down on the earth, on the rock, and on me. Soon the warmth of the rock crept through my clothing, and I was submerged in indolent heat, relaxing, life-giving heat.

The River moved more distantly, more softly, through the darkness of closed eyelids, and the sound of its moving was a gentle blending of swirls and eddies, of impact against rock, of rippling over riffles, of lapping against a shore of sand and pebbles. Birds were singing through the dimness, not with the excited wonder of morning and evening but with midday relaxation and acceptance. A song sparrow rose up the scale and down; a Maryland yellowthroat announced his satisfaction with Pennsylvania; a cedar waxwing spoke in a manner not quite be-

huge gates swung open

142

I am part of a noble company

coming to his tawny beauty. Their songs blended with the murmur of the River. Once there was a whir of wings above me as a dragonfly passed, but I did not open my eyes. And over everything, there was the sound of another river, a river of wind that moved among the hills and trees and rocks and across the singing river and that blended all other sounds into its unity.

Lying with closed eyes on a rock in the sun, our consciousness suspended in space and bound to no philosophy except the nearness of now, we come close to the center of things. We know that the sun is the giver of life and that all things are children of the sun—the bird and the cricket, the river and the stone, the tree, the cloud, the man who lies on the warm rock, all of us brothers under the sun. We are not here alone. We are held to one another by ties of birth and necessity—perhaps, on a warm afternoon in midsummer, by ties of love. I share the earth with dragonfly and mole. They do not weep when I depart nor do they notice my passing; neither do I grieve when they return to earth. I should be poor, indeed, however, if they had never known the sky and ground. And while they live, and the song

sparrow and the sycamore and the river and the cloud, I am part of a noble company.

When I opened my eyes, a buzzard was slowly wheeling against the bright sky. I watched him make two circles and had the uncomfortable feeling that I had been the center of both. I got to my feet,

very close to us

143

stretched, and jumped down off the rock. The buzzard stopped circling and drifted off down the River. I walked back to the boat. Captain Fred, his hands and face smeared with grease, was still tinkering with the engine. "We were beginning to wonder where you were," he said.

"Up the River," I said, "taking a nap on a rock."

Ray began reeling in his line. "It's the back cast," he said. "I can't keep it high enough. Maybe I'll try it again tonight."

"Those clouds," Tom said, "they're wonderful today. Maybe we'll get some sunset pictures this evening. You ready?"

Again we started down the River, paddle wheel sparkling in the sunlight. Through Gray's Eddy we went and past the mouth of Mahoning Creek, where Captain Brady and his avengers, one eighteenth-century morning, killed five Indians as they rose from their beds to greet the morning sun. We passed the three Mahoning Islands and the old Orehill furnace and came to Lock No. 8. While we settled into the abyss of the lock, Captain Fred and the lock master exchanged blithe gossip about old friends and old rivermen.

Out on the River again, Captain Fred swung the "Lady Grace" around to the right below the dam. "There's a wonderful camping site here," he said. "Unless, of course, you fellows are in a hurry." He pointed to a sandy beach, willow bordered. Two

on a blade of grass

fishermen were fishing there, the lazy way, their poles supported by branches stuck in the sand.

"We haven't hurried yet," I said.

"A good place for sunset pictures," Tom said.

In a few minutes, the prow of the "Lady Grace" squished into the sand and a quarter of an hour later, we had made camp. After that, each of us went

beached for the night

144

his own way. Fred worked over the engine. Tom and Ray walked downstream. I went upstream.

Near some coarse grass I found a driftwood log and sat down to enjoy the late afternoon sunlight. It was several minutes before I noticed the grasshopper. We were sitting very close to each other, I on the ground, she on a blade of grass that bent slightly when a breeze I could not feel moved the grass blade. She was a handsome creature in her way, her eyes bright and bold. Though we sat close together, we did not know each other. It would have been better if we had. I knew her name, but she did not know mine. It is possible that she did not see me sitting there, not even with her five eyes, three of them simple, two compound. If she saw me at all, I was but a blurred bulk.

In a few minutes, I should move on or she would fly away, and we should remain unacquainted. Yet life would be different were it not for her and her kind. If it were not for her presence, there would be fewer birds in the trees and bushes around me. And because there would be fewer birds, there would be more mosquitoes. If she were not here, the fish in the streams and the frogs in the marshes would be fewer

and leaner, and because there would be fewer fish and frogs, there would be fewer blue herons standing sedately along the edge of the water in the evening.

The very soil on my hillside at home would be altered, for in the fall of the year, she scoops a shallow hole in the ground, where she lays her eggs. Hundreds of grasshoppers scooping hundreds of holes over hundreds of years will make the soil more friable. Because it is more friable, it is more retentive of moisture, and so, in a small way, the grasshopper has added her bit to soil conservation and to flood control.

Yet the grasshopper, I am told, is an enemy of man. And indeed, this large-eyed insect is hard to defend. She is destructive. She has plagued mankind since before the first Pharaoh, destroying crops and forage and, indirectly, the cattle that would feed on them. To the American farmer alone, she is, annually, a two hundred million dollar liability.

Nevertheless, we know too little about her, I think, to say blandly and firmly that she is an enemy of man. Who are our enemies? Man, of course, is our worst . . . and after him, who knows? Through thou-

a wonderful camping site: sandy beach willow bordered

145

pastures along the banks

sands and thousands of years, this insect with the big eyes and great legs has sifted and aerated and, with her death, fertilized the soil, producing, in the long run, perhaps more vegetation than she has destroyed. For centuries she has fattened quail and grouse for Indian, pioneer, and modern hunter. She has brightened the orchard with more bluebirds and the dark swamp with more red-winged blackbirds. She has increased the number of fish in stream and river and lake. And though she has devastated wheat fields in one country, she has, because she is edible, prevented famine in another. The chain could go on almost endlessly.

The best ecologists, philosophers, and entomologists in the world, working patiently together, could hardly come, at this time, to an accurate estimate of the place that the familiar grasshopper takes in the pattern of living things. We do not know her well enough. If she is my enemy, as she may be, then this afternoon, swaying on a bit of grass, she was a very interesting enemy. And since she seemed to be doing me no harm, I would do none to her.

That night, after dinner, we sat around a blazing fire of driftwood, though all four of us had had to forage far to find it. We listened to the bullfrogs along the River, the tree frogs in the willows, and two melodious screech owls that told ancestral secrets to each other from the hill behind us. The light of the fire brightened the beach and turned the willows gray, and the moon shot quivering spears across the water.

Soon our talk was of the River, and Captain Fred, sprawled on the sand, the firelight on his face, began to tell of things he knew about life on the Allegheny long ago before he was born. He told how logging rafts were "dropped" all the way from Olean to Pittsburgh in the 1840's, rafts that were seventy-five feet wide and two hundred feet long and that were built of white pine logs six feet in diameter. He told of an actor named Booth who left Franklin one day in 1865 saying he would be "gone east" for a few days. He was a queer fellow who owned a small well on the edge of the River. Nobody thought much about the absence of Booth until the telegraph wires announced the assassination of Abraham Lincoln by an actor named John Wilkes Booth. We learned how oil barges were floated down shallow Oil Creek—how a great dam was built above the barges and then blown up so that the barges were actually flushed down into the Allegheny with much destruction and many deaths. He told of Captain Dan Fry's keelboat,

"Great Western," which was poled by hand and pulled along the shore on a regular run from Pittsburgh to Tionesta; and he told of Joseph Fox's dream castle built more than a hundred years ago on a mountain above the River near Foxburg, and of Foxburg itself, how it had been a dream town planned by the son of Joseph Fox as the prettiest and cleanest town on the River.

We listened in quiet excitement until we had used the last of our firewood except for a few pieces that were to be saved for morning. The air was growing cold and fog was settling over the valley. We retreated from the fog into the tent. Inside, before I went to sleep, I could still hear the two owls talking about age-old matters.

Birch bark canoes, grown up, become steamboats and ocean liners, fuels change from wood to oil and to shattered atoms, towns and cities blossom from dreams of wealth or perfection and then fade, the greatness of a man named Lincoln and the folly of an actor from Franklin blend with the subsoil, but tonight two owls, content with being, sing the same mysterious song they sang when the first Mound Builder parted the willows here and wondered whether he should stay or flee.

The Mound Builder stayed for a time and then disappeared. King Shingas listened for a time and departed. The rivermen heard the calls in the darkness and floated on down the River. Tonight we four had heard the cryptic music. Tomorrow we shall not mention it. But all four of us may think about it. The owl is part of the society of living things, content in being so. Tomorrow we may long for his contentment and his assurance. Tomorrow we may achieve them—if we have the time and the good fortune to lie on a warm rock in the sunlight or to watch a grasshopper swaying on a blade of coarse grass.

The next morning we started out in a cold mist for Kittanning and Lock No. 7. We passed Cowan-

canoes . . . become steamboats

a typical river town: an honor to the river

shannock Creek on the left and then, farther down, the great gray rocks that line the shore on the right. In a little more than an hour we were idling outside the lock and waiting for the gates to open. While we waited, we talked to two fishermen, bundled in mackinaws, who said they had started fishing at midnight and were ready to quit. Each had caught a muskie, and between them they had a string of six or seven bass, all taken within a few yards of the Kittanning Dam.

Once through the lock we stayed close to the left shore, for Kittanning is a beautiful little city that takes pride in its waterfront. In 1749 it was an Indian village of twenty-two cabins. Here Captain Jacobs lived, the great Delaware chieftain who waged successful war against the English until he was killed during Colonel Armstrong's savage attack in 1756. Not until fifty years after the burning of the Indian village did the white man's Kittanning rise near the charred ruins of old Kittanning Town. Today it is a clean and thriving little city and an honor to the River.

A half hour later we had passed through Ford City, had skirted the right side of Crooked Creek Island, and were on our way to Lock No. 6. Then, just as we were beginning to look for Glade Run, we heard from behind us the loud moan of a whistle. We looked back. Only a few hundred yards away a towboat was bearing down on us. Again came the tremendous moan of its whistle.

"It's the 'Philo'!" Captain Fred shouted.

The information was interesting, but the towboat was still roaring down on us. "How," I inquired, "do we get out of its way?"

"We won't," said Captain Fred. "We'll wait for it. Captain Brown's an old friend of mine."

The speed of the "Philo" began to slacken. Up in the pilothouse a white-shirted arm waved at us. Obviously, if we were going to be run down, the operation would be an amiable one. Then a man on deck waved. It was all very pleasant. Captain Fred was waving, too. Then Ray waved and gave a short toot on the whistle.

By now the "Philo" was almost beside us and was hardly moving. The pilot leaned out of his window. "Want a lift, Captain? Chicken's in the pot."

Captain Fred looked at us, that hopeful expression on his face again. "He's a wonderful fellow," he said.

Ray said, "Gee, chicken!"

Tom said, "Might get a picture up there."

In a few minutes we were clambering out of the "Lady Grace" and tying her to the side of the "Philo." Fred introduced us to the man who had waved from

148

the deck, Paul Merkel. Then we climbed the stairs to the pilothouse and met Captain Robert Brown. The pilothouse was as neat as Grandmother's parlor on Sunday afternoons—and cozier and more comfortable. I said something about how comfortable it was.

"Yes," Captain Brown said, "pilot houses are a lot different now from what they used to be. Remember, Fred," he asked, "how they used to be? In the winter, I mean, when the ice jams . . ."

That was the beginning of *Rivermen's Reminiscence*, and there were many chapters in the book. They began in various ways.

"Remember the time . . ."

"Jim B - - g died last year. He used to be . . ."

"The year before she blew up . . ."

"How he got off the bar, I'll never know, but . . ."

"When that jam let go . . ."

"Don't suppose you remember Big Bill . . ."

"Big Bill! Why one time we . . ."

And so the chapters went on, disconnected, nostalgic. While they went on, Tom and Ray and I listened or walked around the boat without notice. There was a brief interruption for the best chicken

Capt. Robert Brown

I ever tasted in my life, and then the telling of tales continued.

Captain Brown offered us the use of his houseboat in Tarentum for sleeping quarters that night. We debated the matter, but the lure of the tent and a good campsite on Fourteen Mile Island won out against the novelty of a night on a houseboat.

Regretfully we parted from the "Philo," Captain Bob Brown, and First Mate Paul Merkel. Rivermen *are* wonderful people. An hour and a half later we had passed through New Kensington and Lock No. 3 and were ready to pitch camp on Fourteen Mile Island. There was a broad, sandy beach from which we could see the River flowing over the dam and, below us, a great railroad trestle that stretched across the River and, below that, the Turnpike Bridge. We were getting close to home.

Thirty feet or so from the shore the beach leveled off, an ideal spot for the tent. And someone had presented the island with a picnic table, sturdily set in the sand!

I was starting to unroll the tent when I heard Ray: "Mind if I set it up this time?"

"Of course not," I said. "But why?"

"I just want to do it," he said. "I've been watching you. I know how."

I started back towards the boat, where Tom and Fred were talking, and then I stopped. "I've been watching you," he had said. "I know how." It was as simple as that. Every night since we had arrived at Corydon I had pitched the tent. Now Ray was going

almost beside us

an ideal spot for a tent

to do it. Knowing him, I did not need to look back. He would set up the tent well. He is curious. He is eager. He watches and learns because he wants to learn. The two owls I had heard the night before were not eager scholars. They did what their ancestors did and were as wise as their fathers were but not wiser, or very little. Ray had been learning and would do well with the tent. Tomorrow he would do better. Tomorrow and tomorrow, if he is like most intelligent young men, he would improve upon the work of his elders, in tent raising and in more important matters. In time, he may become a great angler, a great photographer, or a great scholar among books.

He may also be lonely and unhappy, despite his intelligence or because of it. For there is a precious quality of being that often eludes the man of intelligence, even of great intelligence. In escaping, it keeps him from becoming complete. It is that serene adjustment to life of the creatures of instinct, of creatures who do not think, of the two screech owls,

for example, talking contentedly in the fog and doing—without thought—what they were born to do.

What shall I tell Ray when he shows me the tent? If it is set four-square and tight and solid, I could praise his intellect. If it faces the beach so that tonight we can watch the River and hear the owls more clearly, I could praise his desire for acceptance. If both conditions are met, I could quote George Meredith: "Intelligence and instinct now are one." But the best thing, I think, is to say, "It looks good." That way we can remain friends.

I went down to the boat. Tom was saying, "We start with a canoe, move up to a stern-wheeler, and then graduate to a diesel towboat. What comes next?"

Fred laughed. "If the Army Engineers could see the light, we could go all the way to Warren in that towboat. A few more navigation dams, and the whole River to Warren would be opened up to traffic. This valley would grow like crazy."

"Why don't they do it?" Tom asked.

"I don't know. They understand engineering, but they don't understand rivers. What they've done is like building a road halfway to somewhere and then stopping because it doesn't have much traffic on it. Of course it doesn't have much traffic on it. It doesn't go anywhere. But if it went on up the River, past Franklin and Oil City, up through Tionesta to Warren, then you'd see traffic. Man, this valley would grow up over night. It would be worth billions."

"'O Captain! my Captain!'" I wanted to say but didn't, "what would become of the trees and the trout and the deer and the muskellunge? What would become of the ducks on the water and the herons that stand at evening along the shore? What would become of my two owls?"

Instead, I asked, "But the River, Fred. Wouldn't it get to be like the River at Oil City?"

"Nonsense!" he said. "Rivers don't have to be dirty just because they have traffic on them. People have to work together, that's all. There could be beautiful little cities along this river—like Warren and Tionesta and Kittanning. And the fishing could be just as good as it is now—if everybody worked together. Rivers don't *have* to be ugly just because they're useful."

It was the old argument again about the needs of our economy and the needs of our souls. If our economy collapses, there may be no need to conserve our souls. But if our souls wither, of what good is

conversationalists

we cooked our dinner on Fourteen Mile Island

the economy? The balance between economy and conservation is as delicate as the balance of nature herself. Without wise conservation, the economy will corrode and die for want of something to produce. Without a wise economy, we might as well return the land to the wolf and the panther. But there is a balance, and wise men will find it as they are finding it now.

Ray came down to the boat, his face sweaty. "How's it look?" he asked.

I turned around. Among the willows the tent stood square and straight. It faced the River.

"It looks good," I said. "It looks fine."

"That's one more thing I've learned on this trip," he said.

"How about the owls last night?" I asked. "Have you learned what they were saying?"

He grinned. "No," he said, "but I'm trying."

Late in the afternoon we cooked our dinner and we ate it from the picnic table. It was a good table and so were the benches, and we blessed the man who made them and put them there. As it grew dark, a cold wind began to sweep up the valley. We piled more driftwood on the fire and huddled close, saying little. I do not know what the others were thinking, but all I could think of was that this would be our last night on the River. We were only fourteen miles above Pittsburgh.

Twice, long trains of cars rolled across the railroad trestle below us. The sound of their crossings mingled with the rush of wind up the valley and

151

The map labels include:

▲ •Corydon
Cornplanter Indian Reservation
Conewango Cr.
Brokenstraw Cr.
•Kinzua
Kinzua Cr.
▲ Warren

Tidioute• ▲

Pithole Cr.
Oil Cr.
•Tionesta
Tionesta Cr.
Oil City•
Hemlock Cr.
French Cr.
Franklin•
Sandy Cr. ▲
East Sandy Cr.

Scrubgrass Cr.
•Emlenton
Foxburg• Clarion River
▲ Parker
Bear Cr.
Catfish
East Brady ▲ Red Bank Cr.
Mahoning Cr.
▲
Glade Run
Cowanshannock Cr.
•Kittanning
Buffalo Cr. Crooked Cr.
Bull Cr. Kiskiminetas River
Pine Cr. Deer Cr. •New Kensington
•Sewickley ▲ Oakmont
•Pittsburgh
Monongahela River

THE ALLEGHENY

▲ –overnight camp sites

down the Allegheny

152

with the roar of water tumbling over the dam. There was no discord, and after awhile, as if to bid us good-by, the owls began to talk.

When we started out the next morning, it was a little hard to believe that we were only fourteen miles above one of the great industrial cities of the world. The sky was as blue as the sky at Corydon, and the hillsides were tree-covered, bright and green in the sunlight. The River, too, was beautiful —dark green in the shadows, blue and white where it caught the reflection of sky and cloud. Across the River a fisherman sat on a sunny rock, his rod propped up in front of him. Everything seemed much the same as it had at Warren and Tidioute and Tionesta.

But everything was not the same. Slowly, over the miles, the Beautiful River had been turning into an industrial river, though the eye could seldom see the change. The first great source of contamination had been the Clarion. Then had come the acids of Redbank Creek and Mahoning Creek and many smaller streams. Somehow the River had managed to absorb all of these and the untreated sewage of three hundred miles of villages, towns, and little cities. But at last the Kiskiminetas added its tremendous flow of sulphuric acid from the mines, and the River, as we had known it at Corydon and Tionesta and Emlenton and even Kittanning, had changed.

For sulphuric acid from coal mines is the most dangerous pollutant of all. When the President's Water Resources Policy Commission reported on the ten most important rivers in America's future, it said of the Ohio:

Acid mine drainage constitutes the most serious pollution problem. Acid pollution increases corrosiveness, impairing every aspect of water use. It has deterred domestic and industrial organic pollution control, since sewage treatment would not make streams suitable for use.

That news did not come as a surprise to the people of Penn's Woods West. What did come as a surprise to a number of people was another paragraph:

Methods are known for preventing pollution from coal mines and sediment. Some states have inaugurated programs to prevent pollution by coal processing plants, but effective control is prevented where specific legislation exempts these operations, as in West Virginia.

The Commission could have said "as in Pennsylvania" instead of "as in West Virginia."

craft go up and down the river

Yes, "methods are known" to decrease the pollution from mines. They are expensive methods, but someday we shall use them—sooner than many people know. When that day arrives, the Kiskiminetas will become a clean and beautiful stream again. Its water will be safe for public use and economical for industrial use. As purification methods improve, fish will come back to the Kiskiminetas and ducks will nest along its shores. Fish and ducks and industry, we now know, have much in common, for, as even the Sanitary Water Board says, "When water in a stream will not support fish and other aquatic life, the water is not safe for other uses."

As we swung around and started down the River, I turned to Tom. "I wonder how long it has been," I said, "since we saw a heron."

"I don't know," he said. "Days, anyway."

It was true. For several days we had not seen a heron fishing along the edges of the water. The mallards and the pintails were no longer with us. The fisherman on the rock across the River was no doubt fishing for carp or catfish, for we had long since left the waters of the trout and bass and muskellunge. However beautiful the River looked in the bright

153

beyond Lock No. 2—millions of gallons

sunlight, we knew that it was now an industrial river.

If we were foolish, we could grow angry and unhappy about the change. We could become unfair with our contemporaries and with our forefathers. But rivers do change. Once, an industrial civilization, without which we could not have prospered, changed our rivers for the worse. Now, a wiser industrial civilization, without which we cannot continue to prosper, is changing our rivers for the better —and at great cost. It is not doing so for the sake of the bass and the ducks. It is doing so because it already feels the pressing need for water and more water.

"Someday," I said to Fred, "I hope to catch a bass under the Fortieth Street Bridge."

He grinned. "You'll have to live a long time," he said, "but maybe you will. You look pretty healthy."

"I think I'm going to live long enough," I said. "First will come the Clarion. That shouldn't take long. Five or ten years maybe. Then the Kiskiminetas. That may take longer."

"A *lot* longer," Tom said. "Mine pollution is the worst of all."

"Just the same," I said, "I'm going to catch a bass under the Fortieth Street Bridge someday."

And I think I shall, though I may be an old man then. The people of Penn's Woods West cannot long afford the extravagance of the Clarion and the Kiskiminetas. We will reclaim them, and the force behind the reclamation will be not a fisherman's idle dream of bass under the Fortieth Street Bridge but economic necessity. Expensive though it will be, it will come more rapidly than many people think.

Ray gave the whistle a toot. A speedboat was racing towards us. "We're coming to Twelve Mile Island," Fred said. "Pretty soon we'll be at Oakmont, and the boats will be all around us."

Another speedboat came bouncing along in the wake of the first one. "They're a lot more boats on the River now than there used to be," he added. "Mostly because the water's cleaner than it was. We've made a start, anyway. You know, a river doesn't *have* to be ugly."

Oakmont, when we got to it, was as gay as a summer resort in July. White sails puffed in the wind, speedboats twisted hither and yon like water beetles, yachts churned serenely up and down the River. Sometimes when the yachts passed us, they blew their whistles, and Ray was busy tooting back. Speedboats followed in our wake and occasionally drew close enough to call to our good Captain and ask questions about this strange little stern-wheeler, the only one of its kind on the River. And the Captain would beam with pride and would shout comments about displacement and engines with anyone who shouted questions.

As the boats thinned out behind us, I heard Fred telling Tom, "River people are good people." Presently we passed the Nine Mile Islands and then swept into the quiet water above Aspinwall. Again we were reminded that a river city with a sense of pride can be beautiful. Aspinwall, with its factories and its great filtration plant, looked clean and bright.

"My father used to go fishing down here," Tom said. "Sometimes he took me with him."

"For catfish?" I asked.

"No," he said. "For bass. There used to be a lot of bass here."

We passed through Lock No. 2 and looked back at the water pouring over the dam and flashing in the sunlight, millions of gallons of water that will safeguard the health and the industrial progress of Pittsburgh when we stop contamination at its sources.

Ahead of us factories lined both sides of the River, their towers and smokestacks making geometrical

geometrical designs against the sky

Highland Park Bridge

designs against the blue sky, and down the River the Highland Park Bridge swept in a graceful arc from bank to bank. It was strange to think that along these shores white pines once grew in great forests, that the young George Washington walked and slept in their shadows, that almost across from us on our right Chief Guyasuta, the Mingo warrior, companion of Washington, was buried beside his little log cabin. Now the tracks of a railroad siding rest upon his grave.

Past Sharpsburg we went, and Etna and Millvale. Ahead, the great Fortieth Street Bridge curved across the sky. "Better get out your fishing rod," Ray said. "We're getting close."

I was just about to answer him when a streak of blue came towards us from the northern end of the bridge. "Look, look!" I screamed. By then, it was almost over us—the bright blue flight of a kingfisher. On it went to the southern end of the bridge, where we lost it among the rocks.

"Well I'll be darned," Tom said. "A kingfisher under the Fortieth Street Bridge! You know," he said, "maybe you'll get that bass sooner than I thought."

"It's an omen," I said, "the best omen of the trip."

"Except for the owls," Ray said.

In a few minutes we could see the buildings of the Golden Triangle of Pittsburgh towering against the sky and cut by the curves of many bridges. "It's a city of beautiful bridges," Tom said. And under

155

cut by the curve of bridges

them, I thought, still flows "one of the most beautiful rivers in ye world."

"You fellows know, I suppose," said Fred, "that it's the biggest river port in the United States." It will be a greater port, I thought, when the barges float on noncorrosive water and when flood control dams are planned more carefully and when watersheds are deeply forested.

"Look," said Ray. "Some people fishing." We were passing Herr's Island. Three boys and a man were fishing along the shore. Today, I thought, catfish and kingfishers. Tomorrow? I remembered a great blue heron near Warren and mallards that rose from the River at Tionesta and two men with a string of walleyed pike at Emlenton. On some bright tomorrow, the heron, the mallards, the pike, and the fishermen could come back to the River at Pittsburgh. It is not an impossible hope.

Under the Ninth Street Bridge, Fred said, "Let's tie up here and have a bit of lunch." He gave the wheel a turn, and we swung over to the right. In a few minutes we had docked at the little wharf near the Seventh Street Bridge. Then at a restaurant a few blocks away we had our lunch and came back to the "Lady Grace."

As we started off again, we kept looking towards the south, where the new Pittsburgh rose into the sky like castles of a modernistic fairyland. Against the blue they stood, the sheen of the aluminum Alcoa Building, the glitter of the stainless steel in the

the wharf at the Seventh Street Bridge

156

young, poetic, and courageous—the Point

Mellon-U. S. Steel Building, the gleam of the Koppers Building, and, brightly orange, the pyramidal top of the Gulf Building foretelling fair weather. New and young, poetic and courageous, they marched against the horizon, and guided our eyes as we moved under the Sixth Street Bridge to the structures at the apex of the triangle, to the green trees, waterfront bleachers, white boulevard, and mile-long promenade along the Beautiful River. The whole picture seemed too bright and clean to be real.

"You see what I mean," Fred was saying. "A river doesn't *have* to be ugly to be useful. Neither does a river city. Well, here it is. The biggest river port in the country."

And indeed, at that moment, with the sun shining on it, Pittsburgh looked like the loveliest city in the world. But even as I looked, I was remembering the Pittsburgh of a decade before—the red-gray sky that hid the sun, the blackened buildings, the dirty river front, the ramshackle warehouses that filled the lower part of the triangle.

I first saw that dismal part of the city when I was a boy. Fort Pitt was down there somewhere. I had read about it in school and in books about the Indians and the pioneers. I wanted to see it; then when my cousin from New York came to visit me, I could boast about the Blockhouse and take him to see it. In those days there were not many things to boast of if you lived in Pittsburgh.

Somehow I found my way into the district, but I did not find the Blockhouse. It was there, all right, as I discovered years later, but it was so hemmed in by derelict buildings that I could not find it. The street lamps were lighted, I remember, though it was the middle of the day, and soot swirled in little twisters over the streets and sidewalks. The next summer I took my cousin to Kennywood Park instead of to the Blockhouse, but he said that Coney Island was much better.

In those days Pittsburgh was a dismal city. It was also a practical and courageous city. It learned that polluted air was unhealthful and expensive. The

157

City cleaned its skies. The lower part of the triangle was an ugly place of diminishing land values. The City knocked down the warehouses and built skyscrapers and parks there. Land values suddenly jumped from less than seven million dollars to more than fifty million.

Now the City is looking at many other things that need improvement. An immense sewage disposal plant is under construction. After that will come reduction in industrial wastes. And then the mine sealing job will be done. And meanwhile work will continue on forested watersheds.

"What are those bleachers for?" I heard Ray asking. "Those bleachers along the waterfront."

I did not answer him, but I know why they are there. They are a promise, a promise of sailboats skimming the rivers at the Point, of university scull races along the Beautiful River, of kingfishers and sandpipers, of mallard ducks within city limits, of docks for swimming and boating, and of bass fishing for Pittsburghers along the promenade. All these because an enlightened industrial community knows that for its growing population and for its growing economic life, a pure water supply is essential.

"Ray," I said, "I've changed my mind about the Fortieth Street Bridge."

He looked at me.

"I'm beginning to think I'll catch that bass right here at the Point." And I think I shall.

By now we were past the Point and were looking back. Where two sides of the Golden Triangle met, where the Allegheny and the Monongahela mingled into the Ohio, rose the City, white and almost ethereal against the deep blue of the sky.

Our voyage down the Allegheny was over. Already we were on the broad waters of the Ohio, and soon, at Fred's river-front home, we would be docking, saying good-by, and parting. Meanwhile, I kept looking back at three rivers and the City. I did not want to leave them. In a sense, I think I never shall. Pittsburgh and Penn's Woods West—they are my home, and I want to belong, forever.

past the Point and looking back

158

whitecaps in parallel rhythms at Presque Isle

Presque Isle

A COLD WIND IN OUR FACES AND A HOT SUN OVERHEAD, we walked along the beach at Presque Isle. Breakers surged in from Lake Erie, spent their strength, and subsided in quivering lines at our feet.

A little girl came running towards us. In one hand she gripped an empty sand bucket. When she got up to us, she pointed towards the lake. "Big," she said.

I think we should have laughed had it not been for the serious expression on her face. Clearly, she had discovered a miracle and wanted us to appreciate it.

"It *is* big, honey," Tom said.

She looked at him as though she thought he did not understand. Again she pointed to the lake.

I looked with her across that great expanse of water, mile after mile of whitecapped waves rolling shoreward in parallel rhythms until, at last, they ended at our feet in cascades of spray. Above the lake and across the blue sky, clouds scudded towards us as rapidly as the racing waves.

"Big," I repeated after her.

She looked up at me and shook her head no. Then, sand bucket still in one hand, she flung her arms wide.

"*Very* big!" she said.

That was our introduction to the largest lake that touches Penn's Woods West.

It was a good introduction, too, for to one who was not born near the sea, Lake Erie seems to have everything the Atlantic Ocean has except sharks and the taste of salt. If it is less wide than the Atlantic, it does not seem so from the shore; if it is less deep, it does not seem so from a boat. Sky and water meet in that same mysterious, imperceptible line that marks the sea-horizon. Terns follow the troughs of waves and,

159

when weary or satisfied, come back to shore and walk along the beach. And if the Atlantic had its John Paul Jones and "We are just beginning to fight," Lake Erie had its Commodore Perry and "We have met the enemy and they are ours."

After the little girl left us to explain the miracle to her mother, we went on up the beach. Miles and miles of glistening sand lay before us. Except at Atlantic City, no beach along the Atlantic Seaboard is as long as the beach at Presque Isle, and yet much of it is man made. Thirty years ago, it looked almost as it looks now, but for some reason the lake that had deposited the sand over many centuries decided to take it away. Slowly, waves and wind began sucking the precious sand back. The beach was disappearing. All of Presque Isle, it was thought by some, might yet be returned to the lake that had formed it.

a little girl and the lake

Alarmed at the thought that this beautiful hook of land might wander out into the middle of the lake, conservationists, sportsmen, engineers, and state agencies began to lay plans for the reclamation of Presque Isle. The project they settled on was spectacular and expensive. Monstrous pumps would suck sand out of the interior of the peninsula and deposit it along a seven-mile stretch of beach. Elaborate piling systems would keep the sand from washing back into the lake. The cost would be great.

Now the project is a reality. Penn's Woods West has the longest inland beach in America, and the financial gamble is paying off handsomely as tourists, bathers, nature lovers, and anglers flock to the famous peninsula. Each finds the thing he came for: the tourist finds a beautiful resort with neither side show nor honky-tonk; the bather finds bright sun, bright sand, and clean water without chlorine; the nature lover finds abundant waterfowl and rare botanical successions; the angler finds a bay that teems with bass and walleyed pike, perhaps the best walleyed pike fishing in America.

The beach we walked on was a sandy wonderland bordered with green. Because the lake was wild, bathing had been prohibited that morning, and we had the miles of sand almost to ourselves. Terns and sandpipers patrolled the drift line but departed as we approached, the terns out over the lake, the sandpipers along the shore ahead of us. Sometimes we stopped to look at the sand dunes crowned with desolate grasses or a tanker framed by dark cottonwoods, or Tom would stoop and wait for a single wave to break into airy bubbles.

A mile or so up the beach we saw an old man in a mackinaw sitting on a driftwood log. We stopped for a few minutes.

"Next best thing to the ocean," he said. "Did a turn in the Navy during World War I. I come up here every summer and just look at it. That's all I do. I just look at it."

We talked with him awhile and then went back towards the car.

The road around Presque Isle follows in the main the contour of the shoreline, and there are side roads that lead into the forested interior of the peninsula. We drove slowly, for we knew that we were making a strange trip: in less than fifteen minutes we were going to pass through hundreds of years of visible botanical successions.

Six hundred years ago Presque Isle did not exist. A little finger of sand a yard or so in length pointed out from the mainland in a northeasterly direction. A current of water, coming in at an angle from the northwest, deposited sand and pebbles along the tiny peninsula, slowly increasing its length and its width. Year after year the waves added more sand to this finger that reached to the northeast. It became two yards long, ten yards, a hundred. Sometimes the finger made a crook as it moved on, so that a small bay appeared to cut almost across it. Then a storm from the east would seal off the entrance to the bay with sand, and the bay would become a little lake in the interior of the peninsula. In the course of years, many of these lakes were formed.

Meanwhile vegetation was taking hold on the sandy beach. Back from the drift line, clumps of switch grass took root and Artemisia. Panicum grass, bayberry bushes, red cedars, and sand cherries sank their roots into the sand. Inland, around the margins of the lakes, the feathery seeds of willow and cottonwood sprouted.

Many more years passed, and the finger reached farther out into the lake. By now, the sand at the beginning of the peninsula was becoming more like soil, enriched by the vegetation that had lived and died on it. White pines invaded the beginning of the peninsula and, in the wake of earlier growth, began their slow march out towards the tip. The pines, too, altered the soil. After a time it was suitable for the red oaks—the next aggressors, crowding on the heels of the white pines. As the red oaks pushed on behind the pines, they altered the soil still further. Then the climax invaders came to the beginning of the peninsula—the hemlocks, beeches, and sugar maples, and all the other vegetation associated with them. Fol-

framed by dark cottonwoods

patrols of the drift line

lowing the dune grasses and bayberry, the willows and cottonwoods, the white pines, and the red oaks, the new invaders flourished on land that was now six hundred years old.

It is small wonder that the botanists of Penn's Woods West and of many other regions migrate, like Canada geese, to the shores of Presque Isle. Dr. O. E. Jennings says, "Nowhere else in this part of the United States can there be found in the short distance of about three miles such a combination of so complete a series of plant successions as at Presque Isle, with its diversified flora of more than four hundred species."

And so, at the six-hundred-year-old end of the peninsula, which has been broken asunder many times by the fury of Lake Erie storms, we stepped into the car and drove slowly to the northeast. We started among hemlocks, beeches, and sugar maples, passed into the area of the red oaks, then, successively, through the land of white pines, cottonwoods, and dune grass and at last came to the tip of Presque Isle. There we got out of the car and walked to the edge of the water. The waves rolled in, bringing new sand to the beach that was still fighting its way into Lake Erie. A few yards behind us, the dune grasses had already established themselves, and farther away, young cottonwoods were rising above them. Here where the waves washed in to our feet, we could see with our own eyes a kind of creation—a

Tom Jarrett, patient and skilled

new land being born of bright pebbles and shifting sand and new inhabitants moving into their own little niches, their own special Gardens of Eden.

But the botanist knows that their Garden of Eden will not be theirs for long. It will be occupied by a succession of aggressors until at last it will be taken over and *maintained* by the climax community. Peace will not come to the land until that climax community arrives. And what, we might ask, is the nature of a community that can stop aggression and bring stability and peace to its world?

In the world of vegetation, the answer is fairly simple. The community that brings stability to its particular part of the world is the one that adapts itself best to its natural resources and its living companions. Let us suppose that the beech and maple association is the one that will bring order to Presque Isle. To the sun, giver of all energy, the maple and beech raise more efficient systems of branches and leaves than the red cedar does. To water, the sustainer of life and energy, it extends a more efficient root system than the bayberry's. By dropping their leaves in the fall the beech and maple use less water than the red cedar and build up a protective covering of topsoil for the dry days of summer.

dune grasses and bayberry

They share their environment with helpful companions. By furnishing shade in summer they encourage the hemlock, which, in turn, furnishes shade and protection in winter. The protection of the hemlocks encourages enough rabbits to keep the beech and maple seedlings from becoming too numerous, and the presence of rabbits invites the owls that keep the rabbits in check. The summer shade brings songbirds that help to keep the insects from injuring the beech and maples, and the hemlock seeds bring winter birds that feed upon larvae that would emerge in the spring. Sharing their habitat, the maple and beech provide food for squirrels, and the squirrels help to propagate both. Mice and chipmunks and beetles and worms and grubs contribute their share to community growth and prosperity.

At last a minor miracle occurs. The climax community becomes self-maintaining and self-perpetuating, so efficiently cooperative and so tolerant of one another that aggressors are not able to invade its world. Through conservation measures that make those of man seem feeble, the climax community has won its way to stability. Barring fire or a fundamental change in climate or the interference of man, this community should remain much as it is—peaceful and self-perpetuating—indefinitely.

Man, meanwhile, struggles towards peace and stability by other methods and without great success. "It were happy," said William Penn, the first horticulturist of Penn's Woods, "if we studied nature more in natural things; and acted according to nature, whose rules are few, plain, and reasonable."

we drove slowly to enjoy

Kettle Creek spilled over in white froth

Kettle Creek

BY THE TIME WE ARRIVED AT KETTLE CREEK, THE RAIN had stopped. All day we had listened to the click of the windshield wiper, to the hum of our tires on wet concrete and asphalt. Colors had been lost in the fog, and a monotonous gray had washed across sky, mountain, and valley. For two hundred miles we had traveled through a lonely world of dimness, uncertain outlines, and muffled sounds.

Yet the trip had not been unpleasant. Driving in the rain is unpleasant only when the future seems to be more important than the present, only when getting to one's destination on time is more important than enjoying the present moment. Because we were in no hurry, we had enjoyed the gray obscurity —villages hiding in the fog, pastures that looked like Corot landscapes, a farmer on the road riding his tractor and waving us on into the mist. And we had stopped at almost every mountain top to enjoy the drifting world below us.

Now we were at Kettle Creek. As we turned off the paved road and into the camp grounds, we splashed through puddles that were hub deep.

"Better turn in before we get stuck," Tom said.

I slithered the car out of the road and up a little grade into a clearing in the camping area. There was a stone fireplace, near it a small table with a roof above it, all very wet, and thirty feet ahead of us, Kettle Creek, obscure in the murky atmosphere.

"I'll look for the supervisor," I said. "We can unload the gear later."

I walked down the path towards the supervisor's office. After a few minutes I saw a man standing near the breast of the dam, where the swollen waters of Kettle Creek spilled over in a white froth to the rocks below. At first he did not see me. He stood as motionless as the hemlock tree beside him, as erect and serene. At his side, in his left hand, he held a closed book.

He was looking intently at the water seething over the dam. The roar was so loud that I thought I would have to shout to get his attention, but just as I came up behind him, he turned slowly as though he had known all along that I was there. His eyes were bright black, his hair bushy and gray.

165

Kettle Creek, sound and beauty

"I was just listening to the water," he said, by way of explanation or apology. "I like the sound of water."

"I do, too," I said. For a moment I listened with him. The sound was dizzying. "Right now," I said, "there's a lot of it."

"Too much for talking," he said. "You're planning to camp here tonight?"

I nodded.

"Let's go over to the office," he said. He shifted the book from his left hand to his right. I tried to see the title but could not.

We walked silently through the hemlock woods to his office, the roar of the water growing fainter as we went. Inside he made out a camping permit. The book was lying on his desk. It was Thoreau's *Walden Pond*. Near it was a little pile of hemlock cones. I paid him the fee of seventy-five cents.

"You like Thoreau?" I asked.

For a moment I thought he resented the question. He pushed a few straggling cones into the pile. "Yes," he said. He looked down at the book. "Do you?" he asked.

"Very much," I said, and waited.

In a moment he looked up from the book, his face a silhouette against the window. "I have lived in the woods all my life," he said, "and so I understand them. Most people only like them, Burroughs, for instance. But Thoreau understood." He picked up the book. "You have to love things to understand them."

When he turned around, there was a little smile on his face, the smile of the weary or the sad. "My name's Jim Swartz," he said crisply. "If you need anything let me know. I think you'll like Kettle Creek tonight, even if it rains."

When I left him he was looking out the window towards the dam.

166

in the mist by the stream

Back at the car Tom and I put up the tent on the wet ground and started dinner. While we worked and while we ate, I told Tom about meeting Jim Swartz. I didn't tell him about the mysterious smile or about the piercing black eyes because I couldn't, but I told him about how the man looked as he stood there in the mist by the stream. And I told him about listening to the water and about Swartz's distinction between Thoreau and Burroughs.

"I don't get it," Tom said.

"Neither do I," I said, "but I'd like to talk to him some more."

"Maybe we'll see him in the morning," Tom said.

By the time we had finished dinner and had washed the dishes it was almost dark. Tom said, "I'm turning in early this evening, but you do whatever you want."

About half an hour after Tom had gone to bed, I slid into my sleeping bag. It was not quite nine o'clock. A whippoorwill called again and again from across the stream. Crickets said little, tree frogs much. Below us, Kettle Creek spilled over the dam

with a gentle roar that filled the valley, and occasionally a breeze flicked raindrops from trees to tent —a warm, dry, comfortable tent.

I lay there, thinking about other camping trips, memorable all of them but not all of them comfortable. The long-ago camping trips, when I was a boy, were the ones that were often uncomfortable, especially when camp had to be set up in the rain as we had to do this afternoon.

Tenting today is not what it used to be. From my boyhood camping trips, I remembered the trench we used to dig around the tent. In a rainstorm, it looked like a medieval moat, and as the rain continued, the ground inside the tent became more and more like a swamp. I remember the smoky kerosene lantern and the smudge of wet leaves we used in the tent to drive out the mosquitoes and making a fire with wet wood in the morning and the burned or half-cooked oatmeal and the rancid butter and the ham that was faintly green around the edges. And in spite of it all, I loved it.

But today camping in a tent is done in the grand manner of the patrician. A modern umbrella tent can be put up by one man or one woman in five or ten minutes. It has a sewed-in floor through which water cannot penetrate, windows with plastic screening, doorways that are screened and zippered. It denies entrance to slug and salamander, toad and snake, moth and mosquito. You can build a cooking fire if you wish, but the gasoline stove is cleaner and hotter, and the lightweight stove that cooks with bottled gas is cleaner and hotter still. You can get the equivalent of a 100-watt light in your tent with a gasoline lantern or with a lantern that uses bottled gas. And any supermarket has a plentiful supply of varied food in cans that need only be heated. As for beds, you can have an aluminum cot, or a sleeping bag and a rubber mattress that rests on the ground. For myself, I prefer bag and rubber mattress and the ground. I have had worse beds in expensive hotels.

There are still die-hards, of course, who insist upon smoke in their eyes, slugs in their bedding, and fires without matches, but for most campers today, the phrase "roughing it" is downright archaic. They spend less time in setting up camp than the tourist does in inspecting his motel and ordering ice water. They live in earth-scented luxury, dining on better foods than most businessmen get for lunch and sleeping a contented sleep that few city dwellers ever know. And their music is supplied, not by the radio, but by the thrush and the warbler, by tree frog and

through the hemlock woods

whippoorwill, and by moving water and wind among the treetops.

I lay there in a warm sleeping bag on a rubber mattress, remembering and hearing. From somewhere far off, I thought I heard a voice calling, and once from the hill behind us, I heard the barking of a fox. I thought again of Jim Swartz, as much a part of the grove as the hemlock tree he stood beside, and I saw him again, listening, listening to the sound of water spilling over a dam. I wondered if the water said to him things it would not say to me.

When I awoke in the morning, I could hear Tom stirring around outside the tent. A fire was crackling, and the faint odor of woodsmoke filled the tent. There was another sound, too, like the crumpling of waxed paper. I dressed quickly and stepped outside.

Tom was sitting at the table, a package of crackers in front of him. "Watch this," he said quietly, "but don't move fast. This is something to see."

Only a few feet away from him on the table sat a chipping sparrow. It moved about uneasily or expectantly, fluttering its wings and taking little, mincing steps. Tom broke off a piece of cracker and flicked it between him and the sparrow. The bird half fluttered, half hopped towards it, hesitated, moved closer, took it, and finally carried it a few feet away. There he cracked it into pieces and ate the crumbs.

When he had finished, he wiped his bill on his breast and cheeped. Neither Tom nor I moved. "Now watch this," Tom said. He broke off another piece of cracker and placed it on the thumb of his left hand so that the sparrow would have to perch on the palm of the hand in order to reach the cracker.

Hesitantly, almost flirtatiously, the bird came to his hand with much flicking of wings and puffing of feathers. Then he hopped up on the palm of Tom's hand, took the bit of cracker from the raised thumb, and hopped a few feet away.

After the sparrow had eaten this second piece, Tom said, "Now watch him. He's like a puppy."

He got up from his chair slowly and took three or four steps towards the stream. The sparrow cheeped vigorously. Tom took three or four more

168

steps towards the stream. The bird flew down from the table and settled to the ground only a yard behind Tom's heels. Tom kept walking towards the stream and the little bird kept hopping along behind him, cheeping every time Tom stopped. At the edge of the creek Tom tossed the rest of the cracker to the bird. It picked it up in its bill and flew back to the table with it.

"Tom," I said, "how long have you two been putting on this performance?"

He grinned. "About an hour," he said. "I haven't even started breakfast yet. Did you ever see anything like that?"

"At home," I said, "we have tame chickadees, but we worked to make them that way. I never saw a chipping sparrow act like this."

"I didn't work on this one," Tom said. "He began pestering me while I was making the fire."

While we prepared breakfast on the cooking stove, Tom kept talking about the bird. "Why," he said, "are most birds afraid of human beings but not this one? What makes this one different?"

"Maybe the people who were here before us fed it," I suggested.

"Maybe," he agreed, "but I don't think so. There's something different about that fellow. He seems to understand you."

"This plain living," I said, "it could be turning you into a St. Francis. Maybe it's you, not the bird."

"All right," he said, "why *did* the birds go to St. Francis? I think it was because he understood them somehow. And they understood him. It could be. There's a lot that people don't understand about birds and animals."

For a moment I thought of Jim Swartz. "You have to love things to understand them." And I thought of Thoreau's robin-in-the-distance—"the first I had heard for many a thousand years." I thought of the sparrows on John Keats' winter windowsill, so close to his consciousness that he felt he had become part of them. I thought of Wordsworth saying to his skylark, "Lift me, guide me, high and high." I thought of Rossetti's chaffinch, the ghost of the beautiful Siddal.

"Maybe you're right," I said.

After breakfast Tom wandered away with his camera. I washed the dishes and then took the trail up the mountain behind the camping grounds. It was only a little after six o'clock. The birds were still in predawn voice, and a wind was beginning to rise, shaking wetness from every bush and tree. I walked

I took the trail up the mountain

slowly, for the grade was steep and the rocks were slippery. A short distance up the trail, two deer looked at me curiously and did not bound away until I was within fifty feet of them. Around me were hemlock, rhododendron with shiny leaves, groves of cinnamon fern. Blurs of yellow marked the flight of warblers, and as I went on, a yellow chat—clown, gymnast, and coloratura all in one—led the way.

About a half mile up the trail, in a clearing where ferns grew knee-high, I stopped to rest and to look down into the valley. It was a beautiful morning. Sunlight was brightening the ridge across the creek and reaching deeper into the valley. Below, Kettle Creek wound through the gorge, spread out above the dam into a little river, and then spilled to the glistening rocks with a distant rumble. The smoke of our fire still lingered in the valley, a layer of blue drifting upward.

Then, as I stood there, I heard a coughing bark. I did not turn around. I remembered the bark of the fox just before I went to sleep. Slowly, very slowly, I turned my head in the direction of the sound. The corners of my eyes caught vague motion and I turned still farther. A hundred feet up the mountain side a buck moved out from the shadows of a hemlock. He sniffed the air, but the wind was coming from him to me. With stately step he began walking towards the grove of ferns. Once, he stopped to lift his black muzzle into the air, and I was sure he would discover me, for I was still breathing hard from the climb. Again, though, he moved forward, step by fragile step.

Just as he reached the edge of the sunlit ferns, a slender form leaped from the thicket in a high arc, curved down into the ferns, and bounded out again. It was a red fox, disturbed but not frightened. Again and again the red-gold creature leaped clear of the green and caught the sunlight; then, twenty yards away, it leveled off, streaked under a hemlock, and disappeared.

I turned my head towards the buck—too quickly, perhaps, for he sniffed the air again, backed off a few steps, and then sprang up the mountain side. Safe among the shadows of the hemlocks, he turned and looked back, turned again and moved out of sight among the dark shadows.

I stood without moving for awhile, waiting for a new sign of activity. From the general direction in which the trail was taking me, I heard again the coughing bark. I walked on, slowly and quietly. Neither the buck nor the fox had been frightened. If they had been, they would have departed differently—the buck in open flight, the fox in stealthy speed. If the fox had been afraid, I should never have seen the crafty one as he moved among the ferns. Perhaps, if I were lucky, I could discover him and his den. He might have been barking at the cubs. Although the sun was now up, they might still be playing noisily outside the den.

A few hundred yards up the trail, I caught sight of fox spoor. It was on a small rock to the left of the trail. At the rock, I turned off the trail. The wind was still in my favor. Cautiously I picked my way over the heavy knap of hemlock needles. I was doing very well, I thought, not rattling stones or stepping on dry branches, when suddenly a blue jay flew

where ferns grew knee-high

screaming from a tree in front of me. Almost immediately came a series of low barks from a short distance ahead.

My presence was now known, and the fox had won the game of hide-and-seek. Since there was no longer need of caution, I walked on in the direction of the barks. In a few minutes I came to a small clearing, at the upper edge of which two rocks leaned together. Clearly, this was the den, for the trampled area around the rocks was littered with bones and feathers, a most untidy court for such a handsome tenant.

I walked over to the rocks and peered into the hole that was the entrance. No bright eyes shone from the darkness. Fox and vixen and cubs were probably six or eight feet away, far back in the dark safety of their dwelling, though perhaps the fox had given his warning and had left the safety of the den to the mother and the children. Perhaps, even now, he was watching me from some place of shadows and seclusion, as self-effacing in danger as he had been bright and golden in security.

Few animals are more devoted lovers or parents than the fox and his vixen. They mate in late winter and are usually keeping house together before the first thaws. About two months after the time of love the vixen retires to the most distant part of the den and bears her cubs, five or six in the litter.

Then comes the perilous period of child raising. If the den is disturbed, fox and vixen find another home and transfer their children to new surroundings. Some naturalists believe that the vixen seldom leaves her cubs for many weeks after they are born, others that she lives in the den with them for only a few days, preferring to watch the den from a near-by post.

Through the dark nights, she and her mate forage far to find food for their cubs, not wishing to deplete the supply near the den. Unless the cubs are very young, they must leave the den in order to get their dinner, for the parents deposit the bird or rabbit near the entrance but not in it. Then the cubs, not golden yet but gray, come out and eat. After the meal they play near the den, tumbling about, wrestling, nipping at one another like puppies, but a bark from either fox or vixen sends them scurrying back into the dark recesses of their home.

And when at last the cubs are grown and have learned the lore of hunter and huntress, the parents send them off on their separate ways to find their own food, their own dens, their own mates and to

perhaps, even now, he was watching

raise their own families with the ancient cunning of their kind. After the children are gone, fox and vixen remain as mates, finding monogamy more desirable than many human beings do.

Sometimes I hear my hunting friends speak disparagingly of the fox as a *predator*. Having called him that, they think that all is said. But to one who knows the ways of the woods and the streams, to one who knows the ways of nature, *predator* is a term of definition rather than of reproach. Most animals, in one way or another, could be classified as predators. Man, himself, is the most notorious predator of all. Yet predators are not creatures to be hated. They are the balancing agents in nature's scheme of things.

Because of the predator fox, our grouse and rabbits are wiser and healthier, for he weeds out the unfit. Because of him, we are not overrun by mice and rats when we camp in the woods. Because of him, we remember forever the sight of a tawny flame that speeds across a meadow or a grove of ferns.

To exterminate this royal vagabond—even if we could—would be as foolish as to exterminate the bear because he preys on starving deer or the bass because he preys on frogs or frogs because they prey

171

on insects or insects because they prey on other insects or robins because they prey on worms that keep our soil friable. "Let me alone!" is the first command of nature, and he who disobeys that command risks much, including his own well-being. Should it ever seem necessary to disobey, the disobedience should be entrusted not to the hunter nor to the fisherman or farmer or industrialist but to the trained ecologist, who, wise in the complicated balances of nature, will weigh the consequences of disobedience and judge wisely whether the gain is worth the risk.

I left the open glade and started back to camp. If I had been wearing a hat, I think I should have tipped it to Mr. and Mrs. Reynard, who knew from the scream of a blue jay that the two-footed one was approaching and who hid their precious children from the most dangerous of all predators.

When I got back to camp, Tom was gone. If the stream had been clearer, I might have gone fishing, for Kettle Creek is a good bass stream into which trout frequently make their way. I did walk along the path for awhile. A man and two boys were fishing under overhanging hemlocks. Then I built up the fire again, for no reason except that the woodsmoke smelled good, and went to the car to get a book. Tom and I usually put books and magazines on the back seat, just in case we should have to stay in the tent all day. This was not the kind of a day that required tent living, but it was a good day for reading.

The sunlight was warm now, and a few puffy clouds floated through the blue above. The table and bench were almost dry. Laying books and magazines on the table, I settled myself for an hour or so of skimming. The chipping sparrow, I noticed, was not around.

What a hodgepodge of reading material we had collected—a paper-back anthology of poetry, *The Wisdom of Lao-tsze, Birds of Western Pennsylvania, The American Scholar*, Chief Standing Bear's *My Indian Boyhood, Historic Western Pennsylvania*, and Walton's *Complete Angler!*

along the path

puffy clouds floated through the blue

In reading, as in living, we usually find what we wish to find. As I relaxed in the sunshine, I was still thinking of the deer on the hillside, the fox and the yellow chat, the calm valley and the wavering blue smoke from the fire. I was thinking of Tom's chipping sparrow and of Jim Swartz listening to the mysterious rumble of Kettle Creek. Life other than ours is always alluring. If we are curious we want to reach out and share in imagination some part of it, however small—the lilting flight of the swallow, the long, long sleep of frog and chrysalis, the dappled innocence of a fawn among the ferns, the strength and silence and aloofness of a stand of virgin pines. Unconsciously we try to penetrate the worlds that are known to other living things, but it is hard to do, for we are weighed down with a sense of our own importance, with a sense of our superiority to other creatures.

I leafed through the book of Lao-tsze. Out of the simple, sophisticated wisdom of the Chinese, Lao-tsze advised us to "Be at one with all these living things." And again, "Can you hold the door of your tent wide to the firmament?" And again, "Those who would take over the earth and shape it to their will, never, I notice, succeed."

It is not easy to be at one with all these living things. For two centuries we of Penn's Woods West have been so busy clearing land, draining swamps, building roads and factories, digging coal and

pumping oil, taking over the earth and shaping it to our will, that many of us have almost lost the ability to fit into the natural order of things. And yet without that ability we live in a half-realized discontent. In the midst of human company we often feel lonely; in the midst of wealth we feel poor. We do not want to believe that with our birth, "Naked and alone we came into exile," but there are times when we think we must.

Yet this morning standing on the mountain and looking down, I did not feel naked and alone nor did I feel that I had come into exile. I had come, rather, into a community of living things, and after a fashion had been accepted to membership. True, the deer and the fox had fled from me as a notorious predator but not, I think, in much fear, and the yellow chat had had no fear at all. If anything, I think he welcomed me, found me an amusing creature as I plodded along the earth on two clumsy legs.

Below me was the quiet valley, the sunlight bringing out the colors of the western slope. Here, too, I felt that I belonged. I was not an intruder. I felt humble and exalted at the same time, for I was welcome to share the morning with fern and hemlock and rock and rhododendron as all of us were warmed by the rising sun, our common friend and benefactor.

Leafing through the anthology, I found much that I did not wish to read. Today, Lucasta had no charms, Chapman's Homer was for another trip, and

for an hour of skimming

warmed by the rising sun

My Last Duchess, for all her interest in cherry blossoms, did not belong to Kettle Creek. But going on through the book, I came upon a few lines by William Davies that seemed appropriate enough for the events of the morning.

> What is this life if, full of care,
> We have no time to stand and stare.
>
> No time to stand beneath the boughs
> And stare as long as sheep or cows.
>
> No time to see, when woods we pass,
> Where squirrels hide their nuts in grass.

Well, there had been time to stare, and what I saw had been good for the eyes, for the nervous system, for the soul. But somehow, staring or looking is not enough. I had felt for a quick moment, an exalted moment, part of what I looked on, part of the life I witnessed.

Laying aside the anthology, I picked up *The American Scholar* and turned to an article by Joseph Wood Krutch, "Conservation is Not Enough." There I read,

And the thing that is missing is love, some feeling for, as well as some understanding of, the inclusive community of rocks and soils, plants and animals, of which we are a part.

That, I thought, was getting pretty close to the thing I was looking for. *Love, feeling,* and *understanding* are large words, but the earth is large, too, and a mountain range in the fog, and a sunrise, and the look in the eyes of a vixen caught in a trap. And in spite of cynics and the *avant guard,* I believe that the mind and soul of man, also, are large, large enough to find their way home again when, in their loneliness, they feel the need of love and understanding, the need of belonging to the universe.

But to find our way home is not easy. We have been gone a long time. To return, it may be that we shall have to leave the city for awhile—the business-

174

man, the poet, the teacher, the mechanic—if only for a week or two—and stand where the wind blows across the mountains at night and where, in the morning, the sun warms rock and man alike, and the salamander under the rock, and the cedar waxwing in the tree, and the wood shrew who, from under his fallen oak leaf, peers out with tiny eyes at the great world. For these and the beetles and the mites and the May flies are our companions and our helpers in our journey through life to death. Without them the journey would end quickly.

I read the essay twice and laid it aside. Then I picked up a book I had not read for twenty-five years, *My Indian Boyhood*, written by that wise old Sioux, Ota K'te, or Chief Standing Bear. What, if anything, would he say about the Indian's attitude towards life not like his own? Would there be any similarity between his words and the words of the Chinese philosopher? Would he use the words of the essayist—*love* and *understanding* and *feeling*? I started to turn the pages and shortly found the answers to many questions.

Life for the Indian is one of harmony with Nature and the things which surround him. The Indian tried to fit in with Nature and to understand, not to conquer and to rule. We were rewarded by learning much that the white man will never know. Life was a glorious thing, for great contentment comes with the feeling of friendship and kinship with the living things about you. The white man seems to look upon all animal life as enemies, while we looked upon them as friends and benefactors. They were one with the Great Mystery and so were we. We could feel the peace and power of the Great Mystery in the soft grass under our feet and in the blue sky above

to understand, not to conquer

us. All this made deep feeling within us, and the old wise men thought much about it, and this is how we got our religion.

I could have spent the afternoon thinking about the words. But as I returned the books and magazines to the car, fragments of things that other men had said flitted through my mind. I remembered Lear's words whispered to Cordelia, "We two will take upon's the mystery of things"; the words of the Cornplanter, "When I was a boy, I played with the butterfly, the grasshopper, and the frogs"; Jim Swartz's, "I like to listen to the water." I remembered George Herbert:

> More servants wait on man
> Than he'll take note of. In every path
> He treads down that which doth befriend him.

*   *   *

She was sitting beside the stream, a frail, pretty child with brown hair in pigtails. "Hello," she said. "My name's Martha."

"Hello, Martha," I said. "Having a good time?"

She had a little pile of twigs, all about the same length, and she was arranging them log-cabin fashion. "Yes," she said, "I like it here very much."

"You're camping?" I asked.

"Yes," she said, "with my mother and father. I like to camp."

"And your mother and father?" I said.

"I don't know," she said. She placed a twig carefully on two other twigs. "I'm in the third grade."

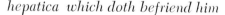
hepatica which doth befriend him

"You're little to be in the third grade," I said. "Why do you like it here?"

Deliberately she placed another twig on the log cabin. She looked up the stream and then, past me, down the stream. "Everybody's nice here," she said.

"Everybody?" I said. "But there aren't many people here, are there?"

"No," she said, "not people. Just everybody."

With her hand she pointed impatiently to the stream and to the trees along the path. "Everybody," she repeated. "You know what I mean."

For the first time she looked up at me. Her eyes were so brown and so lonely that I had to look away—to the stream, to the willows along the bank. From across the creek mourning doves cooed gently to one another, and all around, the tree frogs had begun their twilight conversations. "Yes," I said. "I think I know what you mean."

"I've got to go now," she said, getting up off the path. "I hope we can stay a little longer." Pigtails bobbing, she walked sedately through the grove towards the camping ground. Once she stopped along the way and waved to something in the woods.

It was the next evening before I again saw Jim Swartz. The western side of the valley was already in shadow, and a whippoorwill was calling from somewhere up the stream. I stopped where the water surged over the dam, but he was not there. Then I looked into the hemlock grove, where the last bit of sunlight threw long shadows and speckled the forest floor with bright blurs.

the hemlock grove

I left the creek and followed the path into the woods. He was sitting on a log, dim sunlight touching his white hair. When I came up to him, he rose. "Hello," he said. "I looked for you and your companion yesterday but you were away." His language was strangely formal. He had spoken that way when I first met him.

"Yes," I said, "we went up the stream a few miles. For photographs. It's pretty here," I added. "One of the prettiest places we've visited."

"I knew you would like it here," he said. "I think I told you so."

"You did," I said. "You also mentioned Thoreau."

He smiled. "Thoreau. Yes. He was more than a naturalist. He had a feeling for nature, an understanding of it. It was a kind of religion for him."

The whippoorwill that I had heard was coming closer. It made me think of Tom's chipping sparrow, and I told Jim about how it followed Tom around.

"Yes," he said, "I know the sparrow. He's been coming here for three years. Farther up the stream, by the big bend, there is a towhee. It will light on your finger . . ." He paused and smiled again. "If it trusts you."

"You think they can tell?" I asked.

"I do," he said, as solemnly as if he were taking an oath. "I think many creatures understand us better than we understand them. The dog, for instance. And the beaver. The fox you disturbed yesterday morning was not afraid of you. He understood."

"You were up there?" I asked.

He did not answer. There was no sunlight in the woods now, but the reflected light from the sky seemed to catch in his bushy hair. "There was a beaver once," he said, and then he stopped.

"Tell me," I asked.

"It had been caught in a trap. Illegally. I was a fire warden then. If I had known the man who did it . . ."

"Hurt badly?" I asked.

"His leg. It was a vicious, wicked kind of a trap."

"Could you do anything?" I said. "It must be dangerous to release a trapped beaver."

"I sat down near it," he said, "but not too near. I talked with it for a while."

He ran his hand through his hair. "Be seated," he said. "We might as well be seated."

I sat down on the log beside him. Now the whippoorwill was calling from between us and the stream.

"You talked with the beaver," I said. "What did you say?"

the roar of Kettle Creek

"Oh," he said, "I don't remember exactly. But I told him I was sorry. I told him I meant no harm. I explained to him that I wanted to help him if he would let me."

"You talked *words* to him?" I asked.

"I told him we would have to go over to a tree. I would carry the trap and he would have to hobble along. I wanted the tree between us when I released the trap because . . ."

He hesitated and leaned forward, looking at the ground. "Because sometimes when we are hurt ourselves, we want to hurt others."

For a minute he said nothing but he kept looking at the ground. I could hear the roar of Kettle Creek, but I do not think he heard it. He was thinking of something else. Then he straightened up.

"I took the trap over to the tree, and he hobbled along on three legs. It was a vicious trap, and I had trouble springing it, but after while I did, and he pulled his leg out."

"And then," I said, "he probably went off in a hurry."

"He just sat there for awhile, and so I sat down too, but not too near. I talked with him a little more. I told him I was sorry. I told him I thought the leg would heal. In a few minutes I got up, and he did, too. I went one way and he went another."

By now it was almost dark. He was leaning forward, his elbows on his knees and his hands clasping and unclasping in front of him. I heard the whippoorwill again between us and the creek. Then another whippoorwill answered from behind us, very close, and all around were the gentle night sounds of the woods.

He got up from the log as though our talk was ended, and so I also got up.

"Good night," he said. His hand was hard and calloused. "I would not have told you about it except . . ."

I said good night and started up the dark path to the tenting grounds. Once I looked back. He had left the hemlock grove and was standing near the stream, in the same attitude he had been in when I first met him.

177

"The Lodge" on Spruce Creek

Spruce Creek

THE AMIABLE HOST OF HARPSTER MANOR ON SPRUCE Creek and of the Lodge, also on Spruce Creek, is a man of many talents. He is a farmer, a salesman, a crack rifle shot, a fine fisherman, a conservationist, a practical joker, a deadly poker player, and in the evening when he sits on the steps and looks out over Spruce Creek, a philosopher of the Izaak Walton variety. His wife is a comely woman who likes to bake, to fish, and to put up with the eccentricities of the lord of the manor.

Bob Harpster's home is the Manor, but he spends his idle time at the Lodge on his farm. The Lodge is a roomy place with a great stone fireplace that was once a limekiln and with a second floor bunk room that will accommodate more than a dozen people. The windows look out upon the stream, the level pasture land, and in the distance a wooded mountain ridge.

Tom and I arrived at the Lodge in the middle of the afternoon. Bob was there and so was George

Harvey. George was sitting at the table and was tying some of his famous flies.

"Make yourselves at home," Bob said with a sweep of his arm. "I'll be leaving soon, but I'll be back after dinner."

"And change into your fishing clothes," added George.

"There's steak in the refrigerator," Bob said, "if you're hungry."

"And you'd better wear boots," George said.

"And some cold beer," Bob said.

"And take your landing net along," said George.

A few minutes later, down at the creek, George said, "There's some big fish down by the bridge, above and below. You go down, and I'll go up. Good luck." He started up the creek.

I did not begin fishing immediately, for I wanted to watch George. John Alden Knight calls him the best fly fisherman in America. About twenty yards away he began casting to the creek over high water-grasses, a rhythmical manipulation of rod and line and leader, the line straightening out high behind him, then coming forward and dropping lightly on the water in an effortless upstream curve, rod, line, and angler a continuous instrument. On the third cast he took a trout. "Just a baby," he called back, but I could see that it was at least twelve inches.

I went on down the creek. The water was clear in spite of a week of rain, but high, of course, and fast. In the pool above the bridge I took two browns about eleven inches long on a wet fly. They are well colored, these Spruce Creek trout, and great fighters. I worked them through the fast water, netted them, and released them. After all, Bob had said there was steak in the refrigerator.

Below the bridge I took two more from under a ledge on the far side of the stream, one about ten, one about thirteen inches. Farther down the stream in the riffles below the pool the Harpster cows had taken possession of the water, but they were unselfish creatures and moved aside to let me pass.

Cows, I think, must be numbered among God's elect in the animal kingdom. Their placidity makes me feel ashamed of myself. Except when I am fish-

down by the bridge

ing, I am always in a hurry. I am always vaguely concerned about something I have to do tomorrow or next week. But cows live for now. They exist in the present, and with limpid eyes survey their heaven of pasture, sky, and stream, satisfied to be alive at four o'clock of a summer afternoon.

Leaving the land of the blessed I went on down the stream, taking a little of their contentment with me. I stopped to look at a wild rose bush the cows had not trampled and to listen to the canary call of a goldfinch swaying on a thistle blossom and to watch the swallows skimming over the stream. It was a good afternoon for looking and for listening, and the clouds were adequate excuse for lying down, from time to time, the better to see the airy flight across the blue.

I went on to the wire fence that crosses the creek, picking up two more trout on the way, and then started back. But a Light Cahill fished dry was less productive than the wet fly, and by the time I got back to the bridge I had caught and released only one more, a wonderful fellow thirteen or fourteen inches long who liked the air as much as the water.

At the Lodge, George greeted me with a grin that quickly faded. "Where's the fish?" he asked.

"I didn't keep them," I said. I noticed that there were three beautiful browns lying on the table. The longest must have been seventeen inches or more.

"How big?" he asked.

"Nothing like yours," I said. "Ten, twelve, maybe fourteen inches."

tying his famous flies

179

"Look," he said, "this isn't like most streams. It grows big trout faster than you can take them out. On Spruce Creek you never put a trout back that's more than twelve inches long. You harvest the big ones. You've got to."

"That's slaughter," I said. "I must have caught a half dozen trout down there."

George grinned. "You're used to those free-stone streams," he said. "Spruce Creek's a limestone stream. It's different. It can support more fish because it has more food."

There was a fire in the fireplace, and the three of us sat down in front of it. "Not many people fish this creek," George said, "because most of it's privately owned. That means you've got to fish it hard to keep the population in check. Why, you could go up and down this creek every day in the season and keep all you caught—twenty, thirty a day—and the trout would still be getting ahead of you."

"Somehow," I said, "it doesn't seem possible."

"It's the food," he said. "The stream's alive with it. You have to harvest your trout or you'll throw everything out of balance."

It was the old story of harvesting, of balance, of check and countercheck, and we talked about it in front of the fire for half an hour or so. Clearly, good conservation practices vary from stream to stream, as do the ethics of angling, and the releasing of trout in overpopulated waters may be as foolish as the killing of trout in waters that are almost barren.

Spruce Creek is an ideal illustration of what anglers may expect when they turn their attention away from artificial stocking and towards improving the streams and lakes themselves. There is something a little silly in seeing a small army of men dumping fish into an impoverished creek and a larger army descending upon the creek a few weeks later to take them out. One of these days fishermen will realize that the only way to have good fishing is to have good water, and they will not object when the Fish Commission spends more money on stream improvement and less on artificial propagation. When our streams are protected from siltation by forested watersheds, when spawning beds are available, when there is adequate cover in the streams and over them, when banks are protected from erosion, and when the water runs clean and clear and cool, then we shall have better fishing in Penn's Woods West—and better fishermen.

After George left, Tom and I had the best trout dinner we ever tasted. We washed the dishes, and at about eight o'clock Tom went to bed. He wanted to

the pool above the bridge

180

the Harpster cows

get up at dawn, he said, to get pictures of Spruce Creek in the fog.

I went outside and sat on the steps to the Lodge. The light was beginning to fade from the sky. Presently Bob arrived and sat on the step below me. "They'll be coming out of the woods now," he said. "I like to sit here and watch the deer come out of the woods."

I looked across the valley to the ridge. In a moment three deer came out of the woods. "Accurate forecasting," I said.

"They always do," he said. "I like to sit here and watch them. Look, three more."

They came by twos, by threes, singly. After a time I said, "How many do you suppose there are?"

"Thirty, maybe," he said. "I've seen as high as sixty. They always come out about this time."

It was almost dark now. Frogs were chunking along the creek, and a cow bawled from the meadow. We sat there and listened.

"You love this," I said after awhile.

"More than anyone will ever know," he answered.

"How did you ever come to get it?" I asked.

For a long time he did not answer, and I listened to the whippoorwills in the valley and the frogs and the sound of mumbling water.

"When I was a kid," he said, "I always wanted to hunt and fish and hike through the woods. But I was a poor kid. It was during the depression, and I had to work. I drove a truck after school when I was eleven."

He stopped to remember and to light a cigar. Then he went on. "When I got older I began to make money, a good bit of it. Things seemed to work out right. Now I have what I missed when I was a kid— deer hunting, bear hunting, and a little piece of the best trout stream in Pennsylvania."

"Those beds upstairs," I said. "You must have a lot of guests."

"Most of them have keys," he said. "It doesn't cost them anything. That way we all enjoy it."

I kept thinking of the boy who wanted to go fishing after school but who drove a truck instead. I was thinking of all the boys in Penn's Woods West who

181

uncertain grays

want to go fishing but who cannot, of a whole generation of young folk in cities who have never really known the woods, the streams, the skies.

"Making money," I heard Bob saying, "it's fun at first, especially when you need it badly, but after while it doesn't seem to matter so much. Now, in the evenings, I can come over here and sit on the steps and listen to the whippoorwills and watch the deer come out of the woods."

Late at night, Bob left. I sat on the steps a long time before I went to bed. Once in awhile I thought of the words of an old preacher named Izaak Walton: "We sit on cowslip banks, hear the birds sing, and possess ourselves in quietness." Though the times were different by two hundred years, the story I had heard this evening was much the same as Izaak's.

Early the next morning, Tom and I wandered through the mist that had taken possession of Spruce Creek. The valley was quiet, and such sounds as did drift in seemed remote and unfamiliar. There was no horizon, only a luminous fog against which willow trees wavered in uncertain grays of shifting values. In the morning mystery, the earth seemed very close, and we found ourselves talking in low tones lest we disturb the calm that lay upon the valley.

Quietly we walked the length of the wet pasture, watching elm and willow take hazy form as we approached. Then, after Tom had taken all the pictures he wanted, we went back to the Lodge for breakfast. George Harvey had already arrived, and with him was Eric Walker, the president of Pennsylvania State University. George was dressing a few flies before departing for the stream, flies so delicate, so airy, so realistic that it seemed they might take wing from the table and flutter about the room. After a

for breakfast

Bob, with bent rod

Spruce Creek *is* different. The water is clear, it is cold, it is clean, and so there is plenty of food. Yet with proper management there could be a stream not unlike Spruce Creek in every county in Penn's Woods West. In every county there could be many good streams. If there were, and if fathers and mothers and Scout leaders and members of men's clubs took an interest in them, there might be fewer boys on street corners in the evening, and there might be more boys who would carry with them forever the strangely certain faith of those who know the earth and its ways, the fog at sunrise, the sunlight of midafternoon, the starlight that speaks with all-communicating silence.

Conservation does not stop, as we are sometimes led to believe, with making the world safe for brown trout or for Cooper's hawks. It goes far beyond that. It is a belief in a way of life, of community life, in which we can live happily.

We are the most fortunate and most responsible of living creatures. The boy on the street corner, loneliness and defiance in his eyes, may not know this. But the boy who watches a brown trout patrolling his dark pool or a Cooper's hawk challenging the sky senses that he is an important member of the greatest fraternity on earth. He is not an outcast. He belongs.

"Now I see the secret of the making of the best persons," says Whitman. "It is to grow in the open air and to eat and sleep with the earth."

All afternoon we wandered around the meadow and along the edges of the wood, entertaining ourselves with little things, the geometrical design of Queen Anne's lace, the airy abandon of milkweed seeds, and fungi that grew on a log in the woods. At dusk, on the way back, I picked up a nice brownie. After dinner Bob came down, and we sat on the steps again and talked and watched the deer and listened to the frogs and to Spruce Creek wandering through the moonlit darkness.

time, Charlie Stoddard arrived, and then Moe Silver and a friend, both from Warner Brothers. By the time Bob and Mrs. Harpster, loaded with marketing, opened the door, the room was buzzing with talk of Light Hendricksons and dark pools and the big brownie that President Eisenhower caught on his last trip to Spruce Creek and the ten-point buck that took over the valley at the end of hunting season. There was a quick lunch of steak, fried potatoes, and gallons of iced tea, and then the screen door began to slam as fishermen, their backs to the dishes, departed for the stream. I looked around for Mrs. Harpster, but she too, Lord bless her, had gone. Martyrdom overcoming us, Tom and I washed the dishes. A little later we were out on Spruce Creek.

The mystery of the morning had disappeared. The sun was bright and the shadows were sharp. Up and down the creek we went, watching the early afternoon anglers. Fishing for brown trout in bright sunlight is not usually successful, of course, but below the bridge Mrs. Harpster was bringing in a brownie to net and not far above her, Bob with bent rod was trying to bring a trout up through the fast water. A half hour later we saw them going back to the Lodge together.

183

on a log in the woods

a trout stream has a music all its own

and foamy swirls of water

On Caldwell Creek

THIS EVENING I WENT FISHING. I WENT ALONE. IF I HAD to explain why I went fishing, I should have to say, I suppose, that I wanted to catch a few trout or that I wanted something to eat for breakfast. Neither statement, though, would be quite true. This evening I wanted only to go fishing.

No hatches were on the water and no fish were rising, but trout fishing is pleasant whether the trout are active or indisposed. When they are not rising, we have time to notice things—reflections on a quiet pool, a dragonfly whose motion almost disturbs the peacefulness of twilight, the foamy swirl of water around a dark rock, the scent of hemlock carried along by the faintest of breezes.

A dark form, mink or weasel, slinks along the margin of the stream, keeping to the shadows. Beware, fat frog, and be ready to depart! In the fast current a caterpillar clings to a floating leaf. Will the leaf put into port somewhere and let the caterpillar disembark, or will it discharge its passenger in the riffles for the benefit of trout or redhorse? Upstream, the reflection of a maple wavers into motion. The mink may be crossing the pool. Much is happening while we look, though we can see but little.

And then there is the sound of the stream. This evening, the water was unusually loquacious, per- haps because the birds were rustling bedwards and were quiet. There was a soprano lilt among the rif- fles. Where foam gathered below a boulder, there was bass accompaniment. And indeterminate eddies of sound kept flooding in and receding and flooding back again.

A trout stream has a music all its own, evasive, suggestive, lonely yet self-possessed. We try to un- derstand it, but just when we think we are close to it, the tune changes a little, and then more and more, and we are lost and begin all over again. We feel that there is meaning to the music, and we reach out for it, but it floats through our fingers, through our ears and our brain, and drifts away.

Under its serene hypnosis, we almost lose identity, forgetting the margins of our being, trying to flow out into the music of a trout stream that moves through the dimness. We almost succeed but never quite. In the end, we return to ourselves, which is as it should be, and the trout stream, which had no part in the attempted transfer, goes on about its business.

A trout stream is nature's psychiatrist, a damp rock her couch. We pay no fee, yet we arise refreshed, having seen good things. Tomorrow will be time enough to catch two trout for breakfast. Tonight was for just fishing.

185

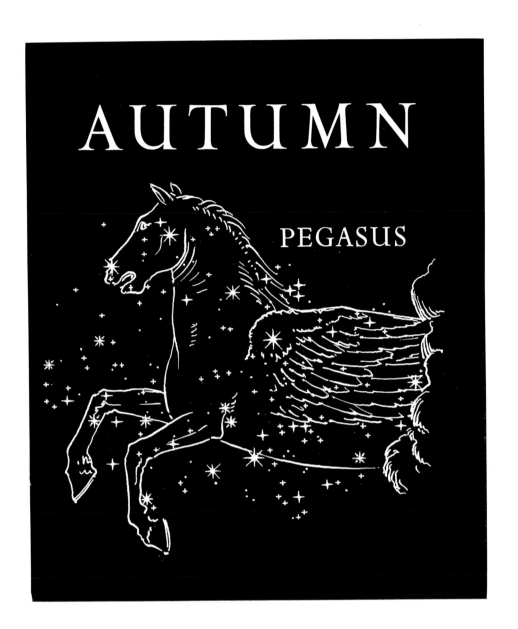

AUTUMN

PEGASUS

THE HORSE

ALL THIS WEEK THERE HAS BEEN A FAMILIAR ODOR IN the air, partly real and partly imaginary, an autumnal odor compounded of burning leaves, of pears in bushel baskets, of apple cider, and of forgotten plums that lie rotting on the ground. For now is the time of year when goldfinches dart among the thistles, when goldenrod brings to barren fields a day-long sunrise, when the dull cicada drones of lusty love, when, setting a color pattern for the weeks to come, the waxy leaves of the sumac turn to scarlet, and when corn shocks stand in rows.

Wild asters are beginning to edge country roads with blue, and flocks of red-winged blackbirds swoop over cattails in the swamp. Although the nighthawks no longer fill the dusk with distant whistling, the white-throated sparrow has returned, bringing with him the pleasant echo of his nuptial song, and the red-breasted nuthatch has come back to visit with his more common brothers.

For some creatures, life and love are ending. In little holes on the hillside the grasshopper has deposited her eggs and waits for death, and the dragonfly has carefully hidden her hopes of racial immortality in mud along the stream. The spider spins his last flurry of silken webs, and the wings of the swallowtail are tattered. But on the upper Allegheny bass and pike and muskellunge, rejuvenated by the cold nights, are chasing minnows through the shallows, and among the second growth, ambitious bucks are beginning to rub the velvet off their antlers in preparation for combat and romance.

As always, though, we wait for darkness and then look to the sky for certainty that the season is about to change. Nor is assurance hard to find. There in the east, early in the evening, is the great square of Pegasus, that winged horse who bears the banner of autumn and who comes to frighten summer from the skies. If for a moment we have trouble locating

189

him, we draw a line from the Pole Star to the most western star in Cassiopeia and continue the line an equal distance, when we come to the star Alpheratz, the northeastern corner of the square. The square represents the body of the horse, but in this topsy-turvy sky of autumn, the horse is upside down and the lowest corner of the square is the beginning of the neck. Three more stars in a line curving to the south and west make up the neck, and the head is a bright star a little to the west of the last star in the neck. From the northwest corner of the square two more stars curve westward to form a foreleg of the celestial horse Pegasus, the winged one, born of the blood of Medusa.

It was the boastful Dauphin, on the night before the battle of Agincourt, who best described this airy quadruped with wings: "What a long night is this! When I bestride him, I soar, I am a hawk; he trots the air; the earth sings when he touches it." Not being a good horseman, I shall leave Pegasus to Dauphin and shall content myself by looking a little to the west, where the retreating Swan glides gently down the Milky Way, taking with her what remains of summer.

And I shall listen, while I watch, to the crickets, very vocal tonight, singing what may be their last song before a hard frost puts an end to their singing forever. Do they have a premonition that the earth is ready to receive them? an aching in the strong legs, a dullness in the tips of the antennae, autumnal fog blurring their once bright vision? If so, then instinct must also tell them that their young are safely nested and that the race of Gryllids will again, some autumn evening, fill the night with music. For sing again they will, as they sang on that October night in France hundreds of years ago when the Dauphin boasted of Pegasus but failed to hear outside his tent the chorus of quick-coming death.

when corn shocks stand in rows

A Back Roads Trip Northeast

I MOVED A LITTLE CLOSER TO THE FIRE. TOM WAS LYING on a blanket, one corner flung across his back and shoulders. From somewhere far off a dog was howling to a sky with no moon, and dozens of octaves above his wail, so high as to be almost indistinguishable, came the monotone of crickets cheeping against the cold and the night of death.

"It won't be long," Tom said. "It won't be long before the summer's over."

"According to the calendar," I said, "it's over now."

"Calendars don't count. Want to make a back-road trip?"

"Where?" I asked.

"A back-road trip. Anywhere."

"What general direction?"

"Maybe northeast? Coudersport? Then south somewhere."

"Friday?" I suggested.

He moved the blanket away from his shoulders and sat up. "Suits me," he said.

And so, on a Friday morning, we started our back-road picture trip in a direction that was generally northeast. Back-road driving is, of course, very different from highway driving. Doubtless there are exceptions, but highway motorists are primarily interested in the foreshortening of time. Their aim is to bring as closely together as possible two points that are distant from each other, the space that lies between having no significance except as it interferes with bringing the destination closer to the point of departure. His objective being what it is, the highway driver looks straight ahead, with flickering glances at the needle of the speedometer to make sure that it is touching sixty, and settles back into an automotive stupor from which he is aroused only by red lights and a growing suspicion that the gasoline supply is low. After minutes or hours of blind flight through space and time, he arrives at his destination, "having seen nothing, still unblest."

Perhaps it was highway driving that caused Robert Lynd to remark some years ago:

Two things are essential to a restful holiday. The first is not to possess a map. The second is not to possess a car. To go anywhere with both a map and a car is to invoke

191

the spirit of unrest and to become the slave of the place where one is not—no longer an idler but an unpaid chauffeur. . . .

But because back-road driving is not deeply concerned with destination, it has none of the faults that Mr. Lynd enumerates. The back-road driver invokes the spirit of rest and serenity from the moment he starts out. He becomes the willing slave of the place he finds himself in—if it be a fit place for willing slavery. And far from being no longer an idler, he uses the car only to find better and better places for idling.

He uses a map, but chiefly to avoid the roads that are marked in red. Because he travels the fine black lines, he seldom drives faster than thirty miles an hour and frequently pulls off to the side of the road so that a highway driver who is off his course can swish past with a honk of the horn and a cloud of dust. Having stopped, the back-road driver usually gets out of the car to see if the spot be a good one for

idling, and it usually is. If the woods are shady or the pasture green, he may climb a rail fence to get better acquainted. If he hears what may be the trickle of water from a rusted pipe into a wooden tub, he goes in search of the sound. Often a tin cup rests on the stone beside the tub, and he suspends his belief in harmful bacteria long enough to quench his thirst with water as cold as the hidden rock it springs from. He spends a few minutes watching the moss wave from the sides of the tub, and then his attention is diverted by the song of a veery, and he follows the song and the bird along a hillside path bordered with ferns. When song and bird have gone, he may walk farther along the path or, knowing that there are many perfect places for idling away an hour of August or September, he may go back to the car and drive on for another mile or two.

Because he drives slowly, he does not have to keep his eyes on the road at all times. On the left a cloud shadow drifts across the valley, ahead a rabbit

past derelict houses

the destination is not important

shadows turn the day to twilight, along streams of no name, and past derelict houses with sagging porches and crumbling chimneys.

Such houses demand that the back-road driver stop and mount the rotten steps and peer through the cobwebbed windows at the faded wallpaper and the painted floors and at the old calendar hanging in the bare kitchen. Once upon a time . . . but now the bats take comfort in the chimney, and the woodchuck lives under the porch, and months before, the robin launched her brood from a nest on a southern windowsill. Thinking many things, the wanderer goes back to the car and continues his journey into anywhere. Sooner or later he comes to a black road and another road of dusty distinction.

To one who has been brought up in the tradition of highway driving the transition to back-road driving is sometimes hard to make. One must not even think of his destination until about four o'clock in the afternoon. The destination is not important. If no adequate lodging can be found, there are always the blanket rolls in the trunk of the car, a gallon thermos jug of water, a box of food, a little stove, and perhaps a tent.

And one must always drive so slowly that he can stop the car before he goes past the interesting thing that he sees to his left or right or straight ahead, for having to put the car into reverse—having, as it were, to back up into beauty—embarrasses the driver and turns adventure into ignominious retreat. If in trying to overcome bad habits acquired on the red highways, the beginning back-road driver has trouble with speed, he might try taking a camera along with him. A camera slows down a car considerably. Every turn of the wheel has a picture possibility, every hill, every valley, every patch of blue sky overhead. And since pictures cannot easily be made from a moving car, it follows that the more times the car is stopped the more good pictures the back-road driver is likely to get. Moreover, unless the car is going slowly, the driver will miss most of the pictures to his right and left and will return with a series of shots that might just as well have been taken through his windshield or bought in the village drugstore.

And finally, the beginning back-road driver should have a good companion with whom to share his vagrancy, one who takes pleasure in little things—puff balls growing on a log, cows lowing at a pasture gate, leaves burning in front of a village store—and who likes to talk about these things when the day and the drive are over.

scampers up the road, on the right gentians show blue against the green. At the top of the hill he is likely to stop the car so that he can look back as well as ahead, and at every bridge that crosses running water he is certain to stop, if only for a few minutes. More often than not, he will pull off the road before he gets to the bridge so that he can have the excitement of discovering the water while he walks instead of while he drives. He can stand on the bridge and look down into the pool that almost always lies beneath a bridge or he may clamber down the path beside the bridge abutment and watch the water from its edge. Old shoes are, of course, a necessity in back-road driving, and old trousers are more suitable than new.

Although roads marked in black are usually more picturesque than the heavily traveled highways, the very best are the dirt roads. They are almost always worth turning aside to follow, and the experienced vagabond will enter them without hesitation, knowing, of course, that he may get lost but that he may also find something more important than his sense of direction. Although these dirt roads are no longer marked on maps, the wanderer searches for them with diligence and follows them wherever they lead —along stony mountain ridges, where the sky is close, into deep valleys, where trees meet overhead and

LOG OF A BACK ROADS TRIP NORTHEAST

Friday morning

From Pittsburgh Route 22 to Murraysville; then black road to left (N) to Route 380 and right on Route 380 to Mamont and Beaver Run Reservoir and on to Saltsburg.

The dreary highway to Murraysville, hot and smelling of gasoline; then the cool back road and relief and trees and fields and farmhouses and the crossroads stores and the signpost to Mamont; the golf course beginning to burn in the September heat, and the dirt road we explored for half an hour; Beaver Run Reservoir, clear and deep, where hundreds of blue gills swam in the shade of the bridge and where swallows darted through the sunlight on the other side; then lunch in Saltsburg, the town that was once famous for saltwater drawn from wells and then evaporated over charcoal fires.

Friday afternoon

From Saltsburg a back road over the Conemaugh Dam to Route 982; then Route 982 to Route 680 and left (N) on Route 680 and 80 to Indiana.

The disappointment of the Conemaugh Dam with almost no water in it and the irony of a sign near the multimillion-dollar structure, a sign above a drinking fountain: Treated Water Please Conserve; the dirt road away from the dam, and all the trees and ferns and blue asters; the abandoned one-room schoolhouse by the hickory tree, an outhouse for the girls and one for the boys and the schoolyard covered with hickory nuts; the dirt road there that led us back into the hills and a quiet valley, sufficient reward of shade and coolness for turning off the

trees and fields and farmhouses

bright in the morning sunlight

black road; and in the late afternoon sunlight the whiteness of the town of Indiana, where we ate dinner and spent the night.

Saturday morning

From Indiana Route 954 to left (N) over Crooked Creek to Willet and on to Trade City; from Trade City Route 210 to the left to Route 119 and left again on Route 119 to Punxsutawney.

A land of farms and gently sloping hills and valleys; the bridge over Crooked Creek with its sulphur water and the yellow mud with raccoon tracks on it; at a crossroad the church and cemetery, bright in the morning sunlight; boys beside a spring creek energetically throwing stones at a snake under a bridge; the long, downhill stretch of road into Trade City; Punxsutawney and Gobbler's Knob, home of the prophet groundhog.

Saturday afternoon

From Punxsutawney Route 119 about a half mile; then left on Route 310 to Reynoldsville; from Reynoldsville Route 322 to left (W) a half mile; then right on Route 950 to Falls Creek; at Falls Creek right to Route 219; at Route 219 right to DuBois.

Farm country again with hills in undulating curves and a blue, September haze beginning to blur the horizon; the future fullback who posed on his front lawn near Reynoldsville; edged with goldenrod, a side road that took us to the sheep; apples in bushel baskets by the roadside; and late in the afternoon near DuBois a good dinner and a comfortable place to sleep.

Sunday morning

From DuBois Route 255 for about a mile; then right on a back road to DuBois Reservoir and on to Route 153; then left (N) on Route 153 about two or three miles to back road into Parker Dam State Park.

DuBois, the December home for thousands of big game hunters; the rolling land of Indiana and Punxsutawney changing to rugged, mountainous country; the winding road through the woods to the Reservoir, blue and calm in the early morning; at the upper end of the Reservoir a contented fisherman sitting in the sun and hoping; the haze still in the air; the swimming pool at Parker Dam State Park and two girls practicing lifesaving holds.

at Sizerville State Park

Sunday afternoon

From Parker Dam State Park the Park road towards Tyler but right at first intersection; then Medix Run road to the Caledonia Pike and left to the town of Medix Run; from Medix Run Route 555 to right to Driftwood; from Driftwood Route 120 left (N) to Route 155 to Sizerville State Park.

The blue haze growing heavier and blurring the distant mountains; the steep Medix Run Road, miles and miles of it, and the heavy shadows, and the trickle of water beside the road as Little Medix Run led the way, and ferns and laurel and huckleberry bushes—as beautiful a back road as can be found in the State; lunch under a pine tree; rabbits darting across the road; at the town of Medix Run the old woman who could not understand why we were lost; the shameful yellow of Sinnemahoning Creek; late in the afternoon, people still enjoying the cold water of the swimming pool at Sizerville State Park; pitching our small tent, a dinner late at night, and later still, the notes of a sparrow in the dark.

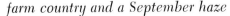

farm country and a September haze

195

the birth of the Allegheny River

Monday morning

From the Park, back to Route 155 and on to Keating Summit and the outskirts of Port Alleghany; then right (E) on Route 6 and along the Allegheny River to Coudersport, still following the river, Route 49 to Gold at Route 449.

At Port Alleghany, the river that we had first met in the spring at Corydon but so shallow here that a boy could wade across it; farther on, the pleasant farms and the corn in shocks and cows grazing in the pastures; at Coudersport, the river smaller even than at Port Alleghany; the winding beauty of Route 49; two girls in a garden patch; a feeling of expectancy as we came closer and closer to the town of Raymond; and at last the birth of the Allegheny River, "one of the most beautiful rivers in ye world," in an ordinary pasture three hundred and fifty river miles from Pittsburgh.

Monday afternoon

From Gold Route 449 to the right (S) through Brookland to Route 6; then right (W) on Route 6 to Sweden Valley and the ice mine; then back along Route 6 almost to Ansonia; then right on road to Colton State Park and Pennsylvania's Grand Canyon; back to Route 6.

The long climb up the heavily wooded mountain side and the late afternoon shadows across the road, and, through gaps in the trees on our left, quick glances at the blue mountain in the distance; white birches increasing in number as we climbed; the lookout point and the dizzying view to the stream and the railroad tracks below and to a tiny canoe drifting through the riffles; the blue jay that swooped out over the canyon and then swooped back; the uneasy feeling in the pit of the stomach; the old woman who said, "I haven't been so scared since I had pneumonia!"; remembering, "In his hands are the deep places of the earth"; and the winding, sunset road back to Route 6 and dinner and a cabin for the night.

Tuesday morning

Route 6 back to Galeton; then left (S) on Route 144 to Germania, Ole Bull State Park, Cross Fork, and Route 120; left (E) on Routes 120 and 144 to Renovo; from Renovo Route 144 to Moshannon at Route 53; left on Route 53 to Snowshoe and Route 220; left (E) on Route 220 to Milesburg and right on Route 53 to Bellefonte.

the stream and the railroad tracks below

196

made beautiful by morning fog

The narrow hillside road with an exciting view at every rise and turn; ours the only car on the road; the silence of the mountain valley where we stopped; at Germania the boys fishing in a spring run across from the church; the bright farm on the mountain side to our right; thoughts of the great Norwegian when he felt he had found heaven here in this valley; Ole Bull State Park and Little Kettle Creek winding through it and hidden among the tall trees the death of a dream; again the winding road and the village of Cross Fork with its combination post office and angler's store; a back road to Hammersley Fork and Ludi's famous lodge for fishermen; Renovo, an unlovely town, made beautiful by morning fog from the Susquehanna River; after Renovo the thirty-two miles of mountain back road without a town, without a gasoline station, but with view after magnificent view of mountains and sometimes of clouds that nestled in their creases; and sixteen more miles of excellent back-road driving to Bellefonte and lunch.

Tuesday afternoon

From Bellefonte Route 550 to Route 350; a back road to Spruce Creek and then Route 45 to Colerain State Park.

Bellefonte, "Beautiful Spring," where trout are almost as important as people; where people stand on the sidewalk of the main street and watch the great trout in Spring Creek and where the fish, in turn, look up at people, who sometimes give them food; the incredible spring that flows eleven and a half million gallons of pure, cold water every day; the old-fashioned buildings; Fisherman's Paradise, where five-pound trout draw only passing comment; Route 550 and a mountain ridge on each side and quiet, red-brick farmhouses and pasture streams and

ours the only car on the road

the surety of autumn

where Spruce Creek joins the Juniata

Queen Anne's lace along the road

cows; the cattails on Route 350; the boys on bicycles where Spruce Creek joins the Juniata on its way to the Atlantic Ocean—while only eighty miles away the Allegheny River begins its journey to the Gulf of Mexico; the old stone house with a story to tell to the wanderer who stops to listen; our evening meal between the tent and the fire; and listening to the high chorus of crickets before we went to sleep.

Wednesday morning

From Colerain Route 45 to Water Street; then left (E) on Route 22 to Route 26; right (S) on Route 26 to Everett and Route 30; right (W) on Route 30 through Bedford to Schellsburg; then left to Shawnee State Park.

Queen Anne's lace along the road; woodchuck hunters roaming across the fields; at the town called Shy Beaver, the old man who explained, "Well, there used to be a colony of beavers down there in the valley, and one of them was very shy, and she came up here to live, and that's why they call the town Shy Beaver"; sitting down on the bank of the Rays-town Branch for an hour or so and talking with a

199

fisherman who was merely idling away his time until squirrel hunting began; lunch in Bedford, old and beautiful, where, according to an eighteenth-century chronicler, "the people are not often sick, and they are sick less because they have no Doctor"; Shawnee Park and on the cliff the house in which John Bowman used to live; the almost deserted beach; the camping ground where we pitched our tent just before the rain began.

Wednesday afternoon

From Schellsburg Route 96 to Route 56 and a back road to Route 869 and Blue Knob State Park; then back to Shawnee.

Rain on the road to Blue Knob, and the long climb up the mountain; rain and mist between us and all other things; the general store where we bought the marvelous slab bacon; the puddles on the road while the rain beat down; the mystery of fog over mountain and valley; the muffled silence every time we stopped the car; the surety of autumn and the fall of leaves; the road back to Shawnee; a sputtering dinner of slab bacon, eggs, steaming coffee, and apple cakes warmed over the fire.

Wednesday night

Remembering, as the darkness closed in and the fire blazed against the dampness, the days and nights I used to fish Shawnee Creek before it became a State Park and lake; the trout and fall fish and small bass; the wise and amiable gentleman who lived on

water tumbling lightly over the dam

the cliff; the ghosts from the Indian village who used to walk along the creek before the lake covered them over completely; and after we went to bed and Tom was asleep, the wind moaning gently in the trees

rain on the road

and singing of things not known to those who drift over the lake in rowboats—the arrowhead maker who lived long ago at Kegg Run, the speckled trout that flashed under the oak bridge, the smell of burning apple wood that came only a few years ago from the house on the cliff, and the good talk before the fireplace after the evening of fishing was over.

Thursday morning

From Shawnee Route 96; then right (W) on Route 31 through Somerset, Kooser State Park, Jones Mills, and Acme to Route 982.

Along the road goldenrod and Joe Pye weed to prove that summer had not gone; a back road to Laurel Hill State Park and a morning walk along the stream in spite of the blue jay that objected to our presence; Kooser State Park and remembering how it looked on a late afternoon in spring when the trillium bloomed and the lake was darkening with shadows; Indian Creek and Jones Mills and the woodland trail bordered with rhododendrons, their leaves shiny with the last night's rain, and the sound of water tumbling lightly over the rocks of the dam.

Thursday afternoon

Right (N) on Route 982 to Lycippus; from Lycippus left on Route 180 to Route 981; right on Route 981 through Latrobe to New Alexandria; from New Alexandria back road to Keystone State Park; from Keystone back to New Alexandria and Route 22; left (W) on Route 22 to Murraysville and Pittsburgh.

Small towns, faded flower gardens, and drab picket fences; the magnificence of the mountains far behind us; ironweed on the edges of fields and dwarf sumac flaming like brush fires; Keystone Park and clear water and the little girl who sat on a log and talked to a wood turtle beside her; the Loyalhanna and the path that led long ago to Keckkeknepolin; then evening and Route 22, blue fumes, eyes looking straight ahead, a hundred speedometers fluttering between fifty and sixty, and the end of a back-road journey—except that back-road journeys never end.

Back-road journeys do not end any more than a book ends because it has been read or a symphony because it has been heard or a painting because it has been seen. In highway driving the trip is ended when the destination has been reached, but in back-road driving the trip lives on for many years, growing both in pleasure and in significance, for back-road driving is a belief in the abiding pleasure of

talked to a wood turtle

blue sky and clouds, of a sparrow's song at night, of a stone house with a story to tell, of an old woman in a country store, a little girl who talked to a turtle, trillium in the spring and sumac in the fall, the taste of huckleberries, the smell of autumn apples, and the exhilaration of being lost and found again on an earth that, to those who love it, is always familiar.

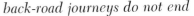

back-road journeys do not end

over gray boulders

Slippery Rock Creek

WHEN I STEPPED OUT OF THE TENT IN THE MORNING, the air was a sharp reminder that November had arrived. In the pallid sunlight Slippery Rock Creek, a hundred yards away, tumbled over gray boulders and in quiet pools reflected the yellow of maple trees and the dark green of hemlocks. Off to the right a flock of goldfinches, drab as sparrows, fluttered over a thistle patch and made the stalks sway as if a wind were sweeping through them.

Tom was walking along the edge of the creek. While I watched him and warmed my hands at the fire he had left, I heard from far off two shotgun blasts. The hunters were already harvesting their share of quail and rabbits before the winter kill. All the day before, we had heard the baying of the hounds and had seen the hunters in bright jackets as they walked across open fields or tramped through thickets. We had listened to the fall of leaves, the chatter of red squirrels preparing for the winter, the chirping of crickets against the time of frost. We

had plucked a few dogwood seeds to take back home, had helped the warty milkweed pods to open and to send their children on their airy way to life in foreign places, and had stopped to look at bird nests, visible now in shrubs that had lost many of their leaves. And we had heard the roar of Slippery Rock Creek as it tumbled down the gorge. What a roar it must have made on the day it was born, eleven thousand years ago.

On that day, though no one was present to hear it, a great rumbling sound suddenly filled the valley above what is now Portersville, Pennsylvania. Glacial Lake Arthur had overflowed its boundaries and was sweeping down the valley. For thousands of years the lake had behaved. Its waters were clear, cool, and quiet. And then something happened. Perhaps the glacial ice melted more rapidly than usual; perhaps the low divide at Alpha Pass weakened. Whatever it was, Lake Arthur, covering much of northern Butler County, decided to become part of

202

the Atlantic Ocean—for in those distant days the watersheds of Penn's Woods West drained into the St. Lawrence River and thence to the Atlantic instead of into the faraway Gulf of Mexico.

As the deluge swept down the valley, trees parted from the earth and floated along like bits of brush. Boulders bobbed in the churning water like corks. The great wave swept in a westerly and southerly direction along the course of a little stream that for centuries had been flowing placidly into Muddy Creek. Now it no longer flowed placidly. Its shallow channel deepened. In a matter of days, it gouged its way so far down into the earth that the land on each side of it seemed to rise up like mountains.

However catastrophic its origin, Slippery Rock Creek is today one of the most beautiful places in Penn's Woods West. Boulder strewn and hemlock scented, the gorge is hundreds of feet deep, and sunlight reaches its floor for only a few hours a day. From Kennedy's Mills, down past McConnell's Mills, and on to Conoquenessing Creek, the valley is filled with a constant roar as water dashes against rocks, swirls and eddies, and then cascades over other rocks.

down past McConnell's Mills

from Kennedy's Mills

203

boulders strewn and hemlock scented

the scarlet wanderers

After Tom came back, we had breakfast and then spent the rest of the day wandering along the shores of the stream. Bass and trout find the creek to their liking, and the cool, shady sides of the canyon are ideal habitat for mixed hardwoods and for graceful hemlocks. In the spring the nature lover who is nimble enough to scramble up and down the sides of the gorge will find precious rue anemone and Jack-in-the-pulpit or perhaps hepatica while it is being visited by lavender butterflies that can almost be mistaken for blossoms. In the summer he may find twinflowers and wild columbine.

Sometimes we stopped to look at the delicate patterns of gray lichens on the rocks. Though small and unpretentious, the lichens are among the oldest living inhabitants of the earth, older perhaps than the giant sequoias. The colonies we looked at had probably begun forming soon after the boulders came to rest in the ravine, thousands of years before. The ability of the lichen to withstand time and heat and cold is due partly to the fact that it is not so much an individual plant as a partnership, a closely united and mutually helpful coalition between an alga and a fungus.

The fungus absorbs moisture from the air and from the damp rock and spreads over the alga a protective mesh that keeps the alga from drying out and dying. In return the alga absorbs minerals from the rock and water from the fungus and supplies its water carrier, the fungus, with carbohydrates necessary for the life of the fungus. So they live, the alga and the fungus, each a necessity for the gray-green existence of the other, in such a close partnership that we know them by their corporate name, the lichen.

But the partnership does more than merely live together. On the rough, moist surface of the lichens, dust settles. Hemlock needles fall from the tree above the rock and cling to the lichens. Insects hide under the hemlock needles and live there and die. Slowly the process of decay furnishes a thin slip of topsoil on the rock. And then the mosses move in among the lichens.

The mosses also gather dust and remnants of death and accelerate the formation of film on film of soil until, after a time, there is enough for ferns. The ferns grow and decay and grow again, and then, perhaps, a hemlock seed drops from the tree above,

and brothers above them

a close partnership

sprouts, takes root, and lives. Though no change was visible, the lichens, mosses, and ferns were at work in a mutual rock-crushing operation that would eventually reduce the boulder to sand and topsoil. Birth and death, destruction and reconstruction, were continuing while we looked on, and our futures as living beings were in some measure being determined by the silent processes taking place upon the rock.

Most of the people who visit Slippery Rock do so in the summer, but there is little doubt that the gorge is at its best in autumn. Then, if the visitor is persevering and fortunate, he may find blue gentians and Allegheny vine, and though neither persevering nor fortunate in his search for them, he is sure to see the rich colors of oak and beech and maple leaves mingling with hemlock-green. On the water, too, the scarlet wanderers drift, in eddies and sudden swirls and in quiet pools flecked with foam. They drift through the reflections of their scarlet brothers above them, through clouds and patches of blue; they scurry around moss-covered boulders, disappear in a cascade of white water, and rise to the surface again in a dark pool shadowed by hemlock boughs.

In autumn one of the loveliest parts of the gorge and one of the most accessible is McConnell's Mills.

205

the hunters in bright jackets

below the mill, a covered bridge

the century-old mill still stands

The old mill still stands, though it has not been in operation for many years, and the water above the dam is deep and clear. Below the mill a covered bridge spans the creek. Everything looks much the same as it did in the 1860's, when Thomas McConnell bought the tract and operated the mill. If anything has changed in the last hundred years, it is not apparent to the visitor—the leaves fall as they fell then, the pileated woodpeckers still search dead limbs for beetles, and the gorge reverberates as it did then with the thunder of rushing water. Presque Isle is lovely in the summer, and the Centre County mountains are startling in the fall, but here within forty miles of Pittsburgh, in any season of the year, is one of the most spectacularly beautiful gorges in eastern United States.

207

puffy clouds from the west

Fee-Fishing Lakes

IT WAS EARLY FALL, AND WE WERE SITTING ON THE shore of Hereford Manor Lake, Tom, the stranger, and I. The morning sun was comfortably warm, and puffy clouds were sailing across the sky from the west. Already the stranger had caught three trout, all of them over thirteen inches long. Now he was relaxed and expansive.

"Ten years ago," he said, "I never thought there'd be fishing like this on the edge of Pittsburgh. I can get here in an hour."

"It's a pretty place," Tom said.

"*Is* the fishing good?" I asked.

"Oh, it isn't like Canada," the stranger said. "It isn't as wild, and you're not alone the way you are up on those big lakes. I used to go to Canada a lot." He plucked a bit of dry grass and put it in his mouth. "My wife's getting older now, and so am I. We come out here once or twice a week."

"I've never fished in a lake like this," I said. "*Is* the fishing pretty good?"

"Not like Canada," he said again. "Too many people, especially on week ends. But if you come out the way my wife and I do, in the middle of the week, like now. . . . And as far as fishing goes, well, last week I caught three trout and two bass in one evening. The smallest was fourteen inches. Sometimes we go over to Perry Lake. That's just a few miles down the road."

He threw away the bit of grass he had been chewing. "When school wasn't on, we used to bring my grandchildren," he added.

"Clouds are good," Tom said. "Let's get some pictures."

"There's a good view up the lake," the stranger said.

We thanked him, said good-by, and started along the shore of the lake, a large lake with a shoreline of three and a half miles. Ten years ago, the area had been strip mined, but careful backfilling, contouring, and planting had restored the productivity of the land and had impounded some sixty acres of water. Hereford Manor is a fee-fishing lake, one of the largest. For a small fee, the fisherman can angle in a fee-fishing lake from early morning until late at night in water that has been heavily enough stocked to assure him some measure of success. He can fish from the shore if he wants to or he can rent a boat. If he needs tackle or bait, he can buy them at the lake. There are open fireplaces, picnic tables, playgrounds for children, and snack bars or modern restaurants. Some of the lakes have beaches for swimming, and some are even lighted for night fishing.

In the western half of the State there are more than a hundred fee-fishing lakes, though a few years ago there was none. Washington County leads with

208

18, then come Westmoreland with 15, Fayette with 13, Cambria with 8, Somerset 7, and Allegheny, Beaver, and Indiana with 6 each. Where many streams have been polluted, as in the southwestern part of Pennsylvania, fishing in the lakes has become very popular. In some places, as at Hereford, the great canyons of the strip mines have been used to impound uncontaminated water and, when properly planted and managed, to provide the fishermen with a day of restful sport and the owner with a profitable business.

But these lakes and small impoundments do more than supply fish for hopeful anglers. They become homes for mink and muskrat, newt and salamander, toad and frog. Early in the morning and late in the evening, deer come down to drink the clear water, and during the long migrations, ducks find them comfortable resting places.

What Dr. Graham Netting said of farm ponds is equally true of fee-fishing lakes:

I am enamored of farm ponds, for they are always multiple-purpose improvements. It matters not what immediate human aim dictates their construction, for, once completed, nature utilizes them as environmental assets so valuable that no expert has yet succeeded in estimating their full worth. Their recreational advantages to the farm family—fishing, swimming, boating, skating—are obvious; but who knows how many insect-destroying toads and skunks they nurture, how many migrating waterfowl find them life-saving havens, how much they moderate the temperatures in adjacent fields, or how effective a nerve tonic the glint of placid water can be to worried mortals.

A few years ago there was considerable opposition to the idea of fee-fishing places. Shortsighted sportsmen fought against the idea because they felt that there was something illegal or immoral in permitting fishermen to fish for trout and bass in the lakes at times other than during the regular season. The Fish Commission was lukewarm to the idea because it felt that the fee-fishing lakes might eliminate many purchases of fishing licenses. State legislators talked of "class legislation."

But as the stripping machines moved relentlessly through the southwestern part of the State, as wildcat operators found it profitable to default on their performance bonds of only $300, as more and more land became desolate and stream after stream turned yellow and sulphurous, public pressure for the lakes mounted. At last the sportsmen, the legislators, and the members of the Fish Commission changed their way of thinking and got behind the movement. When Governor Leader signed Senate Bill 264 he gave his blessing to a movement that has grown in popularity and in importance ever since.

Now fishing has come within reach of every resident of Penn's Woods West who has a fishing license.

fee-fishing lakes are helping nature

where children, too, can relax

It is no longer necessary for people in the southern part of the State to travel long miles to the unpolluted trout and bass streams of the north and east. Since the owners of the lakes stock them at their own expense, good fishing is provided to the public without any cost to the Fish Commission, and since anglers must have a license to fish in the lakes, the income of the Fish Commission has risen. As a result, pressure on public waters has decreased, and money to stock and improve these waters has increased. But best of all, beautiful lakes of pure water are being created, where men and women and children, too, can relax and regain the composure that was lost somewhere among the tall buildings and concrete streets and city playgrounds.

When Tom and I returned to our friend, the stranger, he had exchanged his grass stem for a pipe.

"Any more luck?" Tom asked.

"Funny thing," the stranger said. "Bass are hitting now. Just caught one on a fly rod with a hair bug.

You can't tell what you'll get in this lake." Proudly he showed us the bass, fourteen or fifteen inches long.

"We were thinking," I said, "of taking a look at Perry Lake while we're up here."

"You'll like it at Perry Lake," he said. "Good fishing up there, too. I tell you, these lakes are better than Canada—and cheaper."

We left him and went on to Perry Lake.

Perry Lake is small—about five acres—but when we arrived it was glimmering brightly in a valley formed by gently sloping hillsides. The western shore was dark with the shade of tall trees. Anglers sat in the shade and fished from the grassy bank. Out on the lake, four or five rowboats drifted in the wind and sunshine. In one of them a woman was skillfully bringing a fish to net, but what kind it was or what size we could not tell. There was no loud talk. In fact, from where we stood, we could hear no voices at all, only the subdued chattering of birds among the trees and shadows.

We talked to a few of the fishermen. Three had caught no fish, another had caught two bass, still another two bass and four trout. In fee-fishing lakes as in native trout streams, some anglers are born to the craft and some are not.

After a time we walked over to the grassy side of the lake. There a freckle-faced boy with tousled hair was trying to show a charming young lady how to put a worm on a hook. We watched the lesson for awhile, and then went back to the car. I stood there

and regain the composure lost

the ducks find resting places

Perryopolis and Uniontown, twelve acres of water—and snack bar, picnic tables and boats. Near the Murraysville golf course and off Route 22 is Lake Ro-an, stocked with trout, bass, and catfish. There is also a pond for those who like to fish for carp. Deep Valley Lakes are a quarter of a mile west of the Parkway on Routes 22 and 30. One of the largest is Kings Lake, one mile west of Florence, off Route 18. At Kings Lake there is also fee-hunting in the fall and winter for ducks and pheasants.

Some of these lakes are merely receptacles for fish; others are well planned, wooded, and beautiful. The majority are developments of reclaimed land, and if they are not beautiful, they will become so. Already grass and shrubs have taken hold on the contoured land, and young pines are rising above them. Willows are growing tall at the water's edge. Ducks have found comfortable quarters on the lakes and will assist in the planting of aquatic vegetation. As the years pass, the trees will grow and under them hepatica and rue anemone; mink and muskrat, owl and osprey, fox and frog and deer will return to the land that disowned them and will make the land their home. Fee-fishing lakes are helping nature to restore parts of Penn's Woods West to their earlier productivity and beauty.

a moment looking at five acres of loveliness, the shadows from the trees, the green valley, the boats bobbing in the sunshine, the fishermen along the dark shore, and two other anglers in the sunshine.

"A boy," Tom suggested in the voice he reserves for things photographic, "A boy could have worse company."

Within an hour's drive from Pittsburgh there are many fee-fishing lakes. In addition to Hereford Manor, which is a mile or two west of Zelienople, and Perry Lake, which is about five miles north of the same town on Route 19, there are dozens of others. Barnes Lake, with a refreshment stand and picnic area and five and a half acres of water, is near the Irwin entrance to the Turnpike. Lake Jo-Ann is really two lakes stretching out over twenty acres. It is in Venetia, near Finleyville, and is stocked with trout, bass, walleyes, bluegills, and catfish. Mountain Valley Lake lies two miles west of Greensburg on Route 30. In one place this eleven-acre lake is seventy feet deep. Boats are available. The lake is stocked with trout, bass, panfish, walleyes, and blue pike. Not far from the Monroeville exit of the Turnpike is a small lake called Sunnyhill, spring fed and twenty-five feet deep. Spillway Lake is between

the lesson

211

four-fifths of our population will be living in cities

Students

LAST WEEK I WENT BACK TO THE UNIVERSITY FOR A FEW hours. Students came into my office, students who wanted to know what I was doing. When I told them about the book we were working on, they talked and asked many questions. The talk and the questions left me disturbed.

There is something tragic about watching a generation of young men and young women grow up with little knowledge of the earth and its myriad inhabitants, the earth upon which they depend for sustenance. They have little knowledge and less love. It is not their fault. They are city students whose lives are almost always separated from the earth by a foot of concrete. Their feet do not walk on the naked ground nor do their hands touch it. They spend most of the day indoors, and so they seldom see the clouds driving across the sky. At night, the street lamps blind their eyes to the stars. A mouse is something you catch in a trap; a bird is something brown that flies; water is a treated liquid that comes out of a spigot; snow is wet and dirty, and the highway department shovels it off the streets as soon as it can but never soon enough.

"Tell me," said a pale-faced literature major, "where in the world I can see a nightingale around here. We're reading Keats, and . . ."

A girl, a nursing student, was saying, ". . . in a tent? But aren't there snakes and lizards, and things like that?" She shivered as though a cold wind from the Age of Reptiles had chilled her blood.

A young man who was wise in the ways of conservation announced, "We kill all the sparrows around the house. They kill other birds. You know, other birds—like . . . like the robins, and . . ." His voice trailed off.

"And pigeons," contributed the girl with the Mesozoic chill.

"Yes," I said, "I know, but . . ."

Another girl was talking. She was a pretty girl except that she had hidden the vulgarity of human

212

eyebrows with black grease. "That tree," she said, "the little one at the corner of the chapel. Do you know what it's called? In the spring, it blossoms."

"That," I said faintly, "is a dogwood."

"Is it?" she breathed. "Jesse Stuart wrote a story about one, and an old man too."

"There's a Greek legend about dogwood," said the Classics major. "Something about its red blossoms representing the blood of Christ."

A quiet boy at the end of the table spoke. "Dogwood blossoms are white," he said, "and afterwhile they have red seeds." He is a poor boy who is having trouble working his way through college. "I used to live in the country," he said, "before my dad died."

I made a false excuse about having to see a dean. They understood deans and academic protocol, and so we parted.

Outside, I looked up at the sky, blue except in the west, where clouds hinted of rain. A flock of starlings waddled around on a lawn where no weeds are allowed to grow.

"In twenty years," a sociologist once told me, "four-fifths of our population will be living in cities." The thought did not seem to bother the sociologist and should not, I suppose, have bothered me. But I cannot quite believe that the city will give boys and girls, young men and young women, all that they need. It will give them many good things, libraries, theaters, concert halls, and museums where they may see stuffed animals and pinned butterflies, but something, too, will depart—a way of life that has done much for the spiritual needs of other generations, a way that has taught the *best* men and women, the *best* boys and girls, a goodly measure of humility, acceptance, love. Something precious would be lost on that day, if it ever comes, when boys and girls no longer go barefoot or drink pump water from cupped hands or know the songs of the catbird or pick blackberries in August or watch Orion march across the sky on a December night.

pump water from cupped hands

Young Americans would get along, I suppose, without these experiences. They would still become good citizens, good surgeons, good engineers, good physicists, and, perhaps, even good poets, but I fear that deep down in that solitary place that settles destinies, they would feel alone, unsatisfied, unsure, in a universe that is alien to them because it is not understood.

"We kill all the sparrows." I passed the chapel and the little dogwood tree. "Jesse Stuart wrote a story . . ." she had said in wonderment. "A Greek legend" he had answered her. There is something disturbing about all this, profoundly so, and about, "I used to live in the country," but the universal need for nature will not end in a statistic. The need will be felt so deeply that it will have to be satisfied—even in a changed world.

even in a changed world

from a woodland trail

from an automobile

The Tall Trees

WHEN WE ARRIVED AT COOK FOREST, WE TOOK A HALF-hour tour to get our bearings. The half-hour was enough to reaffirm what we already believed, that Cook Forest State Park is one of the wonder spots in Penn's Woods West. It is a large park of about 8,000 acres. Close by on the east and also bordering on the south are an additional 9,000 acres of Pennsylvania State Forest. The alliance of park and forest is impressive, whether we see it from an automobile, from a woodland trail, or from the height of Seneca Rock.

And the park offers to the city-weary traveler almost everything he could wish for—a pleasant woods for camping, a place to swim in water untainted by chlorine, accommodations for the overnight tourist or for the vacationist, good streams for the trout fisherman, soft trails for those who like to walk one mile or many, dirt roads for the windshield-looker, bridal paths for the saddle-viewer.

Cook Forest is a good place to go to—for a day, a week, a summer. When we come back home, we are easier to get along with. More familiar with the earth, we are humbler and therefore wiser. Our eyes and our minds have a different perspective, and we perceive, almost with a shock, that the apparent security of the city, with its steel and stone, its supermarkets and its copper plumbing, is false and deceptive. We are not independent beings who can perpetuate ourselves forever by plundering the earth and other living beings.

Here, in the quietness of the woods, we look at things more realistically, and we see how dependent we are on other forms of life—on the red squirrel who plants our trees, on the trees that preserve our water, on insects that feed our fish and on the fish that are our food, on the birds that keep our insects from destroying our vegetables and on the hawk that keeps our birds from getting so numerous that we have no

gateway to oldest life in Penn's Woods West

cherries to eat, on bacteria that turn leaves into humus and on the humus that helps to prevent the flooding of our cities, on the earthworm who prepares and aereates our topsoil, and on the wood mouse who, like a good gardener, mixes our topsoil with subsoil. Without these creatures, humiliating as the thought may be, we should perish. In this community of living things, we are only one, and our existence is dependent upon theirs.

Here, as we walk softly through the woods or as we sit on a rock on the edge of a quiet stream, we are close to the earth and all its myriad life, so close that we are likely to agree, perhaps for the first time, with the conclusion of Joseph Wood Krutch: "To live healthily and successfully on the land, we must also live with it ... It is not a sentimental but a grimly literal fact that unless we share this terrestrial globe with creatures other than ourselves, we shall not be able to live on it for long." The tone is ominous, but we human beings are slowly learning. It is not too late.

When our half-hour tour was over, we were near the Cook Forest cabin area. We went to look at the cabins and, for a moment, were tempted to forego our tent. Tom looked at me, and I looked at him. They are clean and rustic and picturesque, these cabins, and all of them have good views for idle moments or for rainy days. But the sky was a bright blue, we had the tent in the car, and most important, a handsome youth on the porch of one of the cabins was making the mountains echo with his cornet. We looked at each other again and then went to the tenting area.

There, a half hour later, we had pitched our seven-by-seven umbrella tent in the wooded camping grounds. As I zipped the door shut, I heard Tom saying, "The light's about right for Longfellow Trail. If we don't wait too long."

In a few minutes we were starting up the trail, and the remembered beauty of it came flooding back; for though I had often thought of the trail, I had not walked among its shadows for many years. Dim and mysterious, it winds through one of the few remaining tracts of virgin timber in Penn's Woods West —a small but magnificent stand of hemlock, white pine, and hardwood. We had been told that the great windstorm of August eighteenth, which Tom had weathered on the bluff at Pymatuning while I slept, had torn down many of the trees. "Two hundred of them," one man had told us. "Three hundred," his friend had corrected. Three hundred, it turned out, was closer to the right figure.

among its shadows

clean and rustic

As we walked along the trail, two things surprised me. One, of course, was the lonely splendor of the trees. No matter how well you have remembered them, you are startled all over again when you actually see them. Back at home, someone says, "They're splendid trees, those hemlocks up in Cook Forest." You answer, "Yes, they are," and you mean what you say, but somehow you never really know how impressive they are except when, a babe in the wood, you walk beneath them and among them. For infants we are, both in years and in fortitude, compared with these giants who started on the earth and reached the sky. They were old before Chief Red Jacket held his first council of war beneath them. They were here before a man named William Penn became the doubtful owner of Penn's Woods West.

The other surprise, an exciting one, was that although three hundred had been lost in the battle, more hundreds, even thousands, remained. It is a grievous thing to see an old pine or hemlock lying on the ground, but it is heartening to see how many of its brothers have withstood one more attack and tower still, crowns high, unconquered through three centuries of time.

But death brings sorrow. Occasionally we passed little knots of people beside a fallen tree. There was no levity along the trail. To many of the mourners, the dead had been old friends.

Once I sat on a rock near a tree that had fallen directly across the trail, and I listened to the talk of a group of people who had stopped there for a moment to rest.

A young man was talking to three older women. "It had to come," he said. "These trees are too old.

They should have been thinned out years ago before they became diseased and rotten."

He looked ruefully at a young hemlock that had been crushed by the fall of the old one. "If they were taken out skillfully and gradually to make room for the young ones, you'd never miss the old ones. In a hundred years you couldn't tell the difference. This is no way to manage a forest," he said. "It's just being sentimental."

Two of the women nodded in polite agreement. The other one, older than any of us, slowly shook her head of white hair. "Just the same," she said slowly, "when your son gets old enough, I want him to see this—before it's too late." She tapped the toe of her buttoned shoe on the trail. "Old things," she said, half turning away, "have a right to live, too."

For a moment, no one said anything. The two younger women looked uncomfortable. The young man was looking down at the buttoned shoe. "Well,"

the great windstorm

217

lonely splendor

he said, "let's be getting back. You women must be tired."

They went on down the trail, the young man first, the two younger women next, and the old woman last. She walked carefully, but she seemed straighter and taller than the rest of the group.

We left the section where the greatest destruction had been done. Underfoot, the trail was soft with pine and hemlock needles, and an aromatic fragrance, sharp and penetrating, filled the air. Once, I looked up as through a funnel to a little patch of sky that the trees did not blot out. There, far overhead, white clouds were racing from west to east. I thought of George Meredith's "A Dirge in the Woods," pine-scented and hypnotic.

> A wind sways the pines
>   And below
> Not a breath of wild air—
> Still as the mosses that glow
> On the flooring and over the lines
> Of the roots here and there.
> The pine tree drops its dead;
> They are quiet, as under the sea.
> Overhead, overhead
> Rushes life in a race,
> As the clouds the clouds chase;
>   And we go,
> And we drop like the fruits of the tree,
>   Even we,
>   Even so.

Here, gathered together in the dimness, they dwell among themselves, the oldest living creatures in Penn's Woods West, their feet, like mine, in darkness, but their crowns in the white light of heaven. I think I can almost understand tree worship and the Druids.

We had walked two or three miles now and were going downhill towards the road, but the shadows and the cathedral silence were as deep as when, an hour before, we had entered them. Only once on our walk did I hear a bird call. That was at the foot of the mountain, just before we reached the road. A blue jay flashed across the darkness, perched on a limb of a shattered pine, and screamed. The bawdy scream still with us, we came to the road and to the end of our journey among the old trees and the dead.

as through a funnel

a dirt road through the forest

On The Way To Seneca Rock

ON THE WAY TO SENECA ROCK WE TOOK A DIRT ROAD that curved through miles of young but sturdy timber, clearly a managed forest, clean and well-kept. At one place along the road, a sign told us that much of the land through which we were going had been swept by a forest fire and that only now, after fifty years, was the land beginning to come back.

The cost of a forest fire, great as we all know it to be, far exceeds the "estimated loss" that the news-papers record. There is, of course, the lost loveliness of the hillside. But let us not count lost loveliness, since we cannot measure it in dollars. There is the loss of humus, of tons and tons of humus, that nature with tireless industry has spent hundreds of years in manufacturing. In the long run, the value of the humus may be greater than the value of the timber. Man might exist without wood, but without humus he would starve to death. Then there is the obvious loss of timber. That is the figure the forest rangers give and the newspapers quote. It is a small fraction of the total damage.

For the greatest cost of a forest fire comes from its aftereffects, a chain reaction that is so costly it is incalculable. Sometime after the fire has destroyed the trees and the humus, rains come. Unchecked by leaf or limb, the rain smacks violently against the bare ground. The impact of the blow is no longer softened by inches of spongy topsoil, nor is there enough humus left unburned to absorb the heavy downpour, nor can the water any longer seep into the countless holes of countless earthworms nor into the winding burrows of moles and wood mice, chipmunks, rabbits, groundhogs.

And so the devastating runoff begins. Puddles of muddy water begin to overflow their rims and to carve little channels into the ground. The channels deepen and become gullies that cut down into the nearest valley stream, where they discharge their muddy water. Now the valley stream is muddy, too, and minnow and trout and crayfish and the larvae of insects sicken from lack of oxygen.

If the burned-over section is large and the stream is normally small, a minor flood occurs. Little islands

the forest floor

lost loveliness

and bottom lands are flooded, rocks that hold the bank up are washed away, vegetation is silted over and killed, the nests of low-building birds are destroyed and small animals and game are drowned, and more topsoil enters the stream.

After a time, the little stream flows into a larger one, and the silt continues to destroy life. At last the muddy water becomes part of the great body of water in, let us say, a flood control dam, and we think the damage is over.

But there in the dam, the remaining silt settles in slow layers to the bottom, reducing thereby the capacity of the dam for the water the engineers meant it to hold. After many years or few, depending upon the amount of uncovered land in the drainage area, the dam will become a great swamp, and a splendid engineering project that cost millions will be a reminder that man has intelligence, but as yet, not enough to assure him of permanent residence on the earth.

Meanwhile, nature, wiser in many ways than man, will be correcting the cause of the damage. Weeds

221

and brambles and wild grasses will begin to move in upon the burned-over section of land. They will slow down the runoff and begin to block the gullies. Then the trees will take over, cautiously, as though they remember the red havoc of the past, and after a great many years, humus will again cover the ground, humus that means the difference between life and death for the vegetable world and the animal world and for man himself. But all this will take decades, perhaps a century, if nature does the job alone.

Once in awhile, as in this shadowy grove this afternoon, we see what can be accomplished when man decides to cooperate with nature as nature almost constantly cooperates with man. Man can help nature salve the wounds, can help her graft new skin upon the face of the earth. He can help nature to reseed the area with grasses. He can block the gullies and let nature fill them up with sediment. He can help the young trees to get started in life and can protect them until they are able to take care of themselves.

Yes, man can cooperate with nature but, perversely, over thousands of years, he has been an aggressor against nature. With supreme egotism, he has tried to control her or to reform her, not realizing

the hawk

trees will take over

that to her the victory will always go, because she is wiser than he, and that if he offends her too much, she will brush her hand across her scarred and ancient face and wipe him off as, for reasons of her own, she long ago disposed of other offenders.

But here, this afternoon, there is no quarrel. Here, nature and man have worked together, nature furnishing the plan and a portion of the labor, man agreeing to the plan, as he must, and furnishing a portion of the labor, too.

Sunlight speckles part of the forest floor with brightness; leafy boughs speckle other parts with shadow. Underground, worms and grubs and burrowing insects are busy manufacturing topsoil. Moles and mice are industriously mixing topsoil with subsoil. They are also energetically feeding upon their co-workers, the grubs and insects, and changing them, too, to topsoil, and will themselves, in due turn, be reduced or elevated to topsoil by the fox and snake and owl. And some sunny afternoon the snake may fall prey to the hawk, and some night, after a tragic mistake, the hawk may fall prey to the

this shadowy grove

On Seneca Rock

HERE, ON SENECA ROCK, WE LOOK OUT OVER THE VALLEY of the Clarion. We are so close to the sky that on another day we might be among the clouds. But there are no clouds this afternoon, only the broad blue of the heavens, the green and yellow of the great valley, and the flash, far below us, of the river that was once —how long ago!—like the Allegheny, "one of the most beautiful rivers in ye world."

When Chief Red Jacket stood on this same rock and looked down upon the river, he knew that in its waters lived sturgeon, bass, and trout, that wild ducks nested among its rushes, that mink, otter, and muskrat built homes along its banks, and that the deer and elk found its waters good to drink. But today the flash we see in the valley is hardly the flash of water. It is the flash of an inky liquid, a contaminated river, on the upper reaches of which the May flies will not lay their eggs.

Could it be that the instinct of the May fly is sounder than the intellect of man? To man and to May fly water is equally important. Without it, both die. Yet man, having added intelligence to instinct, poisons his own well-springs and seems, at times, intent on suicide. For more than a century we did the wrong thing, walked in the wrong direction. Now that we know our mistake, we are retracing our steps and are feeling our way back through the darkness. It will not be long before the Clarion is clean. It will be clean because a growing population and a growing industrial community are desperately in need of its precious purity.

on this same rock

fox. Nature, the eternal creator, knows much, men little. Her ways are dark and inscrutable. Sometimes they seem cruel. But in the end, they bring life.

Shortly, the fall rains will come and drop to the ground not violently as before but gently, the snows will cover the earth, and months later will come blue sky and spring, and out of the death of worm and leaf and hawk will emerge life itself, new and innocent and beautiful, then old and wise and beautiful. It is the way and the balance of nature—with the fox and the frog, with the tree and the toad, and with all things mortal. No living thing can long defy her laws and continue to exist, not even man. We may reject her way and her balance, try to change them to our personal taste, and live and die in loneliness. Or we may accept her way, try to adjust to its wisdom, and live and die in communion with all other mortal things.

For me, the choice is not hard to make. The shadows and the sunlight shift, gently and perhaps with purpose. I am part of them, this afternoon, part of the sunlight and shadows, part of the purpose.

223

on this, our only earth

and soon the river, too, will be like his

On a not distant summer evening, the first May fly will return to the upper Clarion to lay her eggs where her ancestors laid theirs a hundred years ago, and the eggs will hatch under the water, and the larvae will inhabit the bottom of the stream, and the trout and the bass will move in to feed upon the larvae and, in turn, to furnish food for man, and the bandit raccoon will come in some night to share the fish, and the grasses and spatterdock will take root in clean soil, and ducks will stop and find the grasses good, and muskrats will approve the spatterdock, and after mink and muskrat will come trappers who will harvest them for man.

Miles away from the Clarion, barges and boilers will not corrode so quickly, deep wells can be abandoned, steel will be cheaper, and cities will sleep more soundly, knowing that in the morning there will be water.

So varied are the ways of nature, so delicate its balance, that the future of a city such as Pittsburgh may depend upon a hatch of May flies on the upper Clarion. And hatch the May flies surely will, now that we have come to our senses. Some summer afternoon, not far away, they will perform their dance of love and death over the sparkling water. Though no one may be there to chronicle the event, the day on which the first dance occurs will be a good day for the peo-

ple of Penn's Woods West, a day worth waiting for, a day when we take another step not towards death but towards continued life on this, our only earth.

As we stand on Seneca Rock this afternoon, sunlight silvers the river, brightens the eastern side of the valley, darkens the western side, and turns the farthest ridge into high light. Far away, a dog is barking; behind us, a chickadee chatters; and high above, an eagle drifts serenely, in possession of the sky. The sounds, the valley, the trees, and the sky are much the same as when Chief Red Jacket stood here. And soon the river, too, will be like his.

the bandit

WINTER

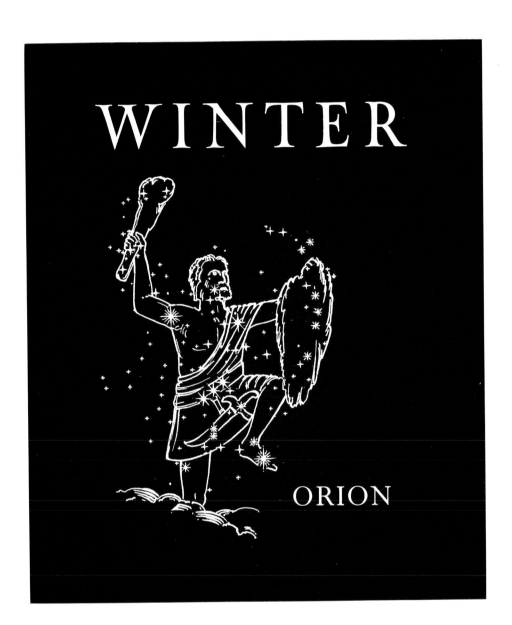

ORION

THE HUNTER

ONLY A FEW WEEKS AGO THE MAPLE TREES WERE flaming against a blue sky. Now, earlier than usual, snow lies lightly over Penn's Woods West, and the maple trees are tangled patterns of black. In open fields, the withered stalks of goldenrod and Queen Anne's lace still stand, and in the woods the ebony spleenwort rises above the snow, but there is little to remind us of summer or of fall.

Winter is the time for remembering, the time for rest. The flying squirrel sleeps in his hollow tree, the bat in a cool, dark cave, and the mole has tunneled below the frost line. The snail has found a rock cranny or a patch of deep moss, the toad sleeps under a log, the frog has dug himself a hibernaculum under the mud beside the stream, and the mourning cloak dozes on the underside of a fence rail but does not slumber soundly.

Weeks ago, with the first hard frost, the ground-hog, earliest of the sleepers, retired to the warmth of his burrow, where with slowing heartbeats he will sleep till the coming of spring. The skunk has taken her whole family into winter quarters and has retired from community life until March. And in a cave in the mountains of Forest County the mother bear, feeling within her the pulse of new life, lies down in natural anesthesia to sleep away her birth pangs and the nuisances of nursing. Less fortunate than the bear, the mother deer is already searching hungrily for buds that will sustain her and the precious burden within her that will be born among the ferns in early June.

On earth, winter is the time for remembering spring and summer and fall, and love and plenty and deliverance from death. It is the time for the slowing of heartbeats, the conserving of heat, the restful preparation for life to come.

Not so in the heavens. There, winter is a time of fierce activity. In the north, at about midnight of an early December night, the Great Bear, forgetting to hibernate, moves in his silent circle southward and westward about the Pole Star. High in the east, Leo, the Lion, crawls over the horizon while Pegasus, of the wings and flying mane, gallops over the opposite horizon. In the Milky Way, south and east of Cassiopeia, Perseus dangles from his hand the bloody head of Medusa; and south of Perseus, Taurus, the Bull, glares with his red, Aldebaran eye at the indomitable hunter, Orion.

But the king of the winter constellations is not easily frightened by the red eye of the Bull. With two equally bright stars—and between them the three bright stars of his belt—Orion faces the Bull and forces him to retreat forever westward.

No modest hunter, Orion is always easy to locate. Early in December, he rises in the east and at midnight is almost due south. The three stars of his belt enclosed within a bright quadrangle mark him as the most spectacular of the winter constellations. He is, indeed, the heavenly hunter, especially when seen from a lonely hilltop on a clear, cold night. Hour after hour he forces westward the red eye of the Bull, the Hyades, the Pleiades; and Sirius, the dog, follows at his heels.

Watching the hunter, we remember a whirlwind voice that spoke one night to Job; "Canst thou bind the cluster of the Pleiades, or loose the bands of Orion?" And we are inclined to answer as humbly and as simply as Job did: "Behold, I am of small account."

Watching the hunter, we gain perspective, see ourselves for what we are, little bipeds standing on a hill in the large night, shivering in the cold, knowing instinctively that there is a last, great cold that will freeze us into the ice of the final glacier, and knowing, too, that long after we have joined the mammoth, Orion will walk silently across the sky.

the ski country

uphill and downhill, around snowbanked curves

Ski Slopes

WE HAD SPENT THE NIGHT IN A CABIN NEAR SOMERSET, toasting ourselves in front of burning logs before we went to sleep. In the morning, dim light filtered through the ice-covered window to the east. Half asleep, I stared at it, a luminous arabesque of ice and sun. Then I heard Tom's camera click.

"I hope, I hope . . ." he said.

After a leisurely breakfast of country ham and country eggs, we started off for Laurel Mountain and the ski slopes. All morning snow had been falling in big flakes. Clean and white, it spread away from us as we drove, flattening rough fields into level planes and steep inclines into gentle rises, growing grayer as it approached the horizon, and at last mingling without definition among the low clouds. In snow time, the world expands, reaches out, blends into the sky in a continuous unity.

At Donegal we put on chains. "At the rate it's coming down," Tom said, "we'll need them."

Leaving Route 31, we began to climb into the Laurel Hill Ridge of the Alleghenies, uphill and downhill, around snowbanked curves. Sometimes at the crest of a hill we stopped to look at the blurred landscape, but the snow was like a dense fog that obliterated outlines and blended with earth and sky. And so we walked through drifts to look at little things: the pattern of wind-blown snow on the bark of young oaks or the trickle of water flowing down a little valley. Unhurried, we looked for trout in quiet pools, heard the great silence of mountains in the snow, admired the geometry of rail fences, marveled at the sturdiness of hemlock.

When driving for pleasure, one may quite properly set a time for departure, but never should one set a time for arrival. The danger, obviously, is that the deadline for arrival might be met and the purposes of the journey missed—acquaintance with the wide, gray landscapes, or with the singularity of a barn

the singularity of a barn

the design of snow and running water

arabesque of ice and sun

glimpse of the split rail fence spilling over with snow, nor should we have seen, in a sudden flurry that descended upon us, the blurred images of horses, wood-sleigh, and mittened driver. But because we had chains on the car we pulled over and let the images pass, all three of them, vaguely as in a dream, while the driver waved his snowy glove; and then we ourselves passed the stone farmhouse. A yellow light shone through the glass panel in the front door, and I wondered whether, if anyone was looking through the glass, we seemed as ghostly to him as the driver and the horses did to us. In a few minutes the flurry stopped, and the world again became clearly visible in black and white.

Shortly, our country road led into a black-top road and the black-top to Route 30. There, just beyond Ligonier, we turned right towards Laurel Mountain. The chains clinked against the bare, concrete highway, and for five or ten minutes we carried on a desultory debate about removing them. Before we could decide, we came to the right turn at the top of the mountain, and our debate ended.

Snow-covered again, the road wound along the ridge through second growth that was lacy and white. Our chains became silent. Once, we saw another car approaching with no sound, and we swung wide to give him the beaten tracks. He waved as he passed, and for a brief moment we heard the crunching of his tires. Then the silence of the snow settled over us again. Twice blue jays flashed across the road, and as we neared the gate to Laurel House three deer looked at us from a clearing. They neither ran nor turned their heads but merely noticed that we were passing.

In a few minutes we were at Laurel House and out of the car. The air was cold enough to make us blink, and a sharp wind stung our faces, but if the

separated from the rest of the world by sunlight that unexpectedly breaks through the clouds, with the black and white design of snow and running water, with the warm brown of a covered bridge.

For pleasure driving in winter, chains are a psychological necessity. Mechanically they may not be needed. They may be a nuisance, and they may be noisy. They may be somewhat humiliating, as a car without chains blows impatient horn for passing. And in spite of the opinions of safety experts, they may even be more hazardous on icy roads than no chains at all. But they give a feeling of assurance, a feeling that you can afford to take a chance on a short cut in spite of six inches of snow.

If we had not had chains we should not, for instance, have dared the side road that gave us a

geometry of rail fences

snow was falling heavily

skiers noticed the weather, they gave no sign of it. Some with shirts open at the collars, others zippered and begoggled until they looked like men from Mars, they took to the slopes in high good humor.

We wandered around and watched. The instructress, petite and graceful as a swallow, was demonstrating her art to a beginners' class. There the slope was gentle enough for feet not skilled in skiing. Most of the time, the snow was falling so heavily that the moving figures were only gray blurs against the white, but for a short time the snow stopped and the sky brightened and we could look far down the main ski lift to the sparsely forested mountain side across the valley. Forty or fifty people, men and women, young and old, were coming up the slope the slow way after going down like flights of erratic arrows.

three deer looked at us

a covered bridge

For a moment or two in the hazy sunlight we saw them coming up, bright spots of color—blues and greens and reds and yellows; then the snow began to fall again, and the colors and the figures turned gray and disappeared as if a heavy fog had settled over the mountain.

For several hours we watched the skiers and the snow and tramped through sturdy second growth. Then we went back to Laurel House for food and cups of steaming coffee. Bill Boardman met us there and, while we ate, told us much about Laurel Hill Ski Slopes. They are his winter loves, and he speaks of them almost tenderly.

There are more than five hundred snowy acres in the tract, he told us, and twelve slopes and five tows. On a busy day, two or three thousand skiers may arrive from places as distant as Pittsburgh, Toledo, Cincinnati, Baltimore, Washington, and Philadelphia, for Laurel Mountain is known as one of the best skiing areas in the East. He told us, too, about

the snow-making machine that is used when nature is not cooperative. Nature is usually cooperative, though, for often when the grass shows green in Pittsburgh and Philadelphia, the snow on Laurel Mountain is two feet deep.

Late in the afternoon we started back. The snow had stopped, and the sun was shining in murky brilliance. After a few minutes of clanking chains on the main highway, we again succumbed to the lure of an unknown road. We turned off the highway and with silent chains followed a little road that led, as

in high good humor

235

far as we could tell, only through white mystery. It was worth following, as side roads almost always are.

Tree trunks were black against a misty sky, and spruce and hemlock sagged under their accumulated burdens of snow. How many millions of the six-pointed, fragile, geometric shapes it must take to bring a hemlock bough to the ground! In depressions and valleys the low sun cast shadows that turned monotony into dramatic plastic life, and deer tracks along the road looked large enough to be the tracks of prehistoric caribou. At the bottom of a long hill we stopped to look at a small stream completely frozen over. The sun was very low now, and its rays touched the stream so that the ice looked like molten metal, golden and fluid.

It was a good place to stop our exploring. We turned the car around. Through the long, dim shadows, hints of saffron on the high ground, we drove back over the road. Again the silence pressed in upon us, and the isolation of a winter landscape after sunset, and then the winter darkness that comes

looked like molten metal

surely and perceptibly, and lonely foreshadowings of the great snow that will someday cover this same valley and these mountain ridges forever and forever, deeper than any glacier ever known to man or beast or lichen on the tundra.

An hour later we were out of the night and were roasting in front of the log fire in the lobby of Fort Ligonier Inn, a good place for warmth, a good place for food and sleep.

down the main ski lift

237

the Scotch pines droop

Christmas

TODAY IS CHRISTMAS. TOM IS WITH HIS FAMILY AS I am with mine. Pine and holly, mistletoe and bittersweet decorate the house, and the Scotch pine, which we cut yesterday, is gaudy with ornaments. Ten years ago we planted this tree, along with others, for harvesting in the years ahead.

We have unwrapped our presents, and the abundant odors of Christmas cooking are beginning to fill the house—cinnamon and pumpkin, mincemeat and date pudding, and, over all, the rich odor of roasting turkey. Throughout the morning there has been in the house a feeling of security and thankfulness, of kindness and good humor, of happy acceptance of our lot—which is not so good as some others, but is better than most, and is surely as much as we have ever asked for. This morning we are content, all three of us.

But now that the excitement of rustling tissue paper is over and our customary peace has begun to flow back into the house, I am standing at a window on the first floor and am looking outside. Last night a fresh snow fell. Our little plot of ground, less than two acres, is covered with white. The maple and haw branches are edged with snow, and the Scotch pines droop under its weight. This, too, is part of Penn's Woods West, a small part but my own, my special corner in a large home.

I shall be gone just a few minutes, I tell my house dwellers. I put on my jacket and step outside.

The world is clean and the sky already blue. As I step off the back porch, an old friend greets me with reproval. A nuthatch on a branch above my head scolds in a voice that might seem rude were it not that we have known each other so long that we talk without deceit. In acknowledgment of his reproach, I pour a glassful of sunflower seeds on the feeding station, but before he can get from branch to station, there is a flutter of small black wings and a chickadee lights on the station, casts a beady glance at me, picks a seed, and flies to the branch above.

The nuthatch comes then, takes his seed, and carries it to the maple, where he wedges the seed into a crevice in the bark. There he hammers at it with his bill in search of the sweet kernel. Now I am in the midst of a raucous, feathery Christmas party as nuthatches, chickadees, titmice, juncos, and sparrows arrive all at once while the lordly cardinal waits in a distant branch for the confusion to turn to quietness. He is not aloof, but much company disturbs him. His Royalty prefers a quiet dining room.

I walk out to the driveway marked by the tires of the milk truck. The ringneck pheasants have found the corn I left for them last night. Their tracks tell that they came down from the shelter of the honeysuckle on the hill and scratched away at the snow until they found their food. All summer and fall we fed them. Somehow they escaped the guns of the hunters. Now, although they do not trust us implicitly, walking away with stately step when we interrupt them, they no longer rush away with whistling wings as they did during hunting season. We are getting to understand one another better, the four hens, the three cocks, and I.

They have shared their meal with rabbits, who came out of hiding during the night and stayed until dawn or after. There are too many rabbits. Their tracks are everywhere. They are having trouble finding enough food. Nature will soon put her regulators to work, and fox and owl and weasel will select the unfit and destroy them, leaving the best—the health-

looking outside

a small part but my own

iest and best adapted. By next May the rabbits who live on the land with me will be numerous again.

They will help to keep the weeds down, they will be fun to watch on summer evenings, they will make the owls like the land better and so improve our nights with music. If, from time to time, they eat a petunia, Helen will scold like a nuthatch. I shall then bring out the rifle, and she will scold like six nuthatches. "Let the rabbit have a petunia or two," she will say. "We don't really *need* them." I shall put the rifle away, as I knew I would, and we shall enjoy the silly sight, some summer evening, of a rabbit eating a purple petunia.

Farther down the road, a red squirrel clicks up an oak tree and squats on a branch, his tail curving up like the spout of an old-fashioned teakettle. He turns the acorn in his paws and proceeds to find the kernel. He is a sociable little fellow, and in the summer he gladly shares the bird bath with catbird and towhee. My friends tell me that if I killed the red squirrels I should have more birds. But I have

239

their tracks are everywhere

enough birds. If I had more, there would not be enough for them to eat on this small plot of land. Nature knows this, and so the red squirrel came. If he varies his diet of pine cones and acorns with an occasional bird egg, he is doing our little community a service by keeping the bird population in check. He had better not try to steal the egg of a thrasher, though, or he will be a sorry advocate of birth control.

My friends also tell me that if I had fewer red squirrels I should have more grays. Perhaps. Gray squirrels do visit us occasionally, but they are voracious feeders, and our supply of beechnuts, acorns, pine cones, and berries is inadequate for their needs. They move on to richer pastures than ours. Since the red squirrel is better adapted to this particular plot of land, I shall let him stay here where he belongs. Besides, I like him.

Between our driveway and the main road is a grove of Scotch pines—not a big grove, of course, but enough to give us a sense of seclusion. Some of the pines are almost forty feet high. I remember when they were so small that the weeds hid them in the summer, yet I have lived here less than twenty-five years. They, too, share this land with us and contribute to our happiness. They keep the hillside from sliding. They cool the summer air and break the winter winds. They furnish food for squirrel and siskin, and the wood thrush likes to flit through their summer shadows. On warm, damp nights they fill the air with aromatic fragrance, and on winter mornings, after a heavy snowfall, they make us stand at the windows in admiration while the bacon burns. If a careless cigarette should ever destroy them, I should be desolate, for I have known them as long as I have known most of my human friends.

I walk on down the ash driveway, looking back, from time to time, at my footprints in the snow. The oak trees are to my left. They have lived here longer than I have, much longer. Back at the house I have a document that says this less-than-two-acres belongs to me. The oak trees know nothing about the document, yet they were living on this land a hundred and fifty years ago. Cornplanter died at about the

240

time these trees were acorns striving to push their taproots into the dark loam, and now their own children, some of them, are seventy feet tall.

They, too, have contributed to the community that lives on the hill. Each year they give a home to the downy woodpeckers; they furnish food for the squirrels; over the years they have prepared a bountiful soil for the rhododendrons I planted beneath them and for the ferns and arbutus. Where the shade in summer is not dense, daffodils, even now, are thrusting their dark way upward towards the light. They approve the soil the oak trees have prepared for them. And under the shelter of leaves covered with snow, the wood mice move, safe for the moment from fox, owl, hawk, and snake. Here their grandfathers lived, and their great-great-grandfathers, and long ago the wolf pawed at the fallen leaves, here where I stand, in order to get his Christmas breakfast.

And under the earth on which the wood mice scamper there are other inhabitants—earthworms and ants and bettles of brilliant hues and centipedes and millipedes and torpid snails and spiders and the eggs of walking sticks and grasshoppers and the larvae of the cicada and perhaps a female bumblebee, fertile and waiting for the spring, and certainly a host of eight-legged mites, thousands and thousands of them, digging deeper into the earth as the frost line lowers--all of them sharing the less-than-two-acres with me and helping me to survive.

As I turn back towards the house, I know that I have much to be thankful for this Christmas morning. I am alive in Penn's Woods West, and I am not alone. When I get back to the warm, sweet-smelling kitchen, I shall find Helen and Peggy—kind and good and mortal. But before I get there, while I am still outside, I must remember and be thankful that here, also, I am not alone, and that if I *were* alone, I should soon die. I share this bit of land and this air with millions of other living creatures, most of whom I cannot see and none of whom feels that I am so important as I sometimes think I am.

I do not own this land, in spite of the document. I am forever a tenant. And the length of my lease will depend upon my good behaviour, a condition I accept this morning willingly.

⁂

As I get up to the house, I see Peggy coming out the back door in her snow suit. "Where were you?" she asks.

"Taking a walk," I say.

"Alone?" she asks.

I hesitate a moment. "Yes," I say, "alone."

It would take a long time to explain, and so I do not, but someday, I hope, she will know that I did not mean exactly what I said.

other life waits with me for spring

241

there will always be homes

other living things

Looking Back

A MONTH FROM NOW IT WILL BE SPRING, AND MY special year among the hills and streams of Penn's Woods West will be ended. In the course of the year I have learned many things, the most important being humility and responsibility—humility when I stand before a leaf or a beetle or a fox, responsibility when I look at them or at land or water.

I know that in many ways I am inferior to the living things around me. Although I am supposed to be superior to them because I have an intellect and they do not, the plain fact is that I am unable to accept the gift of life and adjust to it as well as the simplest leaf on the tree or beetle on the leaf. Intellect alone is not enough to make me feel at home in life. There is something else, some dark, ancestral thing that I have almost lost along the way, and if I am to be content, I must find it and nourish it. Without it I am incomplete.

All other life possesses what I have almost lost. The beech tree grows into its predestined shape as do the huckleberry bush and the maple tree, adjusting to soil, to weather, and to circumstance, content in their identities, not striving to be other than they are. The huckleberry is not envious of the maple nor the maple of the beech. The song sparrow spills out its praise to the morning as it has been doing for centuries, and the thrush, in the evening, mingles its music with the shadows and is not dissatisfied. The red squirrel feeds on the beechnut and the maple seed with an occasional bird egg for variety and does not long for the richer coat of his cousin the gray squirrel. Except for man, all living things seem to approve their lot and their function on the earth. They have "one aim, one business, one desire." They adjust to the universal laws of nature as instinctively as, on a chill day in autumn, the snowy egret at Pymatuning sets feathered sail for the south.

In the eyes of nature it may be that the unintelligent fox in its den is superior to the intelligent man who lives in an artificial, electronic world and is unaware of his relation to the earth. Such a man may take pride in his accomplishments, and they may be truly great, but he has cut himself off from the primal stuff of life and is forever a stranger in the universe. He has drifted away from his only home, the mouldy earth, and he retains no memory of home except, perhaps, in lonesome moments, a dream that once upon a time and in some other place far, far away, he has known peace.

I do not wish to withdraw from life but to belong to it and to accept my part in it as naturally as my companions—fox, huckleberry, sparrow, and beetle. My intellect alone does not show me how to do so. Something else is needed. The truly superior man, I think, has not lost his ancient instincts and approvals. He has managed to retain them and has then com-

243

bined them with his recently developed intellect so that they function together. Saints have this combination in abundance. Poets have it, usually in smaller packages. And, rarely, the ordinary man has it, but then he is no longer ordinary.

Yet accepting my not singularly important place in the earth's great community, I must accept also certain responsibilities that came with the development of man's intelligence. Though I admire the huckleberry bush and the beetle on the leaf for their adjustment to natural laws, I do not wish to be either. Though I am incomplete without Lao-tsze's ability to "Be at one with all these living things," I know that I am also incomplete without accepting my role of the most intelligent of the earth's predators. It is hard to reconcile the two attitudes, one Oriental, the other Hebraic.

Out of his profound quietism Lao-tsze emerges long enough to tell us that "All things spring up without a word spoken, and grow without a claim for their production. They go through their processes without any display of pride in them; and the results are realized without any assumption of ownership. It is owing to the absence of such assumption that the results and their processes do not disappear." And in another place he tells us that in the perfect way of life we "must be free from all self-sufficiency."

On the other hand, the author of *Genesis* counsels us to "Be fruitful, and multiply, and replenish the earth, and subdue it: and have dominion over the fish of the sea, and over the fowl of the air, and over every living thing that moveth upon the earth."

hedgerows for quail

to keep the mouse in check

In a land of boundless natural resources, and the Garden of Eden was just that, the old Hebraic attitudes and injunctions may have sufficed; but today, in a depleted world, there is something troublesome, both economically and ethically, in the implications of the words *subdue* and *dominion* and in the omission of the word *humility*. There is little doubt that we *are* superior to every other living thing that moveth upon the earth. Nevertheless, we, too, are living things that move upon the earth, and, whether we admit it or not, we belong to the great, democratic community of nature and are subject to its laws. We are not separate and self-sufficient, for on the welfare of other living things depends our own welfare. Since we cannot secede from the community, we might as well be sensible about the matter and try, humbly, to be good citizens of the earth, even the leading citizens.

We might begin by getting rid of the ideas of subjection and domination and by replacing them with the more constructive idea of stewardship. Long ago, in America, we subdued our land, and today our eroded hillsides, our strip mines, and our precarious water supply remind us that stewardship would have been wiser than subjection. Long ago we exercised our dominion over "every living thing" and today our vanishing fish, game, and wildfowl remind us again that stewardship would have been wiser.

A good steward is economical and not wasteful, compassionate and not brutal, productive and not destructive. Yet his stewardship must be based on the fact that man is a predator and will remain so to exist. The problem, then, is how can man be a *wise* predator, economical, compassionate, and productive? How can his intelligence direct his predatory instincts so that he can still "Be at one with all these living things"? How can he conduct himself so that he does not eat up his own sustenance and spend his remaining capital?

When Thoreau tells of the felling of the great pine that left an empty place against the sky that would not be filled for two hundred years, I share his indignation—if it is momentary—but I cannot feel that the act was unethical. Our great forests are gone. They will never be here again as they were once— great towering trees that cast a perpetual twilight on the ground beneath. We needed the trees and we cut them. There was, I think, no crime in that except an aesthetic one. Man is a predator and will always behave like one—which is right and natural. As soon blame the rabbit for preying on lettuce as blame man for preying on trees. There is no moral or ethical crime in predacity.

But there was a fault. The fault lay in not being practical enough to replace much of that great forest with young timber that could be managed in a productive way, carefully and lovingly, for the preservation of water and soil and wild life and, therefore, of human life. Because we were not practical we must now waste billions of dollars to conserve the little water that is left. If we are good stewards, and if our climate does not change, we shall have forests forever and forever in Penn's Woods West, but they will be harvested in slow degrees and never faster than they are growing. In them and above them and below them, there will always be homes for other living things. Our forests may never again be as old or as tall as they once were, but they will be here, conserving our soil, conserving our water, and a bountiful life will live among them—life that will make our own life easier and happier.

the fox in its den

the gift of life

So it goes, also, with our fish and game. We have made mistakes, grievous mistakes, by being poor stewards. Our passenger pigeons, for one example, are gone. There are no more in the world. We shot the last one in Penn's Woods West in 1886. Those magnificent flocks a mile wide and sometimes two or three miles long will never again black out the sun. We needed them for food and we shot them. Again I see no crime in the shooting of a bird for food. As soon blame the pigeon for feeding on acorns and insects as man for feeding on the pigeon. Both are predators, and predacity is one of the facts of nature and of life.

If there was a fault, and there was, it lay in our being such poor stewards that we exterminated the valuable passenger pigeon instead of cultivating it in such a way as to furnish sustenance and wonder for later generations of human kind. We were predators against ourselves.

If we are good stewards, we will manage our game, our birds, and our fish with the same care we would use on a well-run farm, harvesting at the right time and rate and planning always, if possible, for a more productive future. That means timber and browse for deer and game laws that are based on biology rather than on chivalry. It means food for the turkey, hedgerows for quail, and nesting sites for ducks and geese. It means clean water, cover, and vegetation for fish.

As good stewards, we shall do these things because we know that, however proud and inde-

245

pendent we sometimes feel, we cannot live without other living things—the worm to till the soil, the lichen to break down the rock, the bluebird to keep the orchard insects in balance, the mould to turn the autumn leaf to topsoil, the May fly to feed the trout, the hawk and the owl to hold the useful mouse in check. Man cannot live if these others die; man cannot be prosperous if these others are poor. Since we are the master predators, our existence depends upon theirs, and the length of time we can live on this aging earth depends not upon our domination and subjection of it but upon the wisdom of our stewardship.

And yet, when we are alone in the woods, when there is no other human being to remind us of our intellects and to bring the intellectual part of our life uppermost, when we can drift gently into the simple consciousness of the rest of the living things upon the earth, we know that in many ways we are not superior. If we excel in reason, they excel in instinct. And they excel in adjusting to the laws of life, which, though neither cruel nor kind, are inexorable.

The wood mouse peeks out from under his leaf and wonders whether the hawk on the branch has seen him and is already started on its arrowy flight of death. And should there come an early frost, the wood aster, beginning to blossom in a sunny spot, may die before its seeds are sown. And the rabbit may fall prey to the fox, and the gentle pewee, having raised her young in a moss-lined nest, must think of her hawk-harried journey to the wilderness of Central America.

Yet each seems to accept and approve its ultimate destination and its present function; each goes about its community business without which the community would fail; each seems to cherish the gift of life that ends in death and further life. And all together they are making life possible for man.

We are not isolated from them; we are part of them. Their life is our life, their death our death. For a brief moment, if we are able to subdue the pride that often accompanies intelligence, we can stand here as their equals and feel the presence of something we have almost lost—a humility that belongs to wood mouse and man alike. In the midst of shadows and leaf mould, of bird song and sunlight, we feel communion with life, not human life alone, but raw, primal life. We are part of it, and for a moment we can at last "Be at one with all these living things which, having arisen and flourished, return to the quiet whence they came."

246

On the Bridge

I REMEMBER HIM AS I SAW HIM ON A SPRING EVENING almost a year ago—tall, lonely, very old. . . .

It was getting dark when I waded up to the bridge, and a hazy moon hung above the mountain. For a moment I was tempted to make a last cast into the pool below the bridge, but there were three trout in the creel and they were getting heavy. I waded up a little farther and then stepped out of the stream.

As I did so, I heard something crunch. I stopped. But I had not stepped on anything. The sound had come from a distance, a strange yet familiar sound. Long ago I had heard that same crunching sound, but where and when? I looked into the dimness but could see nothing unusual, only the fog rising from the water and the faint outline of the pines against the sky. Memories came flooding back, as they sometimes do along a trout stream in the evening. Someone I once knew used to split an apple between his hands with that same sound, and those strong hands and that sound seemed to belong together.

Then something moved at the end of the bridge. I looked more closely and again saw vague motion. "Hello," I said.

"Hello," said a voice.

"Any luck?" I said, for he must be fishing. There was no other reason for his sitting there alone in the early night. I began to climb up the bank to the bridge.

"Any luck?" I heard him repeat in not too friendly a tone. "Any luck? Boy, I haven't fished for fifty years. You won't catch fish in this creek. Not any more."

I was close to him now, and I sat down on the stone wall of the bridge. His hair, almost touching his shoulders, was very white. Between him and the moon, a little cherry tree was tossing shadows across his face. He had half an apple in each hand.

"I took three," I said, starting to open the creel.

"Browns," he said in a gruff voice, "brown trout." Then his voice grew gentle. "I remember," he said, "I remember. . . ."

"When you could catch fifty of them right from this bridge. It was a wood bridge then. All brookies. Eight, ten, fifteen inches . . ." He took a bite of apple.

"And the trees," he went on. "You should have seen them. You couldn't get your arms around them, no, not two of you. They're gone now."

As he talked, the moonlight was sliding on and off his face, as the leaves of the cherry tree shifted.

247

I did not interrupt the silence.

"You know," he said, "God Almighty use to live here. Right here like a neighbor."

He got up stiffly from the stone, his hair white in the foggy moonlight, his shoulders so high that, from where I sat below him, they seemed to touch the mountain rim. "I'll be going now," he said. "I'll be going home."

He stood there a moment, tall and strangely alone. "You'll remember what I told you?" he said. "God and big trees were never far apart."

I got up from the wall.

"I'll remember," I said.

"It's all gone now, just plain gone, unless . . ."

He stepped out from the shadow of the cherry tree, and the moonlight filled his face.

"Yes?" I said, for I wanted him to finish.

"Unless some of you young whips . . . Hell, you should of seen it when I seen it. But it's too late now."

He turned and started down the road. "Good night," he said. For just a moment his step faltered. "And good luck," he added. I watched him go down the road. It was too late, then, but I called after him, "Good night, and good luck to you, too."

For three nights after that, I went back to the bridge in the evening hoping to meet him. But I never saw him again. After that, I asked a few of the natives—old people, most of them—if they knew of such a man, but they looked at me strangely and said they hadn't seen him for a long time. I should like to see him again. I should like to wish him good luck a second time and tell him it is *not* too late.

like a neighbor

ACKNOWLEDGMENTS

So many people and agencies helped us to prepare this book that it is impossible for us to thank all of them personally. We should be shamefully remiss, however, if we did not express special gratitude to the following people:

John Behun for English bicycles and the good company of the American Youth Hostels;

Logan Bennett, Maurice Goddard, and William Voigt, Jr., for advice and for three letters that made our lives easier;

Captain Robert Brown for an afternoon on the "Philo";

The Buhl Foundation for making the book possible;

Bob Harpster for deer spotting trips and for trout fishing on Spruce Creek;

Dick Hartman for a day at a lonely bog and for the things he said about it;

George Harvey for showing us how one of the best fly fishermen in America catches trout;

Leland Hazard and Pete Woods for hours of good fishing on McGinnis Creek;

Jim Hillman for being a great conservationist and for letting us see what can be done with strip mines;

Richard Hoak for information about stream pollution;

O. E. Jennings for kind words in general and for helpful explanations in particular;

Will Johns for helping us to meet our deadline;

the Kempels for hot water, good beds, and pleasant conversation;

Bob Miller for two canoes and two good scouts;

Johnny Mock, Roger Latham, and Chet Smith for lively talks about conservation;

Lois Mulkearn for help on things historical;

Graham Netting for never turning us down when we went to him for advice;

an old man whose name I do not know but whose words I still remember;

Karl Oermann for help in the planning of the book;

Carl and Jane Peterson for being the amiable host and hostess of Twin Lakes;

Roger Reed for pleasant evenings on Pymatuning Reservoir;

Dan Saults for a remembered speech and for other things;

Agnes Starrett for being the kindest of editors;

Arch Tryon for beds, meals, and gentle approval;

Captain Fred Way for memorable days and nights on the Allegheny;

Bill Willis for starting us in the right direction;

Alec Zehner for championing the lost cause of the Senecas.

PHOTOGRAPHIC ACKNOWLEDGMENTS

Most of the photographs in this book were taken by Thomas M. Jarrett. Some were taken by Raymond Cristina. A few were taken by me. For other photographs we thank, wholeheartedly, the following persons or agencies:

Bowen Studios
    the Somerset keeler, oaken and strong, p. 10; steam rose from the eaves of the evaporating shed, p. 11; hollowed out of log, p. 12; pouring the sap, p. 13

Al Church, even in a changed world, p. 213

Dale Gleason, *The Pittsburgh Press*
    where strip miners dug out the coal and left unnatural gullies, p. 44; Dinsmore Dam was being closed, p. 45

Hal Harrison
    among the dead trees, p. 60; only a few feet away, p. 81; dappled with shade and sunlight, p. 101; older than the Senecas—the yellow chat, p. 105; very close to us, p. 143; conversationalists, p. 151; perhaps, even now, he was watching, p. 171.

Ed Morgan, *The Pittsburgh Sun-Telegraph*
    the lesson, p. 211.

Pennsylvania Game Commission
    twin fawns in May, p. 61; R. M. Cady, for a mouse, p. 56; there were Virginia rails, p. 109; frightened eyes, p. 120; the hawk, p. 222; three deer looked at us, p. 234; other living things, p. 243; there will always be homes, p. 243; the fox in its den, p. 245; the gift of life, p. 245

United States Fish and Wildlife Service
    Frank M. Blake, a conducted tour, p. 42; E. P. Heddon, hedgerows for quail, p. 244

United States Forest Service
    deer were diminishing in size, p. 62; Rex Gary Schmidt, the bandit, p. 225

Don Wooldridge, Missouri Conservation Commission, into the air, p. 32; the hunters in bright jackets, p. 206

Many have worked to produce this book besides the writers and the photographers whose names properly appear elsewhere.

The paper is Warren's Lustro Dull. Russell Rutter Co., Inc., bound the book in Holliston linen. The type, linotype Caledonia, was composed and printed by Davis & Warde, Inc. The color plates were processed by Rawsthorne-Cadillac and the black and white half-tones by Pittsburgh Atlas Engraving.

End paper maps were designed by Wendell Gullion, who also helped with the layout of pages. The title page and the seasonal half titles were designed and executed by Theodore Bowman.

The whole was edited, coordinated, and published
under a grant-in-aid from The Buhl Foundation
by the University of Pittsburgh Press
Agnes L. Starrett, *Director-Editor*
in the year of the Pittsburgh Bicentennial Celebration.